THE HISTORICAL PLAYS OF AUGUST STRINDBERG
Translated by Walter Johnson

Queen Christina, Charles XII, Gustav III
The Last of the Knights, The Regent, Earl Birger of Bjälbo
Gustav Adolf

Gustav Adolf

GUSTAV ADOLF

By August Strindberg

TRANSLATION AND INTRODUCTION
BY WALTER JOHNSON

Seattle · University of Washington Press · 1957
New York · The American-Scandinavian Foundation

839.726 - S918 g

163804

NOTE: The contents of this book are fully protected by copyright and no performance or reading, in toto or in part, may be given without the consent of the translator. Inquiries should be addressed to Walter Johnson, in care of the University of Washington Press, Seattle 5, Washington.

Preface

SEVERAL SWEDISH KINGS and at least one Swedish queen have become international figures of importance, but none of the others has ever made as great a positive impression and contribution internationally as Gustav II Adolf, the person who perhaps more than anyone else helped bring the violent strife between Protestants and Catholics to the point where they could with reasonable forbearance coexist in the Western world. Gustav Adolf's grandfather, Gustav I Vasa, had, to be sure, secured the independence of his country and had thereby excited the imagination and aroused the admiration of many a lover of liberty outside Sweden on both sides of the Atlantic, but his achievement was primarily national and domestic. Gustav Adolf's daughter, Queen Christina, promised for a time to play as important a role in European affairs as Queen Elizabeth of England had, but Christina voluntarily gave up her throne when she was twenty-seven in order to become a Catholic and perhaps even more to secure fame and admiration through her personal and primarily nonpolitical qualities. She did become famous or, as many a writer insists, infamous, but her contribution internationally was slight indeed. Charles XII, the great-grandson of Gustav Adolf's half-sister, became internationally known for his military exploits and his heroic qualities, but his foreign nickname, "Madman of the North," while largely undeserved, suggests fairly well Charles's impact on the non-Swedish world. Gustav III, admirer of Gustav Adolf and remotely related to him by blood, would have liked to emulate his great predecessor, but he had neither the stamina nor the adequate opportunity to do so.

vii

Gustav Adolf stands by himself historically. The contemporary admiration for and faith in "the unweary Gilead" from Sweden were such that for generations in the seventeenth century and into the eighteenth he was practically a folk hero for the common people internationally and the object of admiration and study by the learned, the writers, and the devout. Historians have regularly acknowledged his importance to the development of Western civilization.

What his own people have thought of him is clear both in Sweden and among Swedish-Americans. November 6, the anniversary of his death at Lützen, is regularly celebrated; many of the Swedish-American churches have the name Gustav Adolf or Gustavus Adolphus; one of the most distinguished colleges of the Middle West is, significantly, Gustavus Adolphus College. These are merely a few illustrations of the still very much alive admiration and appreciation of the great king.

August Strindberg, the greatest writer of historical plays in recent centuries, had no inherent respect for folk heroes and other glorified figures out of the past. Appreciated by some and criticized severely by many of his fellow Swedes for his irreverent approach to and iconoclastic treatment of such people out of Swedish history as St. Birgitta and Charles XII, Strindberg in *Gustav Adolf* presents a superb realistic interpretation of the king that should not have offended any of his countrymen except perhaps the pedants and the Mrs. Grundys. The merits of the play include a gallery of striking characterizations, a memorable interpretation of the period, highly effective dramatic qualities, and interesting and noteworthy treatments of war and intolerance, perennial problems that apparently will be with us for some time to come.

In its complete form, the translation of which is presented here, *Gustav Adolf* is a play for the study; yet within it is one of Strindberg's potentially most effective historical dramas. Among other things, the complete play sheds a great deal of light on Strindberg's thinking about war and religion at the turn of the century. A judicious and careful cutting to make it possible to present the play within the conventional limits of, say, three hours will reveal a highly admirable play for the stage. As we shall see in the Introduction, there are nondramatic scenes which could be omitted from a stage production; the play carefully cut for the stage would have a compactness fairly comparable to that of *Gustav Vasa*. Since Strindberg wrote for the theater and was acutely aware of its problems, judicious cutting would not be sacrilege. Directors have already done so for both Swedish and German performances.

WALTER JOHNSON

Contents

xi

Gustav Adolf

THE VASA DYNASTY THROUGH GUSTAV ADOLF'S TIME

Gustav I Vasa
(*ca.* 1495; king, 1523–1560)
married

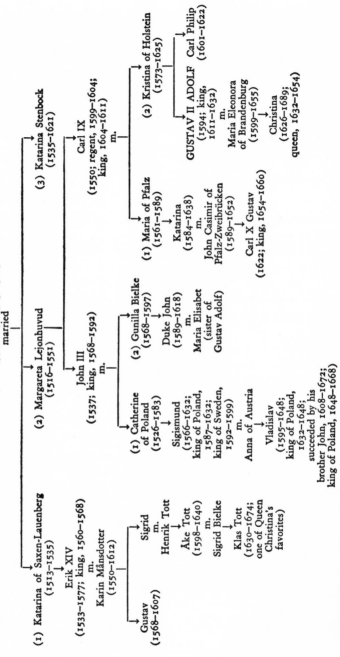

Carl = Charles. Pfalz = The Palatinate.

Introduction

I: STRINDBERG'S INTENTION

Gustav Adolf. A Lutheran saint, who has almost become a school text, had no attraction for me.... In an unpretentious little [booklet] I happened to read that Gustav Adolf, who had begun his career by torturing Catholics (see Cornelius' *Church History*) had finally come so far that he had hanged his own men who had disturbed a Catholic service in Augsburg (or Regensburg?). Then I saw at once his whole character and the whole drama, and I called it my *Nathan the Wise*.[1]

Strindberg might never have written his longest and most ambitious historical play if it had not been for his Inferno experiences[2] in the 1890's, the resultant changes in his thinking and attitudes, various current ideas and events, and the celebration of the tercentennial of Gustav Adolf's birth and the flurry of memorial publications in and after 1894. The Gustav Adolf that Swedish public school textbooks presented to the millions of Swedish school children decade after decade in the nineteenth century was a colorless paragon of the virtues, not the very human being that Strindberg believed any normal human being is, certainly not the sort of man whose life would

---

[1] *Öppna brev till Intima teatern* (*Open Letters to the Intimate Theater*) (Stockholm, 1919 edition), p. 249.

[2] The Inferno experiences consisted of the emotional, mental, and physical agony which led to Strindberg's conversion (see pp. 6-7). For information about the Inferno experiences, see any biography of Strindberg or Strindberg's *The Inferno* (New York, 1913). The major study of Strindberg's Inferno period, Gunnar Brandell's *Strindbergs Infernokris* (Stockholm, 1950), is, unfortunately, not available in English translation.

yield rich material for a drama. What the textbook Gustav Adolf
was like, one typical textbook [3] of the time demonstrates:

> Gustav Adolf was a tall, powerfully built man who in time be-
> came rather fat. His appearance was genuinely Nordic: a healthy
> ruddy complexion; clear blue eyes; and hair and mustache and a
> pointed beard of a light golden color, for which reason he was
> called "the golden king from the North." In his association with
> people he was friendly, gentle, and conciliatory. Like most of the
> Vasas he was hot tempered; he could forget himself in the heat of
> anger to the point of violence, but once having regained his self-
> control he regretted what he had done and made amends for it.
> During the early part of his reign he was not free from youthful
> frivolity, but he soon overcame this fault and in his maturity be-
> came one of the morally purest of historical heroes. It can be
> truthfully said of him, "He was a God-fearing man in all his deeds,
> even unto death." He was enthusiastic about education and knowl-
> edge, understood and spoke several languages, and delighted in the
> study of both religious and worldly books. When he spoke, he knew
> how to put his words so that he swayed the hearts and minds of
> men. As a ruler, he has been surpassed by no [other] Swedish king.
> Yet he was perhaps still greater as a military leader; war was his
> favorite occupation; and he reshaped the art of war.
>
> Toward his closest relatives Gustav Adolf conducted himself
> nobly and dutifully; he was an obedient son, a tender and faithful
> husband, and a good brother. Obeying his stern mother's wishes,
> he sacrificed the love of his youthful days for beautiful *Ebba Brahe,*
> whom the dowager queen instead married off to Jacob De la Gardie.
> He [Gustav Adolf] then married *Maria Eleonora* of Brandenburg,
> famed for her beauty but whimsical and foolish. He married off his
> sister *Katarina* to *Johan Casimir* of Pfalz-Zweibrücken, a German
> prince, who later made his home in Sweden. He was always on
> good terms with his brother Charles Philip and his cousin John,
> but all the same it was a relief for the kingdom that these two princes

[3] The passage is translated from an American edition of Professor C. T.
Odhner's widely used public school text, *Sveriges historia från äldsta till
närvarande tid* (Chicago: P. A. Lindberg & Co., 1906), pp. 188-189.

died without heirs at an early age so that their principalities reverted
to the crown. Charles Philip, who died in 1622, was the last prince
in Sweden to have a principality of his own.

Not unlike the schoolbook characterizations, as late as a generation
ago, of some of our great American men of the past, the passage is
representative and typical of the glorification of the great men of
Sweden's past not only by the authors of textbooks but by the writers
of Swedish historical dramas before and into Strindberg's own time.
Iconoclast that he was, Strindberg could hardly have found the
Gustav Adolf of the textbooks believable, not to say attractive or
dramatically interesting. Gustav Adolf's dutiful regard for and practice of virtuous conduct, even if relieved by the gentle hints of youth-
ful frivolity and a hot temper, were too little in keeping with Strindberg's concept of human nature as an exceedingly complex and varied
combination of good and evil. Strindberg might conceivably have
been stimulated to further investigation into the life of Gustav Adolf,
the textbook paragon, by the implications of his desertion of Ebba
Brahe, the woman he loved; by Gustav Adolf's alleged preference for
war as the ideal activity of a king; and by the textbook author's
cynical gratitude for the early death of Gustav Adolf's cousin John,
who should legally have had the throne, and Gustav Adolf's younger
brother, Charles Philip. But Strindberg's interest in Swedish historical personages became concentrated earlier on Charles XII, whom
so many of his contemporaries idealized and idolized and whom
Strindberg for the most part detested; on St. Birgitta, whom his
favorite historical sources revealed as anything but the model of
sanctity—at least in her earthly existence; and on Gustav Vasa, the
first of the Vasa kings and the king that Strindberg could without
effort admire.

It was not until 1899, when he had completed *The Saga of the
Folkungs, Gustav Vasa,* and *Erik XIV,* that Strindberg read sufficiently widely about Gustav Adolf to find out that the textbook
Gustav Adolf was not *the* Gustav Adolf who had lived between
1594 and 1632 and who, by general admission, had saved the cause

of Protestantism during a period when discussion of the relative merits of religious confessions was as violent and enthusiastic as the discussion of the relative merits of political confessions has been in our own. In 1899 Strindberg was ready to read extensively, if not systematically, about the great Swedish king, and what he discovered or believed he discovered in his reading was remarkably suited to his own thinking and attitudes in 1899 and notably parallel to certain international developments during the last years of the century.

Through his Inferno experiences of the middle 1890's, Strindberg not only had given up every pretence of being an atheist but had arrived at a faith of his own. In his efforts to find meaning in life and in his own suffering, to free himself from his feelings of guilt, and to come to bearable terms with existence, Strindberg had read widely in the literatures of Christianity (both Catholic and Protestant), Buddhism, theosophy, and even Mohammedanism; he had learned that all the great monotheistic religions agree in their central doctrine—that there is one God. He had studied Swedenborg's visions of heaven and earth as well as Linné's *Nemesis divina;* he had been attracted to Catholicism to the point where he contemplated becoming a monk and even spent a short time in a Belgian monastery.

By 1899 Strindberg had secured for himself a personal religious faith which, while it was remarkably free of dogmas, nevertheless had in it certain elements that can be specifically stated. Strindberg believed in *one* God, a God very much like the Jehovah of the Old Testament who, stern and righteous, has a watchful, authoritarian relationship with every human being. He is a God who selects certain men to perform specific tasks; who rewards them when they follow His commandments and His guidance but who punishes them for every deviation from duty and disapproves particularly of the sins of arrogance, pride, and egotistic ambition; and who visits the sins of the father on later generations. Strindberg has illustrated all this, of course, in his three autobiographical plays, *The Road to*

Damascus, and has related his own experiences which led to these conclusions in *Inferno* and *Legends* (*Legender*).

As a result of his thinking about the forms of religion, Strindberg had become a syncretist; he believed that the dogmas and practices which separate denomination from denomination, monotheistic religion from monotheistic religion, were unimportant and not worth either arguing about or fighting about. Strindberg believed rather in the possibility of reconcilation of the various denominations. Implicit in such a point of view was, of course, tolerance of religious confessions other than one's own.

Pastor of the Swedish church in Paris while Strindberg was in the midst of his Inferno agony there was Nathan Söderblom, not only a friend who appreciably understood Strindberg's experiences in the middle 1890's but a man who, before and after he became archbishop of Sweden, was one of the leading spirits in the ecumenical movement of our century in its attempts to bring the various denominations closer to reconciliation and at least to tolerance of each other. Through men like Söderblom, Strindberg had learned about various efforts being made to secure religious tolerance.

Among other matters that excited Strindberg's interest was the International Peace Conference held at The Hague during the summer before he wrote *Gustav Adolf.* For almost a year before the meeting of the conference, lovers of peace and opponents of war had fixed their hopes on the possibility that something would be done to guarantee the preservation of peace and to deliver the world from the scourge of war that had done irreparable harm to mankind throughout its history. The conference made progress toward satisfying such hopes by providing means for dealing with disarmament, the peaceful adjustment of international differences, and the regulation of warfare.

Strindberg shared in the fairly general enthusiasm about the accomplishments of the peace conference. "Disarmament," his answer to George Bröckner's question, "What social reform would

you most like to see accomplished in your lifetime?" is only one in-
dication of Strindberg's hope that at last something was being done
toward bringing to an end the frequently irrational activity known
as war.[4] A loyal Swede but not a chauvinist, Strindberg had never
in all his works glorified or praised war for its own sake. It is not
the military exploits of any of the heroes of his historical plays that
receive major attention; it is not, for example, Gustav Vasa's defeat
of the Danes in battle that he emphasizes; it is Gustav Vasa's character as leader, which permits him to build Sweden from the foundation to the rafters, that Strindberg considers important.

If one keeps in mind Strindberg's interest in religion, tolerance,
and peace in 1899–1900 while he was writing *Gustav Adolf,* and
then reads the play, Strindberg's intention in writing it should be
clear. The passage quoted at the beginning of this section provides
us with Strindberg's own statement of his purpose. It is not Gustav
Adolf, the Lutheran saint of the textbooks, who interested Strindberg. It is rather the Gustav Adolf he saw as a result of his extensive reading about Gustav Adolf and, of course, the period he represents. It is the Gustav Adolf selected by God (*Den Evige,* the
Eternal One) to perform the task of learning the nature of tolerance and of curbing intolerance at one of the most crucial points
in the history of Western civilization—the Thirty Years' War. It is
the Gustav Adolf who becomes the man of tolerance that Strindberg uses as his central character in his *Nathan the Wise,* as his
contribution to the widespread contemporary efforts to forward
both religious tolerance and international understanding and peace.

To present the Thirty Years' War, to demonstrate intolerance in
its various manifestations and nature as well as tolerance and its
achievement, and to present the historical drama of the great king,
Strindberg found it necessary to make *Gustav Adolf* his longest
and, from the point of view of the theater, his most unwieldy play.

---

[4] Quoted in English translation in Elizabeth Sprigge's *The Strange Life of
August Strindberg* (New York: 1949), p. 232.

II: THE HISTORICAL BACKGROUND

Strindberg's study of the historical background and biography was unusually complete; there are in this play relatively few important details to which the contemporary historians and general public could object.[5] Nor is there complete disregard of any of the types of problems that faced Gustav Adolf as an individual or as a public figure: dynastic, personal, domestic, and international, political, religious, and military problems are all represented as they affected the king and his immediate environment as well as his country and Europe as a whole. They all find a suitable place in the play according to Strindberg's own conception of the king and his time.

For anyone unacquainted with the history of Sweden and of the Vasa dynasty in particular, the numerous allusions to Erik XIV, Charles IX, Sigismund, Duke John, the Linköping bloodbath, and the like may prove disturbing. Yet they need not be stumbling blocks if the table on page 2 is carefully considered and, when necessary, consulted. If the fact that in 1544 Gustav I had persuaded the *Riksdag,* the Swedish parliament, to make the throne hereditary in the male Vasa line is remembered, and the table is studied in some detail, the reader can find within the dynasty numerous causes for conflict and the type of family difficulties that Strindberg was extremely sensitive to and interested in. One of the matters that torment Strindberg's Gustav Adolf, for example, is his uncertainty that he has legal right to his throne; Gustav Adolf's respect for law and order as well as his regard for the dynasty were such that he was inwardly troubled by changes in the law of succession for which his father was primarily responsible. Notice particularly:

1. *Gustav,* the son of Erik XIV, was born before the relationship between Erik and Karin was legalized through marriage. Not only did Erik XIV lose his throne through a conspiracy led by his suc-

[5] Of course, Strindberg has compressed and on occasion rearranged the historical material. There are, moreover, details that are historically inaccurate.

cessor, John III, and Gustav Adolf's father, Charles, but historians have given credence to the report that the imprisoned Erik lost his life in 1577 through poison administered to him on the orders of his brother John.[6] One of Strindberg's favorite sources of material for his historical plays—Starbäck and Bäckström's *Berättelser ur svenska historien* (*Stories from Swedish History*)[7]—deals at some length with the unhappy destiny of young Prince Gustav who, feared by his uncle, was taken from his parents and removed from Sweden. The prince lived on until 1607, usually in want and poverty, occasionally a pawn in domestic and international politics, but apparently never—during John III's and Sigismund's Swedish reigns —completely out of the Swedish political picture. Strindberg wisely chose to disregard Prince Gustav: so far as the records go, Gustav Adolf had never been conscience-stricken about the rights of that particular cousin, who after all was illegitimate. Note, however, that Åke Tott, one of Gustav Adolf's ablest commanders, was the son of Princess Sigrid, sister of Prince Gustav.

2. The *Polish Vasas,* particularly Gustav Adolf's cousin Sigismund and nephew Vladislav, had the legal right to the throne, but they were as devout Roman Catholics as Gustav Adolf was a devout Lutheran. The Swedish law eventually provided that the king of Sweden and the heirs to the throne should be Lutherans. Apparently Gustav Adolf had no qualms of conscience about Sigismund's legal right to the throne he himself occupied, but the Polish Vasas never relinquished their claims to the Swedish throne in Gustav Adolf's time. As a result, they and many of the continental rulers refused to acknowledge Gustav Adolf *as king.* What was perhaps even more painful to Gustav Adolf and, before him, to his father Charles IX, was the fact that an appreciable number of Swedes, both lords and commoners, remained faithful to Sigismund —hence, the bloodbath of Linköping (1600), where Charles IX

[6] Odhner says: "It is likely that he was killed by means of poison at the command of John" (p. 158). Less scholarly sources give more specific details.
[7] (Stockholm, 1885 edition); hereafter referred to in the notes as SB.

high-handedly drove through the execution of lords whose major "crime" was that they had remained faithful to their oaths of loyalty to King Sigismund. One of Gustav Adolf's major problems was the struggle with Sigismund both in and out of war; the bullet of Dirschau to which reference is made in Strindberg's play struck and lodged itself in Gustav Adolf's right shoulder in one of his 1627 campaigns against his cousin's forces.

3. *Duke John* (1589–1618), the son of John III and Queen Gunilla, should, according to Swedish law, have succeeded to the throne in 1599 when the Polish Vasas were finally dethroned largely because Duke Charles wanted them to be and because they were Roman Catholics and not Lutherans as the law required. One of the most tragic figures in Swedish history, Duke John was only ten when Charles seized power as regent in 1599, only fifteen when he was persuaded to renounce his rights in 1604, but five years older than his cousin Gustav Adolf when he was again persuaded to relinquish his rights in 1611 in favor of the latter. Duke John disliked his cousin Maria Elisabet, the emotionally unbalanced daughter of Charles IX; nevertheless, the marriage of the duke and his cousin was arranged in 1612. His life became a decidedly unhappy one. It is John that Gustav Adolf is most concerned about; when he feels that he is a usurper, it is the throne that John should legally have had that he has usurped.

4. *Charles IX*, Gustav Adolf's father, cooperated with his older brother John III in deposing Erik XIV and led the opposition to the Catholic Sigismund. In 1595 he persuaded the Estates assembled at Söderköping to swear him allegiance; his actions led to civil war which culminated in the summer of 1598 in direct warfare between Charles's adherents and King Sigismund's loyal Swedish followers and Polish forces. At Stångebro, Charles defeated Sigismund and demanded the handing over of five members of the National Council—Erik Sparre,[8] Gustav and Sten Banér, Ture Bielke, and Göran Posse—all of them members of powerful noble families. Shortly

[8] The father of Axel Eriksson Sparre, one of the secondary characters.

afterward Sigismund returned to Poland. In 1599, Charles had himself elected regent at a meeting of the lords; at a meeting of the Estates in Stockholm in the same year, the Estates deposed Sigismund in favor of his oldest son Vladislav, then a mere child, on the conditions that the child be brought to Sweden within a year and that he be reared there as a Lutheran. Since the prince was not brought to Sweden, he was never acknowledged king, and at the meeting of the Estates at Linköping in 1600 was along with all other descendants of Sigismund declared ineligible for the Swedish crown. It was at the Linköping meeting that the famous Linköping bloodbath took place: at Charles's insistence, four members of the National Council who had remained faithful to Sigismund were executed—Erik Sparre, Ture Bielke, Gustav and Sten Banér, as well as Bengt Falk, one of Sigismund's commanders. Both before and after the Linköping bloodbath Charles had had opponents imprisoned, exiled, or executed; there were few of the powerful noble families that were not hit directly or indirectly by his harshness. It was this sort of conduct that caused the in many ways able Charles to be called "the Bloody." In 1604, after Duke John had been persuaded to renounce his legal rights to the Swedish crown, Charles became king in name as well as fact. A confirmed Protestant with definitely Calvinistic leanings, Charles had qualms of conscience about bypassing Duke John; in his will, he asked that the right of the duke be respected. It is this inheritance that Strindberg has in mind when he speaks of Gustav Adolf as the atoner.

The examination of Table I and the consideration of this necessarily brief account should suggest that the dynastic background of the story of Gustav Adolf was anything but peaceful and pleasant. Blood guilt and open and concealed struggles (in Erik XIV's case even fratricide) for power and place among brothers, cousins, uncles, and nephews within the royal family make the background bloody and cruel. Hence, Gustav Adolf's feeling that he must atone for what his father has committed. It is a record filled with hatred and conniving even among some of the women of the dynasty.

Charles's second wife and Gustav Adolf's mother, Kristina of Holstein, who had in effect been jilted in her teens by his cousin Sigismund, was as proud and ambitious and greedy for power as her husband. Contemporaries and even historians have suspected that she as much as Charles was responsible for the elimination of one rival after the other to make way for her husband's accession to the throne and for the ultimate succession of her older son. Certainly Queen Kristina was the one who above the objections of the clergy arranged for the loveless and incompatible marriage between her erratic and unbalanced daughter Maria Elisabet and Duke John, the cousin who stood at crucial times between her husband and, later, her son and the throne. Queen Kristina was also the one who prevented the marriage of Gustav Adolf with the woman he loved, the beautiful lady-in-waiting Ebba Brahe.

Gustav Adolf's and Lady Ebba's love for each other could not be entirely disregarded by Strindberg. Every Swede has been exposed to the story; many a Swedish writer has used it as the subject of poetry, prose fiction, or drama—Gustav III himself, for example, collaborated with Johan Henrik Kellgren in the writing of a play, *Gustav Adolf and Ebba Brahe* (1786). The daughter of the lord high steward and the great niece of Gustav I's third queen, Lady Ebba was introduced at court in her early teens and soon thereafter she and Gustav Adolf became the object of each other's very genuine affection and love. All the extant love letters and the testimony of their contemporaries support the popular tradition of a sincere and genuine love affair with mutual understanding and agreement about their eventual union in marriage.

But that was not to be, for Dowager Queen Kristina had no mind to see her son married to anyone who was not a princess of royal blood. By furtive scheming as well as both open and concealed pressure, the dowager queen managed to postpone their official engagement and may even have had a hand, as Strindberg suggests, in arranging the temporary liaison between Gustav Adolf and the Dutchwoman Margareta Slots (Cabeljau) in 1615–1616, the most obvious result of which was the king's illegitimate son Gustav Gustavsson of Vasaborg. The king's mother certainly encouraged the suit of Jakob De la Gardie for Ebba's hand, and, above all perhaps, she managed most effectively to keep the king and Lady Ebba from seeing each other except on rare occasions. On June 24, 1618, Count Jakob De la Gardie and Lady Ebba were married in Stockholm. Among the guests was Dowager Queen Kristina. Invited but not present was the king.

Gustav Adolf was allowed to select his royal bride, but both for him personally and for the dynasty his choice was a most unhappy one. A Hohenzollern princess of Brandenburg with as royal a family tree as even Dowager Queen Kristina could insist on, Maria Eleonora was both beautiful and kindhearted. She fell in love with Gustav Adolf, but it was a possessive, demanding, jealous love that brought little happiness to either of them. Erratic and whimsical, the new queen was given to hysteria and unconventional conduct. At no time, according to the records, did she succeed in fully understanding her husband's plans or in supporting his programs. As Strindberg's Queen Maria Eleanora says, she always considered herself a German, not a Swede. Gustav Adolf, for his part, had apparently genuine affection for his unbalanced queen but, considering her objectively, came to the conclusion that he had to protect and shield her as if she were an unpredictable child. A genuine cause of sorrow for both king and queen was the fact that their only child to survive infancy was Christina, a brilliant princess, yes, but nevertheless not a prince who could assure the continuation of the dynasty.

Strindberg pays only slight attention to one other member of Gustav Adolf's immediate family, without question the one to whom he felt most closely linked by ties of affection as well as by blood and on whom he could rely as on no other relative—his older half-sister, Katarina, an intelligent, sensible woman married since 1615 to John Casimir of Pfalz-Zweibrücken and resident since 1618 with her family in Sweden. It was his nephew Carl Gustav, Katarina's son, that Gustav Adolf had most likely thought of as the future husband of his daughter Christina.

The only conclusions that Strindberg's investigations into Gustav Adolf's family and dynastic background could have led to are those expressed in the play: the uncertainty of Gustav Adolf's right to be king of the Swedes; blood guilt and the need of atonement as related to the inheritance of hatred and misunderstanding among the closely related members of the higher nobility—many of whom were, in turn, related not only to the Vasas but to their bitter rivals down through the generations, the Stures; thwarted and frustrated love; adultery and illegitimacy; and the face-saving and kindly settlement for a marriage that had neither understanding nor depth.

To understand Strindberg's play, the reader must also have in mind the essential facts about the religious background of a period that was as concerned with religious controversy as our own is with political. The leaders and many of the adherents of Catholicism, Lutheranism, and Calvinism (not to mention other Protestant factions) were from the beginnings of the Reformation back in the early decades of the sixteenth century violently and fanatically enthusiastic about their own particular sect and the institutions that represented it. In Sweden the relatively mild and gentle Lutheran reformation of Gustav Vasa's reign (1523–1560) had gradually given way to a stricter and more legalistic orthodoxy which bore fruit in such measures as the Statute of Örebro (1617), a law that provided for the exile or death of any Swedish Catholic or Zwinglian (or, as such an adherent was later called, Calvinist). The supporters of each of the religious confessions did not as a rule practice the Christian commandment to love one another; hatred of the Jew was generally no more violent than hatred of the adherents of opposing Christian sects. It was in such a period that Gustav Adolf lived; it was a period when "defender of the faith" was more than a nominal term without content.

Martin Luther (1483–1546) began his reformation largely as a protest against the abuses of the Roman Catholic church; the ninety-five theses that Luther nailed to the door of the church at Wittenberg in 1517 were largely protests against the sale of indulgences and the implications as to church doctrines and practices as they differed from what was stated in the Bible itself. In 1519, Luther attacked the primacy of the pope, about which matter he disputed with Doctor Eck at Leipzig; in the following years he rejected the doctrines that confession and absolution were necessary prerequisites for salvation, that the priests must be celibates, that the pope and his councils were infallible; and even insisted that the priesthood and formal worship were not absolutely essential. In his full development of his religious ideas, Luther shaped Lutheranism into that variety of Protestantism which insists (1) that the Bible alone is the source of the true and valid doctrines of faith; (2) that any human being can attain eternal salvation by accepting the teachings of Christ and believing in him (it is faith, not works that saves); and (3) that the two necessary sacraments are baptism and the Lord's Supper. The Lutheran doctrine of communion needs a comment, perhaps, for it was one of the leading sources of controversy between the Lutherans and the Calvinists. The Lutheran doctrine is that of consubstantiation: Luther insisted that Christ was in the bread and the wine "as fire in the hot iron." Even more than most leaders, Luther in his lifetime became the object of intense admiration on the part of his followers and bitter hatred on the part of his opponents. The Lutherans alone received freedom to exercise their religion at the Peace of Augsburg (1555), but that achievement did not settle the religious difficulties for any appreciable time.

In Switzerland, Ulrich Zwingli (1484–1531) began the reformation much as Luther had done in Germany; his early demands called only for reformation within the church. He laid the foundation for most of the ideas of the second Swiss leader, John Calvin (1509–1564), who, building on what Zwingli had done, taught (1) the Bible as the sole authority on religion, (2) the doctrine of predestination ("He hath mercy on whom he will have mercy, and whom he will he hardeneth"), and (3) the rejection of consubstantiation. The major doctrinal differences between Lutheranism and Calvinism lie, then, largely in the Calvinistic insistence on predestination and its view of the Lord's Supper. It may be said, moreover, that the Calvinistic sect was far more antagonistic to the teachings of Catholicism than was the Lutheran, and that in practice the early Calvinists, unlike at least the early Lutherans, destroyed individual liberty.

Throughout the sixteenth century and well into the seventeenth, there were an appreciable number of men who deplored the practical effects of the religious controversies that raged without let or stop throughout most of the Protestant areas on the continent. Among these men were the syncretists, who believed that the differences among the various sects were slight enough to warrant conciliation and union, certainly not great enough to justify their separation and the bitter hatred and rivalry among them. Strangely enough, the father of Gustav Adolf, Charles IX, was one of them. As interested in theology as his contemporary James I of England, he engaged in learned argument with the ecclesiastical authorities of his own Lutheran country; his avowed purpose was to reconcile the various Protestant faiths. But the fairly new freedom to argue about religious questions captivated many, and conformity to an ever narrower creed, and an ever more mechanical interpretation of the doctrines taught by the reformers became the contradictory practices of a time that led to one "religious" war after the other.

Religious reformation and politics had early become mixed. The numerous rulers of the fairly independent little states of badly split Germany had from the time Luther appeared become either his defenders or his bitter opponents. The picture is highly complex and confusing—princes with sincerity as to faith and sincerity as defenders of the faith are indeed rare in sixteenth- and seventeenth-century Europe, when religion was frequently intentionally confused with political and personal interests. Certain it is that both the Prot-

estants and the Catholics used political means to forward their
ends; the formation of the Protestant Union and that of the Catholic League in the early years of the century for the defense of their
respective religious rights were only indications of the use of political means for religious purposes. Note that Fredrik of Pfalz,
Winter King of Bohemia, one of the characters in Strindberg's play,
had been head of the Protestant Union.

The political background of *Gustav Adolf* is, of course, both
national (i.e., Swedish) and international. Since Strindberg chose
the closing years of the king's life as his subject, little more need be
emphasized here about political developments within Sweden beyond what has already been said above about Gustav Adolf's dynastic
and family difficulties. Strindberg does, to be sure, hint at the
strengthening of Sweden within its own borders by such great
leaders as the chancellor Axel Oxenstjerna, frequently called the
greatest statesman in Swedish history; there are hints, too, of the
political moves that Gustav Adolf had made to strengthen Sweden's
position in the Baltic area, and to place it in a position to assume its
brief but brilliant role as one of the great powers of Europe in spite
of its relative poverty and scarcity of manpower.

The major portion of the political background of the play is
necessarily European rather than merely Swedish. The Thirty
Years' War (1618–1648) or, more exactly, the first twelve years of
it and especially the last three of those twelve years are the primary
setting of Strindberg's play. The Germany which existed under the
rule of the Hapsburg emperors was not a closely knit, unified nation but rather a loose and chaotic confederation of small states
and free cities; it was a Germany torn by religious controversy and
bitter political rivalry as well as marked by intellectual and artistic
achievement and wealth. The war which started as a religious
struggle between the Protestant and Catholic princes of Germany
developed, perhaps largely because of the Hapsburgs' greed for
power, into a bitter struggle for political power and territory; it

developed, too, into a struggle that involved eventually practically all the countries of the continent.

Highly significant in the background of the play is the German military policy, "War must support war"—the idea that troops were to be quartered by the people of occupied territories and supported by them either in the form of war levies or through plunder. Even the composition of most of the armies merits attention: the majority of the soldiers fought for pay and plunder, not for a cause and rarely with any sympathy for the inhabitants of the conquered cities and rural areas that they plundered. Strindberg amply illustrates the technique of maintenance through the plundering and ruination of conquered or occupied German territory.

The Swedish armies were usually, as Strindberg explains, notable exceptions to the rule. Not that Sweden had a sufficiently great population to man its armies with native Swedes and Finns [9] alone, but the careful organization of the army and its strict and usually maintained discipline along with the innovations in military techniques—appreciably the products of Gustav Adolf's own mind—made the Swedish armies, whether composed of natives of the country alone or of Swedes and Finns mixed with foreign mercenary troops, the objects of admiration and amazement on the part of the German people, on whose soil the war was fought.

The background of *Gustav Adolf* includes the outstanding events and personalities of the Thirty Years' War between 1618 and 1630 when Sweden entered it. Strindberg has allusions to the episode of May 23, 1618, when Bohemian Protestants forced their way into their Catholic King Ferdinand's palace at Prague and seized the king's regents, Martinitz and Slawata, and their secretary, and threw them out of the window, an episode that may be said to mark the beginning of the war. Strindberg not only refers to the Bohemians' election of the Calvinist Fredrik V of Pfalz, head of the Protestant Union, as king of Bohemia in 1619, and his disas-

[9] Finland was an integral part of Sweden until 1809. Throughout historic times, both Finns and Swedes have inhabited Finland.

trous reign until 1620 when Tilly, the Bavarian commander, defeated the Bohemians at White Mountain outside Prague, but also
makes Fredrik a character in the play.

The Catholic conquest of Bohemia and the restoration of Catholicism there, the extension of the war into Germany with one
Catholic victory after the other, and the growth of the Hapsburg
emperor's power in the early 1620's as well as the disunity and envy
of the Protestant princes are important for an understanding of
what Strindberg says of the action in the play. The attempt on the
part of Christian IV of Denmark to come to the aid of the Protestants in 1625 was more than balanced by the appearance of the
brilliant military leader Albert von Wallenstein at the head of his
own personal army of fifty thousand men in support of the imperial
and Catholic cause. In 1626, Tilly defeated Christian; in 1627, Wallenstein joined forces with Tilly and drove Christian out of Germany. In 1629, after having forced his way to the Baltic, Wallenstein had perhaps made plans to conduct a naval campaign against
the northern countries; then in May, 1629, he concluded peace with
Christian, who promised to give up all claims on German lands
and not to interfere again in German affairs. The same year the
emperor issued the Edict of Restitution, which restored to the
Catholic Church the lands and other property that had been in lay
hands since the Peace of Augsburg (1555).

In 1630, when Sweden was preparing to enter the war, the pros-
pects for the Protestant cause were bleak indeed. There was no
leader worthy to be mentioned with the imperial generals Wallenstein and Tilly; and the jealousy and envy of the Protestant princes
among themselves; the violent antagonism between Lutherans and
Calvinists, both princes and people; the ravaging and plundering
of most of the Protestant lands; and the continued successes of the
Catholics made it seem inevitable to many Protestants that their
time was running out and that the imperial as well as Catholic
power would be extended to take in not only Protestant Germany
but Protestant Holland and Lutheran Scandinavia as well.

Sweden alone was in a position and had the interest to interfere. By 1630 the Church of Sweden had succeeded in making itself thoroughly orthodox Lutheran, and on the throne was one of the ablest men of the time, a man who was, moreover, a sincerely enthusiastic believer in the Lutheran form of the Christian religion as well as an able administrator, a natural-born leader, and a military genius. Although he was king of one of the most extensive countries in Europe, he had had to face certain facts realistically in the preceding nineteen years of his reign. Though Sweden was a large country, it was sparsely populated; it had exceedingly great limitations not only in manpower but in material wealth with which to finance military expeditions; it had bitter enemies to the west, the south, and the east—Denmark, Poland, and Russia. In the nineteen preceding years, Gustav Adolf in spite of handicaps had fought with all of them, and by 1630 he had concluded either peace or armistices with all of them. He had extended Swedish possessions across the Baltic; he had gained control of strategic ports in Polish-controlled northeastern Germany; he had brought greater efficiency into his government and had placed able men in it; he had brought the Swedish people to support him and his programs in an unprecedented way; he had reorganized the whole Swedish military establishment; and he had surrounded himself with the ablest men available, many of them—far from incidentally —related to victims of his father's purges.

Gustav Adolf's reorganization of Sweden's army explains in large part how the Swedes could accomplish what they did. He inaugurated an army organization that covered the whole country, organized his regiments by provinces, provided for the peacetime maintenance of the soldiers at a minimum cost to the nation, instituted regular periods of training, drew up and usually managed to enforce articles of war which made the Swedish armies the best disciplined and least cruel of his time, and succeeded in giving his troops the conviction that they were fighting for a cause. It was a national army, strikingly different from the large mercenary armies of his opponents.

In addition to his reorganization of the army which made it, as some authorities say, the most effective military force of the time, Gustav Adolf did much to revolutionize military tactics and equipment which helped make it possible for his usually numerically inferior forces to defeat overwhelmingly superior forces.[10] Among the innovations were such matters as the substitution of mobility for momentum (light detachments for slow-moving forces in great depth), lighter, more rapidly firing guns for muskets, and light field cannons for heavy artillery pieces. In addition, his theory included keeping one third of his army ready for battle but in reserve until it became plain where it was most needed; the provision of a regular supply system; the gradual and slow occupation of enemy territory; the protection of his lines of communication to the rear; and the reduction of the number of mercenary troops under his command to the minimum made necessary by the limits of national manpower.

The reputation of Gustav Adolf had spread beyond the boundaries of Swedish territory by 1630; his military successes against Poland and the gradual expansion of Swedish territory as well as his reputation as a devout Protestant had become known on the continent as well. Many a German, exposed to the horrors of a war waged largely by mercenary troops and based on the theory that war must support war, seized eagerly upon the reports that a deliverer would come from the north; fervent Bible readers that many of them were, they seized, too, upon Biblical passages that without too great an effort could be made applicable to Gustav Adolf.

The action of the play, it will be noted, deals primarily with se-

[10] For information about Gustav Adolf as a military genius, see such books as A. A. Stomberg's *A History of Sweden* (New York, 1931), Nils Ahnlund's *Gustav Adolf the Great* (New York: American-Scandinavian Foundation, 1940), and Ingvar Andersson's *A History of Sweden* (New York, 1956).

Gustav Adolf's campaigns, 1630–1632

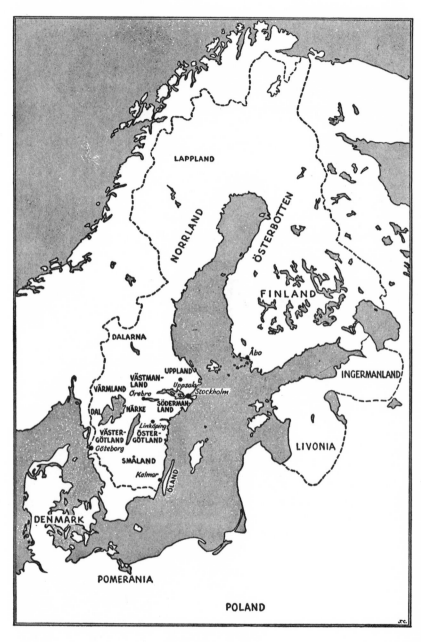

LAPPLAND

NORRLAND

ÖSTERBOTTEN

FINLAND

Åbo

DALARNA

VÄSTMAN-
LAND

UPPLAND

VÄRMLAND

Örebro

Uppsala

Stockholm

INGERMANLAND

DAL

NÄRKE

SÖDERMAN-
LAND

VÄSTER-
GÖTLAND

Linköping
ÖSTER-
GÖTLAND

LIVONIA

Göteborg

SMÅLAND

Kalmar

ÖLAND

DENMARK

POMERANIA

POLAND

Sweden in 1630

lected episodes from Gustav Adolf's less than three years in Germany (1630–1632), from his initial landing with his troops at Usedom to the start of funeral services at the castle church in Wittenberg just after the Battle of Lützen in November, 1632, the battle which firmly established Protestantism in Europe and made Sweden one of the great powers of Europe. See, for reference, the table of dates below and the maps in this section.

A LIST OF MAJOR DATES

1630

Midsummer	Landing of the Swedes at Usedom
July 18	Capture of Stettin
August 7	Imperial dismissal of Wallenstein

1631

January 18	Signing of treaty with France
April 3	Capture of Frankfurt an der Oder
May 4	Alliance with Brandenburg
May 10	Destruction of Magdeburg
August 21	Tilly's invasion of Saxony
September 1	Alliance with Saxony
September 5	Union of Swedish and Saxon armies
September 7	Battle of Breitenfeld
September 27	Crossing of Thuringia Forest
November 17	Swedish entry into Frankfurt am Main
December 7	Crossing of the Rhine
December 19	Capture of Mainz

1632

March 21	Entry into Nuremberg
April 14	Entry into Augsburg
April 29	Battle of Ingolstadt. Wounding of Gustav Adolf; death of Tilly

1632

April 30	Death of Sigismund of Poland
May 7	Entry into Munich
July 16	Wallenstein encamped at Altenberg
August 18	Arrival of Oxenstjerna
August 24	The battle at Alte Veste
October 8	Gustav Adolf's departure from Bavaria to go to the aid of Saxony
October 22	Wallenstein's capture of Leipzig
November 6	The Battle of Lützen. Death of Gustav Adolf

III: DRAMATIC STRUCTURE

I called it my *Nathan the Wise*.[11]

Strindberg never wrote a play about Swedish history that is more ambitious or more theatrically unwieldy than *Gustav Adolf*. While each of his historical dramas of character such as *Gustav Vasa* or *Gustav III* is concentrated primarily on the central character, *Gustav Adolf* has the three closely related and interwoven themes of war as illustrated in the Thirty Years' War, the problem of religious intolerance, and the development of the king in his struggle against intolerance both in his environment and within himself. To demonstrate and illustrate these, Strindberg has done what he tells us in the above quotation; that is, he has followed Lessing's example and written a play designed first of all for the study; he has constructed his play without his usual regard for the limitations of the theater.

In the 1903 edition, the five long acts of *Gustav Adolf* consist of thirty-one, fifty-two, thirty-four, forty-two, and twenty-eight pages, respectively. There are sixteen scenes and well over sixty characters. Almost seven hours would be required for the stage presentation of the complete play. As we shall see later, at least three of the acts contain scenes that in whole or in part contribute a great deal to

[11] *Öppna brev till Intima teatern*, pp. 249-250.

the clarification of Strindberg's concept of the Thirty Years' War and his ideas about religious intolerance but do very little to advance economically the action of the play as it centers in the development of the central character. If one considers *Gustav Adolf* as a play for the study, one can object very little to the inclusion of these relatively undramatic portions, however; they do clarify the war in its many facets and they either explain or illustrate in detail what Strindberg has to say about both war and intolerance.

The dramatic technique that Strindberg uses is the naturalistic—or, as many Americans prefer to call it, the realistic—technique explained in the preface to *Lady Julie* (1888). To illustrate his themes, the dramatist has built a plot consisting of (1) crucial episodes centering about Gustav Adolf during the period when he developed from a leader intolerant enough to be unwilling to shake a Catholic's hand to the point where he "hanged his own men who had disturbed a Catholic church service" and of (2) representative episodes from both military and civilian life. The scenes, the dialogue, the exposition and foreshadowing, and the characterization are all in essential keeping with what Strindberg says about technique in the preface of 1888.

Act I. In a superb first act, Strindberg introduces the reader and the audience at once to his themes; the religious, racial, political, military, and personal conflicts; and many of his characters with a naturalness that is his own. To provide the extensive background needed for his massive subject, he paints boldly, creating sweeping effects and almost unlimited panoramas without neglecting, however, the characteristically telling Strindbergian detail.

The opening part of the act conveys both the physical setting of the coming action and the brutalizing and anarchic effects of war, the latter being revealed through an environment of plundering, starvation, want, and brutality. From the beginning Strindberg intimates that the utter despair of the Germans is relieved by the hope that deliverance is at hand in the person of Gustav Adolf. The despair expressed by the Lutheran miller against the background of a country plundered and devastated by mercenary armies is in sharp contrast to the hope expressed by his Catholic wife that a deliverer will come who will bring order out of chaos.

The quiet entry of the Swedish herald who reads Gustav Adolf's initial proclamation, with its two promises that he will protect the personal freedom and property rights of the German people and secure religious freedom for the persecuted Protestants, further emphasizes the difference between what they have already suffered and what they may hope for through Gustav Adolf himself.

Strindberg increases the dramatic effect by having representatives of the common soldiers and the noncommissioned officers enter in a quiet and orderly fashion to demonstrate the correctness of what the king has promised in his proclamation. Strindberg makes clear that the men conduct themselves well because they have a firm and respected leader who not only has set up standards of conduct but enforces them. Strindberg demonstrates, too, that Gustav Adolf's humbler followers grasp only in general and varying degrees the cause that their king represents and that they have come to Germany to fight for.

The orderly entrance, one by one, of Gustav Adolf's commanders, specialists, and Erik Rålamb—the man closest to the king and the one through whom we learn to know the king's ideals, hopes, and fears—heightens the dramatic effect, confirms our faith in the correctness of the king's promises, and conveys effectively how very human Gustav Adolf's supporters are. Aside from Erik Rålamb, they are no paragons or dedicated fanatics; they admire their king but understand him and his cause only in part.

Against this background of a devastated Germany with its embittered and oppressed people whose hope has been awakened by the arrival of the Swedish king, and against the background of the ordinary humanity and great poverty of his own people, Gustav Adolf makes his first appearance. His demeanor and confident bearing convey his idealism, his firm faith in God, and his belief that he is a man chosen by God to perform a great mission. All this gives a sense of reality to his mission and a feeling that it will be accomplished. He becomes the embodiment of the people's hope. Yet Strindberg injects a note of doubt, which serves as a premonition of impending difficulties:

KING: Well! Now I am here! . . . How are you? . . . So quiet! Have you had dinner?

HORN: No, Your Majesty . . .

KING: Why not?

HORN: Because there isn't anything to eat.

KING: Then we'll have to go to bed hungry for once; and still be thankful after such a splendid start.

HORN: Splendid?

KING: Isn't it splendid that we could complete our landing without the slightest opposition? Isn't it good fortune without compare that the enemy withdraws? I am so delighted that . . . I am afraid, afraid as always in good fortune that it won't last long . . .

There will be no plundering; there will be order and discipline. Gustav Adolf himself confirms the hope of the people and demonstrates that his promises are sincere.

By means of the conversation between the king and Erik Rålamb, Strindberg further demonstrates that the king thinks of his mission as a clear-cut Lutheran crusade, but through the touching meeting with the miller's Catholic wife Strindberg shows that the king not only is very human but also has the capacity for growth.

By means of one long, carefully constructed scene against a broad and extensive background, Strindberg succeeds superbly in setting the mood, introducing many of his characters, making us aware of his three themes—the war itself, the problem of intolerance, and the character of Gustav Adolf, and foreshadowing the coming action. It is a brilliantly conceived and executed opening act.

Act II. In five long, leisurely scenes, Strindberg demonstrates and illustrates (1) the progress of the war, (2) the complexity of the whole matter of religious intolerance (and introduces his own solution—syncretism), and (3) the development of the king as he is forced to face a bewildering array of difficulties. Strindberg presents masses of material to show that neither the war nor the religious question was a simple and clear-cut Lutheran crusade for the protection and security of the Protestants. He succeeds in demonstrating this by showing both Swedes and supposedly friendly Germans in action; by introducing highly intelligent men of various faiths who prefer either not to discuss religious differences or who insist, "Has not one God created us all?"; by showing Calvinist opposed to Lutheran, Lutheran employed by Catholic, and Catholic serving Calvinist; and by showing the Lutheran crusader allying himself with Catholic France.

The self-confident, dedicated Lutheran hero could say in Act I:

> I hate the Catholics . . . You know I can smell a Catholic within gunshot, and when I've had to take one by the hand I've felt as if I were taking hold of a snake! That's why I didn't need any declaration of war, that's why I needed no alliances, because the sheep know their shepherd, and the shepherd knows the wolves! And the one who is not with me is against me!

The Gustav Adolf of Act II is no longer as naive as that: he has been forced to break his promise to protect the rights of the Germans; he has learned that the religious issue is not simple; he has been forced to compromise his Lutheran-Protestant ideals by allying himself with Catholic France; he is no longer certain that he clearly knows what his mission is. Rålamb, the idealistic guardian of Gustav Adolf's conscience, says:

> The great goal, the holy cause, everything forgotten for the enemy's gold! What have we become but the abomination of our brethren in the faith and the scorn of our enemies, a band of plunderers of strangers?

Strindberg makes it abundantly clear that this is an exaggeration and motivates every compromise that the king makes or is tempted to make; he also introduces the imperial thought—political unity of the Germans—and Gustav Gustavsson, the king's illegitimate son, both preparatory to action in later acts.

As part of such a massive drama for the study, Act II is impressive for its development of the themes of the Thirty Years' War, the problem of religious tolerance and intolerance, and the steadily deepening characterization of Gustav Adolf.

Act III. The two long scenes—the first with its setting in the churchyard next to the battlefield at Breitenfeld and the other a victory celebration that ironically becomes anything but a celebration—are not only highly colorful but also further clarify the themes.

In the churchyard scene Strindberg demonstrates both the bitterness of religious antagonisms over what he considers petty differences and the solution of the problem of intolerance. By means of the argument between the two simple gravediggers, Strindberg illustrates the futility of all arguments about the details of religious faith. By means of his presentation of the confession of faith by representatives of the Mohammedan, Romany, Jewish, and Christian (Catholic, Calvinistic, and Lutheran) religions, he demonstrates the essential identity of all these faiths in their basic doctrine of belief in *one* God who is the father of all mankind and presents syncretism as one solution to the problem of religious intolerance.

The increasing complexity and brutality of the Thirty Years' War are clarified largely by means of expository dialogue on the part of observers or commentators. The significance of the Battle of Breitenfeld is particularly important; as Johan Banér explains, that victory should have been followed by peace, for through that victory Gustav Adolf had won for all practical purposes the initial goal of his mission—securing his fellow Protestants the right to worship God according to their own desires.

But the king, who appears ten years older as Johan Banér says, has succumbed to the temptation of yielding to selfish ambition. As victory has followed upon victory, the king has become less and less the dedicated crusader who has a noble mission to perform and more and more the arrogant fighter for power. Unfortunately, we learn all this only through the discussions of the great commanders, for Gustav Adolf appears only briefly at the end of this act. Wallenstein's thought of unifying all Germany becomes—for Gustav Adolf—speculation about securing the imperial crown for himself; for that reason he begins to isolate himself, directly or indirectly, from most of the talented young Swedes who have served the young crusader well.

Act IV. Strindberg continues the development of his three interwoven themes, with his central character receiving more direct attention than in any of the previous acts. In scene 1, Strindberg suggests that the renegade Gustav Adolf the Great has finally rejected his intolerance toward non-Protestants. In scene 2, the commanders review the progress of the war which not only has brought Gustav Adolf to the height of his power and worldly glory but has increased his personal ambition and isolated him from his own people. In scene 3, the corruption in the Swedish camp is illustrated in close relationship to Gustav Adolf's growing tendency to think in terms of wider areas of personal power rather than of his own countrymen and his own role as a deliverer. In a highly effective part of this scene, Gustav Adolf comes in after being wounded at Ingolstadt:

> I thought . . . that I was the chosen one, but then I had to learn better. My time has not yet come, but I'm grateful for the warning.

He has learned that he is "a blind subordinate of the Lord, whose plans we are never permitted to understand." In scene 4, Strindberg demonstrates that Gustav Adolf has become a man of tolerance. At last he understands that his role is that of deliverer from oppression, but, even in his inner distress and isolation, he only approaches the humility and the resignation that the Eternal One demands of him.

As part of a drama for the study, Act IV is notably effective. It not only advances the dramatic action and the development of the three-fold theme, but it makes clear Strindberg's basic ideas about war and about religion.

Act V. In scene 1 Strindberg demonstrates that the Eternal One is chastising the man He has chosen to combat oppression; corruption, death, and disease have struck the camp of the chosen one as never before; Gustav Adolf still is toying with his arrogant and selfish ambition to become the arbiter of power throughout the empire; he has turned from his own Swedes and Finns to Germans.

> KING: I don't possess myself; I can't control myself. You know, the worst . . . God, whom I used to reach in prayer, has turned His back on me, and I cannot find Him any more!
>
> STENBOCK: Really? Turn home to your tabernacles, Israel, for you have gone astray!

In the highly moving second scene—the scene of the trumpeter's death—Gustav Adolf is brought to resignation; he *wants* to go home, not to pursue his selfish personal ambition.

Scene 3, with a setting in the cold, foggy rainy morning before the Battle of Lützen, presents the humbled Gustav Adolf who knows that he can do nothing without God's guidance and help and that he must do what he is called upon to do. It is a chastened chosen man of God who goes into the battle to win the goals of the mission God has set and chosen for him.

The final, cathartic scene is a dignified, subdued presentation of what is less mourning or preparation for mourning than it is a highly suitable celebration of the victory in death of the heroic chosen man of God. He has become the sacrifice that made possible freedom of conscience for everyone in Protestant Germany and the Protestant North. Resigned and humbled and purged of arrogance, pride, and selfish ambition, Gustav Adolf has become the atoner for blood guilt and the deliverer from oppression, the blind and obedient subordinate of the Lord whose plans he was never permitted to understand fully.

Exposition and Preparation. As usual in his historical plays, Strindberg provides information about the background of each part of the action in a thoroughly realistic manner. He prepares just as realistically and carefully for what will take place later. Note this excerpt from scene 2, Act II, as an illustration:

KING (*draws with chalk on the map*): Now I'll cross out Frankfurt an der Oder with red: It is taken! (*To* HORN) What do you say, old man?

    (HORN *remains silent; distressed.*)

KING: Nothing? . . . Well, young Lennart, what does St. Paul say about this?

TORSTENSSON (*hurt*): Your Majesty! (*Someone pounds on the door.*)

KING: There, there, forgive me. (*To* BANÉR) Johan, what would you do now if you were in my place?

BANÉR: I'd rather not say!

KING: Haven't you sent Rålamb up to the palace?

BANÉR: Yes, I have, Your Majesty. (*The pounding on the door increases.*)

KING: Well, I sent him away so I could talk and act freely. That youngster has won my heart so fully that he looks after my conscience like a jealous woman. There are moments when I'm afraid of him! (*General silence answers the* KING's *speech.*) He actually tyrannizes over me . . . that's how it is; why I don't know, but that's how it is! What is that noise out there? . . . Speak out, Johan . . . you're the bravest.

BANÉR: It's the soldiers, of course, dissatisfied because they haven't been paid . . .

KING: Always their pay!

HORN: All they've had to eat during the last seventy-two hours is dry bread . . .

KING: Supplies from Hamburg are expected at any minute.

HORN: The wagons have turned back and gone to the enemy outside Magdeburg instead, because the notes haven't been redeemed.

KING: How much you know that I'm never permitted to know! . . . How is my friend, Marcus of Hamburg?

HORN: He's not exactly suffering, for Tott is treating him to both food and drink, but he's dissatisfied and will no doubt avenge himself.

BANÉR: And he's joined forces with that Jew from Wolgast and other Israelites; and they say when there are ten of them, they'll hold divine services or read the Torah, as they call it!

KING: What is Torah? Do you know, Lennart?

TORSTENSSON: The Torah rolls? The five first books of the Old Testament, the Pentateuch, the same holy book as our . . .

KING: Almost the gospel! So they're unbelievers! I certainly can't let them celebrate divine services, can I? . . . But this noise . . . it makes me ill! . . . Johan, go and find out about it, and have Fabricius come right away.

(BANÉR *goes out.*)

KING: My friends, you know I feel how someone has taken me by the hair to drag me where I don't want to go. Those cries out there . . . they're not the cries of want or suffering; they're the evil passions that war has let loose . . . I know where it will lead; I know I don't want to go there; but I'm being dragged there. (*Gets up; moved*) For twenty years I've been at war, but I can never get used to the horrible smoke of powder; it smells of the devil, sulphur and saltpeter, and it makes people evil as if it rose from hell to mock the thunder of heaven; but it brings only showers of blood and tears instead of blessed rain for the crops of the field!

Typical of most of the exposition and preparation, the passage not only tells us what has happened but prepares us for what is to come. It illustrates very well Strindberg's skill in presenting necessary explanation and foreshadowing naturally and economically.

A sort of exposition and preparatory passage of great length, which can be found only rarely in Strindberg's other historical plays, occurs frequently in *Gustav Adolf*. Note the lengthy discussions of religious and other questions by the quartermaster and the sergeant major and the discussions by the men about Gustav Adolf of primarily military and political matters and their possible significance. (See pages 77 ff. and 168 ff., by way of illustration.) In a play for the study the leisurely and frequently repetitious discussions—particularly of the religious questions—have some value in clarifying the action and the ideas Strindberg presents, but in a play designed for the stage they have little or no justification.

Dialogue. The dialogue in *Gustav Adolf* is the sort used almost exclusively in all Strindberg's historical plays. In the original, his Swedish is the modern and generally colloquial Swedish of his own day. Aside from an occasional expression, he does not attempt to create a historical atmosphere by means of the archaic Swedish of the seventeenth century; it is instead the living, colloquial language, adapted as far as possible to the personality and mood of each speaker and to the occasion. It is the natural, often haphazard, dialogue of the sort that is discussed in the preface to *Lady Julie.* Note the following excerpt by way of illustration:

> BRAHE: And here is Lützen!
>
> STENBOCK: What do you mean?
>
> BRAHE: This is the place where it will happen! . . . The battle, I mean . . . It's a horrible hole, where the ground is like waves as after an earthquake . . . I wish we were somewhere else.
>
> STENBOCK: What is horrible . . . is this terrible darkness . . . Why, the sun has been up two hours, and it's still dark! It's the last of the plagues of Egypt; the first were the flies and the angel of death at Alte Veste!
>
> BRAHE: So you, too, have thought of that? . . . But it's as if things were bewitched in this darkness and fog that postpone the battle! If we could start before Pappenheim gets here from Halle, the game would be ours . . . Did you see the king?
>
> STENBOCK: Yes, I saw him. He had slept in his carriage for a couple of hours. But it wasn't any fun to look at him. The bullet from Dirschau was moving, and he was freezing so that he shook. Ugh, this fog! And it smells like lye. Have you noticed that?
>
> BRAHE: Like salted cod, I think! (*Pause*)
>
> (*They go up to the fire to warm their hands.*)
>
> BRAHE: What are you thinking about?

STENBOCK: And you?

BRAHE: I'm not happy.

STENBOCK: It does look a little difficult.

BRAHE: If Duke Bernhard is to form the left wing with nothing but Germans, and I'm to command the center . . . then I don't feel as confident as I'd like to feel . . .

STENBOCK: That may be, but you'll have the king to your right and, with him, me, Axelsson, Sack, Soop, and Stålhandske . . . It will go well, you'll see . . . oh, yes . . . and we'll all get together tonight in Auerbachshof . . . I hope the host has his *boniments* about Luther's cask of five thousand tankards, or whatever it was . . . and . . .

BRAHE (*listening*): What's that?

STENBOCK: Your . . . anxiety!

BRAHE: Perhaps!

STENBOCK: Nils!

BRAHE: Fredrik! What was that?

STENBOCK: Listen, my friend, you're making me anxious!

BRAHE (*abruptly*): Can one depend on Kniphausen?

STENBOCK: Absolutely!

BRAHE (*paces the floor*): Four, five, six . . . Six! (*Speculates*)

STENBOCK: What is it?

BRAHE: Nothing, nothing! Imagine, I can hear my watch ticking inside my coat!

STENBOCK (*puts his arm about* BRAHE's *shoulder*): Is it your heart?

BRAHE: Well-l. I just happened to think about Margaretha . . . and little Elsa whom I haven't seen yet.

STENBOCK (*brusquely*): You have the right to have one thought only today! One! (*Slaps him on the shoulder*) Chin up, Nils, or we're marked by death!

Strindberg's dialogue is as naturalistic as possible in a play. The haphazard, wandering, fragmentary, repetitious qualities of normal or real conversation dominate the dialogue so effectively that a reader might easily fail to grasp the careful art behind it.

Characterization. The preface to *Lady Julie,* various comments in *Open Letters to the Intimate Theater (Öppna brev till Intima tea-*

tern), and Strindberg's own accounts of his Inferno experiences are all useful to an understanding of his intentions in characterization in *Gustav Adolf*. The first two emphasize Strindberg's conviction that simple central characters are usually, if not always, unrealistic because of the very "fertility of soul-complex." For Strindberg, human beings like Gustav Adolf are both highly complex and dynamic; they are what Strindberg calls "characterless characters," i.e., human beings who have not ceased to grow and who are so complex that they are "hard to catch, to classify, and to keep track of." The accounts of his Inferno experiences and the *Open Letters to the Intimate Theater* contribute a conviction not mentioned in the preface (Strindberg was a declared naturalist in 1888). This is the conviction that not only does the Eternal One exist but that He is so concerned about His creatures that, like Jehovah of the Old Testament, He watches over them, disciplines them, directs them, and even calls upon the ones He has chosen for special tasks to sacrifice themselves for the accomplishment of those tasks. The combination of Strindberg's ideas about characterization in the late 1880's —the interpretation of dynamic and complex central characters in terms of environment and heredity—and the ideas about the two-sided relationship between God and the individual acquired in the 1890's is the key to the characterization in *Gustav Adolf*.

Strindberg, furthermore, distinguishes between the so-far-as-possible well-rounded characterization of the central character and the somewhat less complete individualization of secondary characters: they are characterized as fully as is necessary to the understanding of the play and of the central character. Furthermore, in *Gustav Adolf*, there are minor characters who are not individualized but are shown only in the static role of their work (e.g., Pastor Fabricius) or their conventional role in history (e.g., Torsten Stålhandske).

In the following sections, I shall discuss Strindberg's applications of these ideas to Gustav Adolf as the central character, to representative secondary characters, and to certain minor characters.

IV: STRINDBERG'S GUSTAV ADOLF

The blond man with the gentle spirit, who always had a joke on
hand even in dark moments, very much a statesman and a little of
the musketeer, the dreamer about a universal kingdom, our "Henri
Quatre" who likes beautiful women as much as a good battle, half
Swedish and half German, with a mother from Holstein and a
wife from Brandenburg, related to Pfalz, Prussia, Hesse, Poland,
Hungary, Bohemia, and even Austria, sufficiently sinful to be a
human being, who has inner conflicts that make a drama rich and
interesting. Supplied by Cardinal Richelieu with 400,000 a year on
condition that he would not disturb the Catholic League, he partici-
pates for [over] two years in the Thirty Years' War against the
House of Hapsburg and involves himself—as a dramatic character,
that is—in unsolvable difficulties since it is a matter of distinguish-
ing friend from enemy, and only his death on the battlefield can
restore the harmony and cut the tangled threads.[12]

Strindberg's Gustav Adolf is not a character fixed and firm
early in maturity but a highly dynamic being, rich in his variety,
constantly changing, not always predictable, and frequently difficult to catch and to analyze. A characterless character—i.e., a
highly complex and humanly dynamic one—Gustav Adolf is revealed, as realistic characters in a play must be, through what he
does and says and through what others say about him and do because of him. Strindberg's interpretation is presented, as he says in
the preface to *Lady Julie*, through the use of "material which is
. . . worked up, admitted, repeated, developed and built up, like
the theme in a musical composition." There is one difference in
emphasis: Strindberg in 1899–1900 saw Gustav Adolf's participation
in the Thirty Years' War as a pilgrimage. In other words, Strindberg emphasizes the inner development of the king from the time
of his arrival in Germany to his death at Lützen in order to show
how Gustav Adolf, as a man chosen of God for the performance of

[12] *Ibid.*

a great task under adverse circumstances, became a heroic man of tolerance.

By means of exposition and demonstration, Strindberg makes it clear that "the blond man with the gentle spirit" is a person with a charming and winning personality. His good nature, kind-heartedness, thoughtfulness, consideration for others, sense of humor, quick temper, and other personal qualities are quickly apparent after his men start talking about him and certainly after he makes his first appearance. The qualities as reflected in his actions are, as Strindberg says, "repeated, developed and built up."

Strindberg also shows Gustav Adolf in various roles, among them those of the brilliant military leader capable of inspiring his staff and of disciplining the men in his service, the gifted statesman, the husband of a beautiful but not highly endowed woman, the father of an illegitimate son and a legitimate daughter, and the conqueror and military ruler of an occupied territory who must deal with natives that are not always friendly. All these matters are important; together they give a sort of realistic case report on an intensely interesting human being. With the information supplied in one way or another, this report explains in naturalistic terms why Gustav Adolf has become a Lutheran crusader with a deep sense of inherited blood guilt and the resultant need for atoning for the sins of his father.

When Strindberg wrote of "inner conflicts that make a drama rich and interesting," he had in mind the inner conflicts that torture Gustav Adolf as he progresses from intolerance of non-Protestants upon his arrival in Germany to full religious tolerance, on the one hand, and his inner conflicts in terms of his own struggle with the Eternal One, on the other. The keys to Strindberg's characterization are therefore to be found primarily in (1) Gustav Adolf's relationships with Erik Rålamb, the young idealist who serves as the guardian of the king's conscience and in whom he confides his thoughts and fears; and with the brilliant Swedish staff members as he "involves himself . . . in unsolvable difficulties," and

(2) his isolation. The relationships change and the isolation increases as Gustav Adolf makes his pilgrimage and reaches the point where "only his death on the battlefield can restore the harmony and cut the tangled threads."

At the start of the pilgrimage Gustav Adolf is very much in rapport with both Rålamb and the great commanders. What these men who know him best think of him, Strindberg demonstrates quickly. Brahe speaks of "the king's happy self-confidence and firm faith"; Horn, reminded by Torstensson of the many unfavorable aspects of the situation, says simply, "Don't worry! When the king comes, he'll blow on the skein, so that it can be wound up! Where we see absolute darkness, he'll see pure light, for he brings light with him and is born of light!" Rålamb adds, "I always think of the sun or of gold when I see my hero approach." Against such a background of faith and confidence, the king makes his first appearance, expresses his delight over their successful landing, but admits, "I'm afraid, afraid as always in good fortune that it won't last long." This foreshadowing of difficulties which the optimistic Lutheran leader vaguely senses, linked with earlier information that he has started out on his crusade without adequate resources in supplies, finances, and manpower, is supplemented toward the end of Act I when, after having reported to and consulted with his staff, he confides to Rålamb: "May He see in my heart that my love for my fellow-believers is as boundless as my hate for the papists." He has convictions—he is chosen of God to deliver his fellow Protestants, the task will be simple, the issues are clear. German Protestants will rush to his assistance, and he will know his enemies without difficulty. Naive as some of these convictions are, Gustav Adolf faces his first real test on German soil when he does not smell the miller's Catholic wife within gunshot and finds her handshake as warm as that of any Protestant. Presented in the unhappy environment in which he will have his pilgrimage, Strindberg's Gustav Adolf is interesting because of what he is and interesting because of what he can become.

In Act II, Gustav Adolf wins victories but has to face difficulties, temptations, and revision of his thinking about his crusade, the religious faiths, the significance of the whole war, and himself. His first difficulty stems directly from his naive assumption that the Lord would provide and that therefore he did not need to prepare adequately in advance for feeding and quartering his troops. He compromises out of necessity by exacting a war levy from the people of Stettin even though he has promised to protect the Germans' property rights. Confronted with his first real temptation—the offer of a subsidy from Catholic France—he rejects it with the assertion that the Swedes would sooner eat bark off the trees than accept money from the hated papists. Yet his attitude toward the non-Protestants broadens to the point where he insists that they, too, are people.

The imperial thought—Wallenstein's thought of unifying all Germany under one temporal ruler—is the second really serious temptation and the most important one for the Gustav Adolf who struggles with the Eternal One. The effects of this thought—the temptation to attain temporal power for himself—do not become evident in this act, however.

The relations between Gustav Adolf and his Swedish commanders are still excellent. Strindberg develops his characterization of the king by presenting what they think about him and what they are willing to do for him. To them he is God's fair-haired boy, the chosen of the Lord, the man selected to accomplish great deeds. They admire him, respect him, believe in him and his cause, but at the same time they know that he is humanly fallible:

> HORN (*to* BANÉR): Why did he send for the pastor?
>
> TORSTENSSON: Why, he always does when he intends to commit a wrong.
>
> BANÉR: He's like a lovable child or a beautiful woman; everything is becoming to him, even his less attractive deeds.
>
> HORN: That's why he has been called . . .

TORSTENSSON: Even to sin, for without sin he would become self-righteous . . .

BANÉR: I think a little sin is very becoming to him; otherwise, he'd not be human . . . he'd be too great and superhuman.

HORN (*listening to what is happening outside*): This won't end well, though.

BANÉR: Everything ends well for God's fair-haired boy.

TORSTENSSON: And it'll end with his taking the French money, too!

They respect him for his basic integrity; they admire him for his capacity for leadership and action; they like him for his kindness and friendliness, for his thoughtfulness and consideration, for his ability to joke and his optimism, and for his human weaknesses.

When the king is forced by his lack of money and the soldiers' insistence on getting paid to accept a subsidy from Catholic France, the commanders see the necessity for the action but insist that the king must be spared from the humiliating negotiations:

KING: . . . So I'll go to the French ambassador now!

BANÉR (*stations himself before the door*): No! Not the king! Our king shall be as pure as the flag we follow! Gustav Horn, show us that you can wear a dirty shirt for your king . . .

HORN (*gets up*): Well said, Banér; let us touch the dirt, but not he! To the French ambassador, then! We already have the authority!

KING (*childishly happy as if he had got out of something unpleasant*): Thank you, my friends! It takes greater courage to do an evil deed than to capture a fortress! (*When* BRAHE, *too, wants to leave*) No, Nils, not you! Not you!

(HORN *and* BANÉR *leave.*)

KING (*sinks down on a chair*): That was where I did not want to go. Thy will be done, O Lord!

Yet when the king rationalizes about his keeping Spandau and Küstrin after the disastrous fall of Magdeburg, and thus fails to keep his promise, both Horn and Banér refuse to accept his decision. There is a great deal of the musketeer in his commanders, who speak of his "bright, easy nature that usually follows his clear conscience" and his "divine lightheartedness" and who try to protect him from committing avoidable error. They are self-respecting men as well; while they believe in him and his "call" to save a cause, they also see in him a human being, weak and sinful and not too different from themselves.

Gustav Adolf faces other highly disturbing difficulties. His German fellow believers have not seen the issue as clearly as he has; his Swedish soldiers conduct themselves no better than others except when they have to; instead of making the best of it and putting up with privations as he does, they insist on getting their pay and being fed; the German Protestants are so sharply and bitterly divided that they prefer Catholicism to each other's faith. In fact, the whole political and religious picture in Germany is confused.

With the firm belief that he is one of the chosen, "an anointed of the Lord" selected for a very special but limited task, he reluctantly signs the agreement with France, providing him with money but threatening to change the whole nature of the war from a crusade to gain for his fellow believers security to worship God in their own fashion to a war of a purely political kind. He has a feeling that the God of Hosts may be forcing him to walk a path that he himself had not planned to walk.

He tends to rationalize actions of which he does not inwardly approve; he refuses to acknowledge to himself that he is rationalizing; he childishly feels relieved in not having to negotiate with the French directly; he is distressed when he discovers that his Swedish soldiers could turn even temporarily against him; he sends Rålamb, the guardian of his conscience, away when he does not want to face the truth completely; he summons Pastor Fabricius when he contemplates an action that does not measure up to his ideals; he avoids reading the agreement with France; he has an impulse to compromise with the Jews about their religious services when he needs money; and he feels acutely the need for admiration and approval.

These reactions are all illustrative of very human facets of the highly complex character who is at the same time an idealistic dreamer and a man of action. He has not given up his goal, however; he has implemented his articles of war; he is able to learn quickly and, after inner conflict, to change his mind; he has no illusions about the nature of war or of its effects on human beings; he admires good fighters, gentleness, wisdom, and agreeableness; he understands people and has sympathy for them; he is no out-and-out egotist; and he is confronted with an idea basic to religious tolerance—the Eternal God does not seem to love the one child more than the other.

Against a background of increasingly difficult and complex factors, the further revelation and development of Gustav Adolf's character take place in Act III. In scene 1, Strindberg makes it abundantly clear that the situation in the Swedish camp has not become easier: there are ever greater losses in manpower, gradual increase in corruption, and pathetically bad conditions for the women camp followers and their numerous children born in want and privation and reared under most unfortunate circumstances. Strict rules designed to keep his camp thoroughly Lutheran and Protestant in spirit—as originally planned—have given way to the toleration of Mohammedans, gypsies, and Catholics as well within the Swedish area. The strife between the Calvinists and the Lutherans becomes more bitter. The political alliances with German princes, both Lutheran and Calvinist by faith, have proved empty: the allies are little men, envious and jealous of each other as well as guilty of duplicity to and lack of cooperation with the man who has come to Germany to secure their religious freedom.

Erik Rålamb has had an exalted notion of Gustav Adolf and his cause; to Rålamb, Gustav Adolf has been a well-nigh superhuman being fighting the good and pure fight for a great cause. After the great and crucial victory at Breitenfeld, Rålamb denounces him:

> King of Babylon! . . . "Art thou also become weak as we? Art thou become like unto us? Thy pomp is brought down to the

grave, and the noise of thy viols: the worm is spread under thee, and the worms cover thee . . . How art thou fallen from heaven, O Lucifer, son of the morning! how art thou cut down to the ground, which didst weaken the nations!"

It is after this denunciation of his pride, arrogance, and selfish ambition that Gustav Adolf dismisses Rålamb, who has been the guardian of his conscience.

To clarify the changes in Gustav Adolf's actions and thinking, Strindberg has three of the great commanders consider the victory and what is likely to follow it:

> BANÉR: The goal is won; North Germany and the shores of the Baltic have been cleared of the emperor's forces, of Italians and Spaniards; the north has driven the south back within its borders, and the balance has been restored. After a victory like this, what usually follows? Gustav?
>
> HORN: Peace!
>
> BANÉR: Lennart?
>
> TORSTENSSON: Peace!
>
> BANÉR: Johan? Peace! And if peace doesn't follow now? What can we justifiably call the victor then? Johan? A lover of fighting and honor, who likes war for its own sake, perhaps for the sake of booty, and above all for personal reasons.
>
> TORSTENSSON: Don't talk like that; the king might hear us!
>
> BANÉR: No, he has quit listening to us . . . ever since his wife came. And the lady of the house doesn't like us. It seems to me our best days are over, and what's coming is merely dull! Think of it . . . on this day of victory and success I look back with sorrow on the time of want and adversity, the time of young enthusiasm, when we came like tramps but were filled with courage and hope and faith.
>
> TORSTENSSON: You're right, Johan; most people can take adversity, but no one can take success!

The crusader who came to serve a great cause and to attain definite but limited goals has changed. The goals of protecting the interests of Sweden in the north and of gaining security for his fellow believers in Germany have been secured, but the king who "looks ten years older today" is dreaming about further exploits, perhaps, as Banér suggests, because of love of "war, for the sake of booty, and above all for personal reasons." The king has turned away from the old advisers who served him well when he moved their hearts and minds to support him and his original objectives, and has turned to new advisers who will serve his less unselfish goal, merely hinted at, the selfish and arrogant realization of Wallenstein's great idea. Gustav Adolf has set out to serve not as the willing and obedient servant of the Eternal One but as the servant of his own ambitions to solve for his own glory and power the difficult and complex political and religious problems facing the Germans. But only the chosen one who bends in humility before the Eternal One can realize his objectives; he who in arrogance and pride takes things into his own hands will be disciplined by the Eternal One and forced back into the path He had chosen for him. As Rålamb says, "The man who wants to take the rudder out of the hands of Providence runs into the shallows."

In Act IV the characterization of the king is further developed by a consideration of his plans and his attempts at realizing them. These have changed so much that Gustav Adolf has dreamed of becoming the emperor of a vast area in which he would wield the power over a united Germany as well as over an expanded Sweden, so that he would have become not only the political arbiter of Europe but also the guarantor of religious and racial tolerance:

> OXENSTJERNA: Heraldry is a fine art, but government is a science! (*Gets up*) My king, permit an old friend . . .
>
> KING: . . . to block my plans? No! No one may, not even an Oxenstjerna!
>
> OXENSTJERNA (*sits down again*): So it's true that success has so intoxicated our king that he's begun to dream he'll be a second Alexander the Great?
>
> KING (*violently*): Chancellor, no more!

OXENSTJERNA: King, no more . . . Stop here! and turn back to the
    little country where God placed your cradle.

KING: It's too limited for me!

OXENSTJERNA: Is it too limited . . . our large country, whose borders
    and extent no one yet knows, where there is one man per square
    mile who longs for neighbors? Our forefathers, the Goths and
    the Northmen, emigrated because they found it too limited, but
    they were soon crushed by the streams of emigrants, were swal-
    lowed up, and didn't leave a trace after them! No, our land is
    big enough for the one who has a mind and spirit great enough
    to fill the empty expanses, and with great thoughts to populate
    the empty wilderness!

By way of commentary on the way in which victories have affected
Gustav Adolf and his Swedes, Marcus says: "The stay on these
vine-clad hills has done the Swedes no good! The sleep of victory
and drunkenness! Ring the dinner bell; then they'll come! . . . It's
going downhill, Your Majesty! Downhill!"

The king's inner conflicts concerning the expanding dream as opposed to his relatively clear-cut original ideals are clarified along
with the explanation of the growth of his understanding and thinking about the war. He says after he has been wounded at Ingolstadt:

No, Johan, I can't joke any more, for I have walked through the
valley of death. I thought when Tilly fell that he alone was in our
Lord's disfavor, and that I was the chosen one, but then I had to
learn better. My time has not yet come, but I'm grateful for the
warning.

And, a moment later, when Gustav Horn, the king's *"best"* man,"
has said that he has not always understood the king's plans and
objectives, the king bursts out vehemently:

My plans, *my* objectives, which haven't been mine and which I'm
just beginning to understand . . . as I understand that I have been
only a blind subordinate of the Lord, whose plans we are never
permitted to understand!

Gustav Adolf, the chosen one, was being led by the Lord of Hosts along a pathway he himself had not chosen, encouraged on occasion, and struck and disciplined whenever he became proud or arrogant or self-sufficient.

"Unmerciful to law breakers and desecrators," Gustav Adolf has come far, however, from the narrow orthodox Lutheranism and anti-Catholicism of his earlier days. He has learned that "there are many mansions in the kingdom of the Lord. And for everyone his own!" In his analysis of the war directed at the Calvinist Fredrik of Pfalz, the one who "could light the fire," the man who has to extinguish the fire explains:

> You were once king of Bohemia, and you misused your royal power to plunder the churches and to oppress the Catholics, but your intolerance forced you into cruelty against Protestant sects other than your own! To me, you have never been a martyr, and your exile, your sufferings I have always considered the clear results of your acts. This whole terrible war, this irreconcilability, this beastly hatred which we ascribe to the enemy really stem from you.

From having been a hater of Jews and Catholics, Gustav Adolf has developed into the champion of tolerance—religious and racial:

> I have finally heard the defendant, something I ought to have started with; and I have learned something! Out of those unsolvable contradictions in which I had been caught at the beginning of this war, I have finally worked my way; I have found myself and my task, which I didn't understand until now. This has restored my strength of decision and courage of action . . . From now on it will be the deliverer against the oppressor!

Nevertheless, the hero who has learned that his task is not "to collect a wagonload of crowns" but to gain security for his own land and for northern Germany against oppression of every kind is not a happy man. He is a human being beset by worries and inner turmoil that go beyond the present and its problems, back into the dark and shadowy past and into the uncertain future. He is distressed about the possible significance of the Pfalz family to the future of Sweden and that of his daughter Christina; he is concerned about the long and bloody struggle between his Vasa dynasty and the rival Sture family, and the blood guilt he has inherited from his father Charles the Bloody; he feels that he is a usurper on the Swedish throne; he is distressed over the gradual dispersal of his Swedish staff of friends and kinsmen; and he senses his impending death so keenly that he must set his house in order.

The final act makes unmistakably clear Strindberg's interpretation of Gustav Adolf. In scene 1 appears a Gustav Adolf who has well-nigh reached the end of his pilgrimage. Smitten by the Eternal One with one Job-like trial after the other, Gustav Adolf still refuses to bend in humility and give up completely his arrogant dream of the imperial crown or, as Fredrik Stenbock puts it, of "a wagonload of crowns." He is still afflicted with the very human desire for power, position, and honors. The Lord of Hosts chastens him by placing his enemy Wallenstein in a position of vantage; disease and vermin strike down twelve thousand of his men and thousands of his horses; his Swedish camp that he had tried to make a model has sunk to the level of his enemies:

> QUARTERMASTER: I'm ashamed . . . because we've become a disgrace to Sweden, because from having been the soldiers of the Lord in discipline and honor we've become as bad as our enemies. All vices, all crimes flourish in our camps, and we have just as many pagans as Christians, but we have still more corpses than we have living men. The whole country about us stinks, and our friends curse us!

Ever shorter of supplies, the soldiers and their following of women and children are starving; the sick and the wounded are without medical care and medicine; corruption flourishes. As Nils Brahe phrases it, "I don't believe human beings are born any more, only wild animals." To make the situation even worse, the great commander Torstensson is captured by the enemy; the brilliant Johan Banér is wounded; the king has become isolated.

In two conversations—the one between Marcus the Jew and the king and the other between the king and Fredrik Stenbock—Gustav Adolf is forced in what is a turning point in his career as a chosen one to face the truth. The Jew speaks like an Old Testament prophet when he explains that Gustav Adolf is no longer engaged in a war against oppression, that the only justifiable thing he can do is to conclude an honorable peace, and that "what has been was great and splendid; what is coming. . . ." When the isolated Gustav Adolf again turns to one of his Swedish commanders, Fredrik Stenbock, he boasts a little about the crowns he might have had, but he admits that he is tortured by evil dreams. His error has been made plain to him; he knows that the Lord of Hosts has turned away from him:

> KING: Command me, then, and I will obey! For two months I've been here as if bewitched, unable to move. I want to get away, but I can't! It's as if Wallenstein were a sorcerer—who can silence swords and people and people's will power. I don't possess myself; I can't control myself. You know, the worst . . . God, whom I used to reach in prayer, has turned His back to me, and I cannot find Him any more!
>
> STENBOCK: Really? Turn home to your tabernacles, Israel, for you have gone astray!
>
> KING: That's what Oxenstjerna, too, said in Mainz! Well then, I will go home to my fatherland, to my lakes and forests, to my child . . .
>
> STENBOCK: Fine! If only the road to Leipzig is open . . .

The Lord of Hosts is not yet done with disciplining His favorite; the chosen one who could have made a peace after Breitenfeld that would have secured his initial goals must be further chastened.

In scene 3 the king is farthest down emotionally and mentally. Handicapped by the fog, the cold, wet, shivering king sees and understands the restlessness and uneasiness of Brahe and Stenbock and forces himself to appear cheerful and confident. The effort is supreme; the results, incomplete:

> KING: Well, shall we have supper in Leipzig today? . . . and dinner in Wittenberg tomorrow? It will be fun to see Wittenberg! No, this is terrible! The sun is gone, and the great darkness has come!
> (SMITH *comes up, falls to his knees, and kisses the* KING's *foot.*)
> KING (*gets up, furious*): Get up, man, or I'll strike you!
> SMITH (*to the others*): He is a martyr and a saint!
> KING: Saint? I thought only Catholics believed in saints! I'm a poor, miserable sinner, I'll have you know!

Without the protection of armor (the bullet of Dirschau is giving him pain) and in anguish, after having bowed completely in humility before the Lord of Hosts, the king goes into his last battle.

The final scene—in sharp contrast to the preceding ones—presents the final estimate of Gustav Adolf:

> QUARTERMASTER: Think of it, I can hardly feel the sorrow; for me, this act is the most beautiful and the most worthy celebration of victory, for the hero has given himself as the sacrifice of thanksgiving to the God of Hosts.

In winning his great victory at Lützen, Gustav Adolf ironically loses his life when he wins everything he had set out to win for his fellow believers and for his country—an application of the Biblical admonition that he who would gain his life shall lose it. In everyday human terms, the expiation through death of Gustav Adolf's personal sins of pride, arrogance, and selfish ambition, and of his inherited guilt is tragedy; in the religious sense, victory.

In Gustav Adolf, Strindberg has created a memorable "characterless character," the figure of a great but human hero, dynamic and complex. Part of the explanation of Strindberg's success certainly lies in his understanding of the historical Gustav Adolf; as much lies in his life-giving use of the results of his own personal spiritual and religious experiences from the middle 1890's.

V: THE SECONDARY CHARACTERS

Of the more than sixty characters in the play, over twenty are secondary characters, i.e., characters whose roles are important enough to receive sufficient interpretation to make them come alive. Queen Maria Eleanora, Gustav Horn, Johan Banér, Åke Tott, Lennart Torstensson, Fredrik Stenbock, Nils Brahe, Erik Rålamb, the Lutheran miller, his Catholic wife, the bailiff, the sergeant major, the quartermaster, the provost, the schoolmaster, Marcus the Jew, Rudolf, the cooper and the members of his family, Gustav Gustavsson, the trumpeter Nils, Fredrik of Pfalz, and Leubelfing are all individualized sufficiently to make them stand out as individuals who affect the characterization of Gustav Adolf or the dramatic action. The consideration of what Strindberg has done with Erik Rålamb, Johan Banér, and Nils the trumpeter, three representative secondary characters, will show what his technique is.

Erik Rålamb and the Swedish commanders are the phalanx of Swedes the king keeps close to him, partly because he wants to atone for what his father had done to them and theirs, partly because he likes them very much as the attractive human beings they are, but primarily because he knows that each of them has a great deal to give him in the achievement of his goals. In his happier moments, the king can give his warm appreciation and understanding to these men who dare to speak their minds to a king whom they either love or admire but whom they consider not too far above them; in his unhappier moments, he can blurt out in his anger, "If I have fostered little kings who think they've outgrown me, my stern father has taught me the cure."

Erik Rålamb, the queen's chamberlain who becomes the king's adviser, the nephew of one of the great nobles executed at the Linköping bloodbath by Gustav Adolf's father, is remarkable proof of Strindberg's insight into the nature not only of mature people but of the very young. For Erik Rålamb, the twenty-year-old, is the very young idealist and perfectionist who can say, "I always think of the sun and of gold when I see my hero approach . . . and the day I find a spot on his pure, warm soul, I'll no longer believe in what is good." Rålamb is devoted both to the queen, whom he loves for her beauty and her charm, and to the king, whom he considers the incarnation of the heroic and the good. The king understands him and appreciates him as "a dreamer, knight of virtue and honor"; Rålamb serves as the defender of the king against criticism, as his confidant, as the guardian of the king's conscience by holding up the vision of the ideal before the king and rebuking and denouncing him as only the very young can on the occasions of departure from the ideal. The king says:

> Well, I sent him away so I could talk and act freely. That youngster has won my heart so fully that he looks after my conscience like a jealous woman. There are moments when I'm afraid of him! . . . He actually tyrannizes over me . . . that's how it is; why I don't know, but that's how it is!

Erik Rålamb is not merely a young idealist who smacks a great deal of the self-righteous, moral prig. His very human infatuation with the beautiful Maria Eleonora, his serving as confidant to her, his knightly protectiveness toward Luise, his jealousy of both the king and the queen, his exchange with Åke Tott, and his treatment of Gustav Gustavsson testify to other human qualities as well. The youngster who had inscribed on a funeral wreath, "A foolish young man, Erik Rålamb, who kneels at his fatherly friend's bier and with tears of humiliation begs for forgiveness for his lack of understanding," is a far more complex character than a cursory reading would indicate. The final comments on him show us what Strindberg thought young Rålamb was:

> FABRICIUS: Erik Rålamb! The youngster with the great heart and the hot blood!
> GRUBBE: In a word, the youngster with the high standard for low things!

FABRICIUS: With fresh memories from the heavenly home of man that make him dissatisfied with old people's feeble attempts to establish heaven on earth.

The man among those closest to the king who receives the fullest characterization is Johan Banér, kinsman of Gustav Adolf and the son of one of the men executed by Gustav Adolf's father, Charles IX:

SERGEANT MAJOR: Johan Banér!
FINNISH ENSIGN: Surely that's the king?
SERGEANT MAJOR: No, but he looks a lot like him. The son of Kristina Sture and Gustav Banér, who was beheaded at the bloodbath of Linköping.

In Act I, it is Johan Banér who knows how to control Åke Tott; in Act II, it is Johan Banér who is reprimanded by Gustav Adolf:

Yes, Johan, you're a fighter, not least in drinking bouts . . . but learn a little gentleness from Lennart, and I'll like you better . . . And a little wisdom from Gustav Horn . . . A little agreeableness from Nils Brahe.

By means of little actions and speeches, Strindberg succeeds in making Johan Banér come alive as a noisy, frank, open general who likes his bottle and who has little use for the amenities of a court; an officer who understands both the king and his deeds; the bravest of the brave on the field of battle but a little unversed in the art of approaching the members of the fair sex; a man of action and a man with a keen mind. It is Johan Banér who says: "No! Not the king! Our king shall be as pure as the flag we follow! Gustav Horn, show us that you can wear a dirty shirt for your king. . . ."

Not only does he know his military science—both theoretical and practical—but he understands the people about him and the implications of what is happening to them. He approves of religious tolerance, and he has no use for the nicer, finer distinctions between the various sects ("I suspect they're lying, both of them. I'm a syncretist, as you probably know!"); he has no hesitation about pointing out the king's errors bluntly ("A king believes only what he wants to!"); he can analyze correctly and come to logical conclusions that may not tally with what are supposed to be the "correct" analysis and the "correct" conclusions:

> The French alliance is our king's greatest act as a statesman, because he then quit being a narrow-minded general for one sect and became a statesman who is a credit to his teachers, Hugo Grotius and Petrus Ramus. But he should make peace now! That's to say: I don't personally have anything against war, but I hear something in one ear which tells me: So far, but no farther! Now I have to have a drink! . . . Yes, the devil take Luther and the pope and Calvin and all the other wranglers; I'm a Christian and would preferably be a syncretist if I should be anything. A syncretist is one of those who think it's all one, if you can only say the Lord's prayer with a fairly clear conscience . . . I said fairly, Lennart, and you're not to quibble about my words.

It is Johan Banér who understands Maria Eleonora and her daughter Christina (he likes neither of them); it is Banér who understands that Brandenburg will reap what Sweden has sown. Tall, blond, and handsome, Johan Banér resembles the king physically, but, unlike the king, he is the rough-hewn soldier who rejects the amenities of social life. Nevertheless, as Strindberg makes clear again and again, Johan Banér is "our dear old Johan" as well as the loquacious genius and the rough-and-ready soldier.

One of the most moving characterizations is that of Nils the trumpeter. Strindberg effectively introduces the ten-year-old:

> SERGEANT MAJOR: Well, gosling, you'll stay where you're put, eh?
> TRUMPETER: Yes, of course!
> SERGEANT MAJOR: How old are you, Nils?
> TRUMPETER: Ten, going on eleven!
> SERGEANT MAJOR: You're half dry, as we say in Borås! Do you know what that means?

TRUMPETER (*impudently*): Yes, but, if anybody but you had dared to say it, I'd have let him have it!

SERGEANT MAJOR: Fine! Put the trumpet away; put the badge on your arm! Then you're in the army! (*Puts a yellow badge on the boy's right arm*) Now, boys, you're to go, but give your Nils a cheer first!

BOYS: Hurrah! . . .

SCHOOLMASTER (*to Nils*): Say good-bye nicely to your comrades now!

TRUMPETER (*swaggers a little*): So long, kids!

SCHOOLMASTER: That wasn't nice! Not nice at all! . . .

SERGEANT MAJOR: That's right, maybe, but it was very human, above all very boyish. March, old man!

And a little later: "Go up there to the cannons and be quiet. Don't forget that you're an important man and that Europe's waiting for you!"

Strindberg has very nicely caught the boyish qualities of Nils in his brief appearance in the Auerbachshof scene. It can be safely said, moreover, that in Swedish literature, which has many oustanding interpretations of children, none of them surpasses scene 2 in Act V, the scene in which the trumpeter dies comforted only by the aristocratic young page and the king. The youngster who says, "I was born on a drum in Livonia, I have been cradled on a transportation wagon though Poland, and finally got under the schoolmaster's cane in—let me see—Brandenburg" has no parents and has never seen his country. He knows some of the legends and superstitions of Sweden, he has heard about the great blue lake called Väner and the mountain that resembles a church roof; he has never been given affection. Proud of his trumpet, he admits, "It isn't fun any more to be in a war"; he wants to go home. The touching exchange between the two youngsters is only one of the many little techniques by which Strindberg makes Nils come alive:

LEUBELFING: Boy!

TRUMPETER: Do you think I'm dying?

LEUBELFING: Are you afraid to die?
TRUMPETER: No, why should I be? I haven't done anything wrong!
LEUBELFING (*puts his hand on the boy's forehead*): You, boy!
TRUMPETER: Do you think I'm going to die?
LEUBELFING (*weeps*): Yes, I do.
TRUMPETER: Don't cry . . . I'll manage! (*Falls asleep*)

Along with the portrait of Gustav Adolf, the portrayals of all these secondary characters are proof of Strindberg's genius for convincingly individualizing characters of both sexes, young and old, of all classes and ranks, and of various nationalities and races. That is indeed a noteworthy achievement.

VI: MINOR CHARACTERS

The great majority of characters are, of course, minor or incidental. Distinction can be made between the silent characters such as Erik Soop, Torsten Stålhandske, Karl Hård, and Axel Lillie and speaking characters such as Fabricius, Grubbe, the bailiff's assistants, the Danish ensign, the soldiers' wives, Hrasan, the schoolboys, the gravediggers, the book printer, the sculptor, the painter, the cantor, the smith, the rat catcher, the farmer, and his wife. The silent Swedish heroes merely appear as part of the historical background. The others mentioned, however, do speak and do affect the action of the play or the characterization of more important figures. Fabricius, for example, appears only in his role as Gustav Adolf's personal chaplain and spiritual adviser; Strindberg makes no attempt to characterize him as a person. The Afghan Mohammedans, to cite another example, are static figures that help illustrate the point that the great monotheistic religions agree in their fundamenal doctrine of a God who is the father of all mankind. All of these minor and incidental characters are at best types.

VII: THE PLAY FOR THE STUDY VS. THE DRAMA OF CHARACTER

As a play for serious consideration in the study, *Gustav Adolf* is undoubtedly an impressive fulfillment of Strindberg's intentions in writing his *Nathan the Wise*. Strindberg succeeds in his interpretation of the Thirty Years' War, in presenting clearly his ideas about war and peace as well as intolerance and tolerance, and in giving us a gallery of interesting character portrayals, above all, a convincing one of Gustav Adolf himself. As Gunnar Ollén aptly says in his *Strindbergs dramatik* (Stockholm, 1949), "When a person has once read or seen the play, it is that [work] which illustrates the Thirty Years' War in his memory" (p. 309). The play is, moreover, an important document for anyone who wants to understand Strindberg's thinking during the crucial years at the turn of the century.

But *Gustav Adolf* is, theatrically considered, an unwieldy play. Seven hours are too long a period for most theatergoers to sit through a stage production even if every one of its elements is thoroughly dramatic. Strindberg undoubtedly knew what he was doing when he wrote his *Nathan the Wise;* he included too many passages that are acceptable and even useful to a reader but that simply will not do in a theater.

Liberal but careful cutting of more or less undramatic and frequently repetitious elements will, I believe, reveal a historical drama of character that not only will go on the stage but will compare favorably with Strindberg's major plays of that kind. Act I might well be left intact, but the following sections could be cut:

Act II, scene 1 (to the king's entrance)

Act III, scene 1; scene 2 (to the entrance of Horn, Banér, and Torstensson)

Act IV, scene 1; scene 2 (to the king's entrance); scene 3 (to the king's entrance); scene 4 (to the king's entrance)

Act V, scene 1 (to the king's entrance).

Further cutting could be done in the king's long speeches on pages 192-197, for example; they are packed with historical details, many of which are dispensable for the stage. If all this were done and what remains of Acts III and IV were united, there would be left a unified and compact historical drama of character eminently suitable for presentation in the theater within the conventional limits of time. Moreover, *Gustav Adolf* could easily be adapted for the movies, for it has everything that would provide a producer with the opportunity to create an excellent historical movie.

Gustav Adolf · A Play in Five Acts

Characters

KING GUSTAV II ADOLF, *36 years old*

QUEEN MARIA ELEONORA, *31, his consort and sister of the elector of Brandenburg*

AXEL OXENSTJERNA, *47, chancellor*

FABRICIUS, *court chaplain*

GRUBBE, *the king's secretary*

GUSTAV HORN, *38, field marshal (cavalry)* *

JOHAN BANÉR, *35, general* *

ÅKE TOTT, *32, major general (cavalry)* *

LENNART TORSTENSSON, *27 (artillery)* *

FREDRIK STENBOCK, *23 (Småland Regiment)* *

NILS BRAHE, *26 (Yellow Brigade)* *

ERIK RÅLAMB, *20, chamberlain*

THE MILLER, *later driver in the baggage train, a Lutheran*

THE MILLER'S WIFE, *later midwife, a Catholic*

THE BAILIFF, *a Jew from Wolgast, later head of the fire brigade*

BAILIFF'S ASSISTANTS

THE SERGEANT MAJOR, *formerly a student at Uppsala, native of Västergötland*

THE QUARTERMASTER, *native of Småland, a Zwinglian*

THE PROVOST, *a gipsy and a pagan*

THE SCHOOLMASTER, *an ex-soldier and a native of Östergötland*

AXEL ERICSSON SPARRE, *a Finnish ensign in the Swedish army and the son of Erik Sparre, who was beheaded during the reign of Charles IX in 1600*

A DANISH ENSIGN

THE COOPER

THE COOPER'S WIFE

LUISE, *their daughter*

RUDOLF, *a student at Wittenberg, her cousin*

* See pp. 232-233.

GOVERNOR OF MECKLENBURG, *a 70-year-old Lutheran, appointed by Wallenstein*

SCHWARZENBERG, *minister in the government of Brandenburg, a Catholic*

MARCUS, *a Jew, the representative of the banker Israel in Hamburg*

GUSTAV GUSTAVSSON, *the son of Gustav Adolf and Margareta Cabeljau, now a student and* rector illustris *at Wittenberg, 15 years old*

HRASAN, *Jews' reader at their divine services*

GEORG WILHELM, *elector of Brandenburg, Gustav Adolf's brother-in-law, a Calvinist*

JOHAN GEORG, *elector of Saxony, Syncretist (supporter of the fusion of all Christian churches)*

GRAVEDIGGER I

GRAVEDIGGER II

NILS, *10, a trumpeter*

FREDRIK V *of Pfalz (the Palatinate), the "Winter King," the former king of Bohemia, whose election to the throne was the most immediate cause of the outbreak of the Thirty Years' War*

THE HOST *in Auerbachshof*

THE BOOK PRINTER *(in Munich)*

THE SCULPTOR

THE PAINTER

THE CANTOR

LEUBELFING

GROOMS ERIKSSON *and* JÖNSSON

THE SMITH

THE SMITH'S BOY

A RATCATCHER

A FARMER

A FARMER'S WIFE

TWO SENTINELS

   Silent characters

ERIK SOOP

TORSTEN STÅLHANDSKE
KARL HÅRD
AXEL LILLIE

Settings (1630–1632)

ACT I: *The shore on Usedom*

ACT II: *A wealthy burgher's home in Stettin; a room in a farm-house; in the camp outside Frankfurt an der Oder; the palace park in Berlin; in the fortress at Spandau*

ACT III: *A churchyard on a hill; in Auerbachshof in Leipzig*

ACT IV: *A pass in Thuringia; the terrace of a palace outside Mainz; the market square in a village near Ingolstadt on the Danube; in Munich*

ACT V: *The camp outside Nuremberg; the same; a shed at Lützen; the castle church at Wittenberg*

ACT I

The shore on Usedom.[1] Sunlight on an ancient oak forest; under the trees, grass and flowers. Through the forest can be seen a strip of the light blue sea. Tower-like clouds in fantastic shapes above.

To the right a cloister in ruins—now a mill. Outside the gate is a long table with benches under white and violet lilacs. Behind the corner of the building can be seen the large water wheel and the milldam with a bridge at the sluice; reeds and yellow waterlilies edge the millrace. The mill is shut down, and only the murmur of the water can be heard. At the middle of the stage is an image of the Madonna under a chapel.

MILLER'S WIFE comes up to the Madonna with a lighted candle, which she places in a tube on the picket fence; crosses herself and then kneels. MILLER comes in; stops still and waits. MILLER'S WIFE rises.

MILLER: I certainly didn't intend to disturb you, dear . . .

MILLER'S WIFE: I know, dear. Even if war has raged during all the years we've been married,[2] we've kept peace in our home—you with your Lutheran beliefs and I with my Catholic faith.

MILLER: Each and every one is saved by his faith—I learned that from my mother . . .

MILLER'S WIFE: That's what many people say, but, when you're pressed for both room and food, it's not too easy to keep peace!

MILLER: Listen—it's midsummer day; the sun is shining, and we

65

should celebrate with our friends. But, of course, there's nothing to put on the table; the mill wheel has stood still for a year for want of something to grind, because where Wallenstein's [3] horses have tramped no seed will grow, and they've tramped for twelve long years; the millrace is choked with weeds, and the only thing we've got out of it is some flowers... Our son's at war, and our daughter ... Well, better to say nothing ...

MILLER'S WIFE: What are you getting at?

MILLER: If I only knew! To get away from this boundless misery!

MILLER'S WIFE: Where in the world would we go? Pomerania is desolated, Mecklenburg laid waste, Brandenburg barren. Where would we go?

MILLER: To war, with the others! Better to plunder than to be plundered!

MILLER'S WIFE: That's not so! Better to eat acorns with the beasts than to steal a steak for oneself—we'll have to take the bad days with the good.

MILLER: Oh, I don't know. How did you take the evil day when the Croatians threw your daughter on horseback and rode away? You took it so hard, you had to be taken to the asylum in Wolgast ... [4]

MILLER'S WIFE: Sh-h! sh-h! The Lord punished me for my sins by making me walk through the valley of death and see what I had never suspected; perhaps it was a consolation, too. I've never been able to remember that horror, quite, or to miss her.

MILLER (*looks toward the back*): I can hear the rustling of the underbrush and the rolling of pebbles (*lies down listening with his ear to the ground*) ... hoofbeats and clashing of weapons ... Evil is at hand, dear! Worse than the year when the Croatians murdered people upstream so that the falls became red, and the big wheel whipped blood as at an autumn slaughter. Do you remember the body that got caught in the paddles and rolled up and down, up and down? I can still see it, and there's still a mark on the shaft from it ... they say that's why the waterlilies are red this year ... and the eels in the pond are fatter than ever, but no one dares to eat them, for they smell like dead men and are blue as the dead. (*Three acorn pickers, emaciated and ragged, enter. They gather acorns under the oaks and put them into bags.*) They're the acorn pickers, the only birds wandering about this year! The starlings have never come; there are no rooks or wild doves on the unsown field, which only bears thistles and thorns; no pike leaps among the reeds, no perch in the stony shallows; the fish in the river and the brook have wandered out to sea, frightened by gunshot and the thunder of cannons. My country! My poor German country! What have we done that we should suffer so?

MILLER'S WIFE: We have sinned!

MILLER: Which we? Why, it hits both the bad and the good, both Lutherans and Catholics, both the emperor's people and the elector's. Tilly quarters and levies contributions even from his own Catholics; and Wallenstein, that horrible Friedlander, plunders his own duchy of Mecklenburg. Why, it's the Babylonian confusion, it's the flood of sin, the last days! (*Pause; he listens.*) See, there: the horseman of the Apocalypse!

(*A Bavarian cavalryman, called a Kronberger, rides into the background from the left; his horse is black, his riding saddle black trimmed with silver; the rider is wearing black armor with a white death's head above the closed helmet; he has a lance with a little white banner. He rides slowly and looks searchingly out to sea; stops in the center of the back stage; opens his visor and again looks at the sea; lets the visor drop and rides out to the right.*)

MILLER (*and his* WIFE *have concealed themselves behind the Madonna*): The forerunner of death? Who's coming now? A Croatian! (*A Croatian comes in from the left; knapsacks, dead geese and chickens, articles of clothing, a basket, etc. hang behind him. He follows the Bavarian and looks straight ahead as he goes. Be-*

hind the Croatian come the acorn pickers, who can be seen picking up something.)

MILLER: See, the crows follow the sower! The sower's the horse— Oh God, to be a horse in these days! (*Beggars and marauders come in, follow the others, silently and stealthily.*)

MILLER: The rear guard—misery, hunger, theft, sin! . . . all the vices! and infamy! Everything for the sake of honor, and of virtue and religion!

(*Two Walloons enter on foot; they climb a hill and stand observing the sea.*)

MILLER: Tilly's [5] Walloons! What are they looking for? Those cloud formations over the sea mean thunder. But those people fear neither the thunder of heaven nor the fires of hell! (*The Walloons hurry out.*)

MILLER's WIFE: Evil is at hand!

MILLER: New evil! Is there any evil that isn't old for us? A new crime, a new vice, it would take a genius to think of a new one.

MILLER's WIFE: Don't blaspheme! You must have noticed that, in the days of good fortune, misfortune stood back of the door; and, in the hour of need, help sat by the fire waiting—(*ecstatically*). Look to the north: those golden clouds do not bring thunder, for behind those clouds the sun shall rise; from the north shall come the unweary Gideon, for the Spirit of the Lord is resting in the northlands!

MILLER: Where did you get that? The northern cuckoo is the cuckoo of sorrow! The Danish Christian IV [6] came tumbling down here from the north, to help us, as they put it, but he was so badly defeated at Lutter by Tserklas Tilly that we've had it seven times worse since.

MILLER's WIFE: Farther to the north! Farther to the north!

MILLER: Up where the Swedes are? People have talked about them, too, since they were down ravaging Polish Prussia, but they stay politely at home . . .

MILLER's WIFE (*looks out to sea; shades her eyes with one hand*):

Believe me! Believe me! I see crosses in the sky, one cross, four crosses, five, eight, nine, more than anyone can count, and they are like yellow rye, and under them I see white sea gulls as big as ships; and the good blond man stands at the prow and lifts his hands in blessing over the water and the lands—I can't tell if he walks on the water, but thousands of people stand on the shores and greet the good and blond man: blessed is he who cometh in the name of the Lord!

MILLER: Where do you see all that?

MILLER'S WIFE: In my eyes when I raise them to the clouds.

MILLER: Yes, you're seeing a vision! I see nothing! Yes, I see the bailiff in Wolgast riding with his assistant ahead of him. (*Looks to the left*) Go in, dear, for there'll be a rough session here, I suspect.

MILLER'S WIFE: He's a dark man, the bailiff; but after him will come the blond one. (*Goes into the house. The* BAILIFF *enters riding on an ass which is led by the* ASSISTANT.)

BAILIFF (*dismounts*): God's peace, Martin Miller.

MILLER: God bless you, bailiff. Please sit down.

(BAILIFF *sits down at the table; thinks for a while.*)

MILLER: Is it bad news or good news?

BAILIFF (*hastily*): Martin, have you heard of the edict of restitution?

MILLER: Re-sti-tu-tion? Must have!

BAILIFF: Restitute, *hoc est:* to replace, to restore to the original owner. Well, then: when the Protestant movement began to spread here in northern Germany, the Lutherans confiscated all church properties, among them the cloisters, which they said had no owners, or were *res nullius*. Among these cloisters was even this Cistercian one, which you bought and converted into a mill. (*Takes up a document*) On the basis of the imperial edict and in my capacity as *confiscator imperii,* I am forced to declare your property restored, and so it is taken away from you.

MILLER: The emperor uses religion, then, to seize property?

BAILIFF: Exactly like the Protestants that time when under pretense of faith they stole the church silver and the cloister lands.

MILLER: Which action was approved by the religious peace of Augsburg? . . .[7]

BAILIFF: And was nullified by the battle of the White Mountain.[8] You see: shame strikes home! and what's wrongly seized is easily lost. You have bought stolen goods, and now you have lost them.

MILLER: Is it to be a cloister again?

BAILIFF: No! It's going to be an imperial supply house for the troops.

MILLER: Excuse this question: Are you a Catholic?

BAILIFF: We have quit putting such questions for good reasons, because the hundred-year religious struggles were settled, and we learned to live next to each other with Christian forbearance. Why do you want to raise the two-edged sword of dissension between us?

MILLER: I don't want to . . .

BAILIFF: Well, then you're not going to know my faith, either! Changing the subject: Have you seen that cloud over the sea?

MILLER: Yes, of course.

BAILIFF: Some say it's gunpowder dust; others that it's a thundercloud. We have heard thunder, seen lightning; and old women say they have seen signs—you understand . . .

MILLER: My wife said something like that a while ago. What do you believe?

BAILIFF: I do not dare to believe, but I hope . . . hope that the great war will see an end, that our fields will be sown again, and that our children may see better times.

MILLER: Our children, my children, who have gone astray—I had expected to welcome them back sometime under their parental roof . . . which isn't mine any more! To tell the truth, I haven't anything to hope for. And my wife!—she'll never live through this!

BAILIFF: Martin, if you knew what I and mine have lived through

... if you knew! (*Rises; speaks to his* ASSISTANT.) Put up the notice!

(ASSISTANT *takes up a paper, which he pastes on the* MILLER's *door.*)

BAILIFF: Remove your belongings before the executors come . . .

MILLER: Where? I can't do it alone, and my wife is sick; she'll get worse. And, if I put my belongings outside, the Croatians will come!

BAILIFF: What's wrong with your wife?

MILLER (*his* WIFE *appears on the porch; the* MILLER *points at his forehead*): Sh-h!

BAILIFF: My errand is done; don't be angry with me, for I have only done my duty. (*Pause*) Do you know this is a festival day? No? Yes, in Wolgast they're celebrating the hundredth anniversary of the Augsburg Confession,[9] which gave the Protestants freedom.

MILLER: Freedom?

BAILIFF: Yes! Come to the festival. It will amuse you, strengthen your courage, and your faith.

MILLER: Thanks very much. But since my wife can't be along—she's a Catholic—I'll stay away.

MILLER'S WIFE (*looks at the notice*): What does it say?

MILLER: It says: The Lord gave and the Lord has taken away; blessed be the name of the Lord! And that is interpreted: We have lost everything we had.

(MILLER's WIFE *falls down, unconscious.*)

MILLER: That was more than she could bear. Help me! (*The* MILLER *and the* BAILIFF's ASSISTANT *approach the* MILLER's WIFE.)

BAILIFF (*calmly*): Is she dead?

MILLER: No! But why are you standing there like a dead man?

BAILIFF: Because I've seen so much misery that I can neither suffer nor feel any more.

MILLER (*sits down on the bench*): By my soul, you're right! It's all the same if she lies in there or out here. I think I'd prefer to see her at the bottom of the sea, and me, too. Strange! I'm almost happy—that things are as they are! (*Walloons race across the back of the stage.*) Why are those men rushing like that?

BAILIFF: I've asked myself that all day. Something's happening in the distance, which we don't know but which these birds of carrion have smelled . . . Aren't you going to help your wife?

MILLER: No, I can't move a finger, even if my heart were to break; my misfortunes have paralyzed me, and I'll never see a happy day again; but I can't weep, either. There lies the bride of my youth, the only woman I have ever loved . . . my son in the war, my daughter raped—think of it, raped . . . my poor, poor, country, what have you done?

BAILIFF: A country divided against itself cannot stand.

MILLER: Yes, you can say that!

ASSISTANT (*to the* BAILIFF): Look, sir, look—the mirage over the sea!
    (*They look at the cloud over the sea, which has now assumed the form of an old city with towers, gables, battlements, and spires—shadow images in the color tones of the cloud.*)

BAILIFF (*to the* MILLER): What is this?

MILLER (*without turning around*): It's a mirage or an illusion! People say it is Vineta,[10] the city which was plundered by Danes and Swedes and sank to the bottom of the sea afterward.

BAILIFF: Oh, was that out there?

MILLER: On the island of Wollin. The people in it hated Christ— that's all I know. (*Smoke pours from the mill building.*)

ASSISTANT: The mill's on fire! For Christ's sake, put it out!

BAILIFF: Open the millrace, miller, and turn on the water!

MILLER: What's the use?

BAILIFF: Save your belongings, man!

MILLER: Nah! They'd only be taken by the Walloons, those incendiaries!

ASSISTANT: Look, bailiff, it's haunted out there again! Look, the crosses! The golden cross! (*In the mirage can now be seen a large number of masts with flags; the yellow cross on a field of blue.*)

MILLER'S WIFE (*awakens and gets up*): Vineta has sunk, and its heathen houses have collapsed before the symbol of the cross. The gold king is here; the savior has come. Blessed is he, who cometh in the name of the Lord! Hosanna!

BAILIFF (*to the* MILLER): What is she raving about?

MILLER: Since she got crazy, she insists her soul is out wandering while her body lies as if dead. That may be, but something has happened out there! (*Noise off stage*)

VOICE: The Swedes are coming!

VOICE II: The Swedes are coming!

BAILIFF: The Swedes are coming!

MILLER: The Swedes are coming! (*Walloons rush from left to right, followed by acorn pickers and marauders.*)

BAILIFF: Farewell, then, Martin; I'll go back to town to get information.

MILLER'S WIFE: Why is there smoke in the mill?

MILLER: Because it's burning, and it's burning because the Walloons set fire to it! . . . Let the emperor's house burn; it will be a midsummer fire to direct the Swedes! See, the rats are deserting the burning house. Come, wife, and we'll do the same. Out into the wide world! (*Now the blue-and-yellow flags can be seen more plainly, and under them the topmost sails.*)

ASSISTANT II (*enters hastily*): Mr. Bailiff!

BAILIFF: Out with it!

ASSISTANT II: The Swedes landed this morning; they've been busy putting up their camp; and now they're here.

BAILIFF: And the imperial forces?

ASSISTANT II: They're withdrawing without putting up any resistance!

BAILIFF: Strange! But everything's strange in this war, where no one knows who is a friend and who is an enemy. What do our people think?

ASSISTANT II: They're celebrating the arrival of their deliverers! (*People—farmers and city dwellers—have gathered on the stage.*)

BAILIFF (*to the people*): The mill is burning! Put out the fire! Put out the fire! (*Some of the people rush into the mill, whereupon the smoke gradually comes to an end.*)

BAILIFF (*to the* MILLER): The sun has come through the cloud; now you can disregard the emperor and settle down under your own roof again. Life is like that, Martin.

(MILLER *goes up to the sluice; opens the millrace.* MILLER'S WIFE *goes to the left.*)

MILLER (*comes down from the sluice, up to the* BAILIFF): Is it right that one pays taxes to the emperor?

BAILIFF: Pharisee! Grant unto God what is God's; the emperor will always get what is rightly his.

MILLER: Whose friend are you?

BAILIFF: I am Cato's friend and Plato's friend, but preferably the friend of justice. (*A Swedish* HERALD *enters, preceded by three trumpeters and three kettledrummers; followed by the* QUARTER-MASTER *and the* SERGEANT MAJOR.)

BAILIFF: There! Now we'll find out! (*The trumpeters blow a fanfare and the kettledrummers beat their drums; the people gather about them.*)

HERALD (*reads from a notice*): "Gustav Adolf, King of the Swedes, etc., hereby proclaims and makes known to all the people of the German nation and the evangelical confession that he has landed in Pomerania only as a friend and protector to rescue brethren in the faith from the papists' intolerable oppression and to secure freedom of conscience for the adherents of the pure evangelical faith. And we assure the inhabitants of this country personal freedom and property rights, encouraging each and every one to report to the commanding officer that person caught stealing, plundering or illegally extorting, so that he may without delay be brought to suitable punishment.

"Issued in Wolgast at our headquarters.

"Gustavus, as above."

(*Trumpets and kettledrums. The* HERALD *leaves; the* SERGEANT MAJOR *and the* QUARTERMASTER *stay and begin to measure up the ground.*)

BAILIFF (*to the* MILLER): Well-l?

MILLER (*scratches his head*): Yes. That is good, very good, but . . .

BAILIFF: There was a jarring note . . . Listen, your wife is a Catholic; so the Swedes will be defending you against her!

MILLER: I would have liked to have had it a little different . . . but one has to be satisfied, be satisfied.

QUARTERMASTER (*has read the notice on the door of the mill*): Is this the emperor's mill?

BAILIFF: No-o.

QUARTERMASTER: Belongs to the Catholics, according to what it says here. (*To the* SERGEANT) It will do for quartering our generals. Record that.

BAILIFF: Excuse me, sir, but the stranger came as a friend this time, didn't he?

SERGEANT MAJOR (*bragging*): Stranger? The king of the Swedes isn't a stranger in this country. The elector of Brandenburg is his brother-in-law, just as the prince of Siebenbürgen, Bethel Gabor, once was; the elector of the Palatinate is his kinsman; he's related to the dukes of Mecklenburg, Lauenburg, and Holstein; with the landgrave of Hesse, too, and note carefully that his cousin King Sigismund of Poland makes the king of Sweden a relative of Emperor Ferdinand II himself. Besides my king is a German prince in the general government of Prussia in the principal areas of Braunsberg, Elbing, Pillau, and Memel. So not really much of a stranger! Is he? Eh? Huh!

BAILIFF: Welcome, then, gentlemen, to your brotherland. I hope the trip over was good.

QUARTERMASTER: So-so.

BAILIFF: I present myself as the city bailiff of Wolgast and recommend this friendly-minded people for your best consideration.

(*Swedish soldiers and baggage people come in; set up tents, put up booths, make fires with cooking equipment; set up a field smithy, a shoe stall; move in tables and benches, etc. It has become darker over the sea; the wind is sighing through the trees, and the breakers can be heard.*)

BAILIFF (*to the* MILLER): Now you've lost the mill again, for the time being, but this is the surest way of getting it back.

MILLER: Dreams! No, I'd prefer to enlist and roam about the country to settling here and having nothing to grind while the water runs in vain. Here are kettles, and, if you're on the rolls, you always get something to eat.

(*Swedish banners are set up by the mill door, where guards are also placed.*)

BAILIFF: Good luck, Martin! A new time is coming, bad for some, good for others! Good luck! (*Goes out with the* ASSISTANTS *and the ass*)

(MILLER *goes to the right; is thoughtful. The* SERGEANT MAJOR *and the* QUARTERMASTER *sit down at a table.*)

SERGEANT MAJOR: That was really a—hm!—of a trip . . . mustn't swear in the service . . . three weeks of contrary winds . . . do you know, that was a bad start? And then they ate up all the provisions; so that we had to exact contributions from Öland; [11] that was a nasty thing, and the Ölänningar aren't enthusiastic about us! Well, we're here! But we have nothing to eat; I don't want to talk about drink (*yawns and licks his mustache*); not a horse for the baggage train, still less a driver! The generals, who're expected any minute, will have to sleep on empty flour sacks with empty stomachs. *Sapperment!* A lot of religion's needed for a campaign like this!

QUARTERMASTER: Good thing to have a little religion, and you could use some more!

SERGEANT MAJOR: And you a little more good nature! We haven't come here to convert redskins or to baptize Turks!

QUARTERMASTER: The Turk, my son, is in your heart; look for him there, and you shall certainly find him.

SERGEANT MAJOR: So you're off like that, old man?

QUARTERMASTER: I'm not off, but I'd like to ask a question, a vital question, young man; a question for your whole life (*accentuates slowly*). Do you know what makes a Christian (*more quickly*) what he is? No, you do not know that. I will tell you! It is election by grace!

SERGEANT MAJOR (*turns his back to him and goes toward the back of the stage*): Go home and go to bed, and put on something old!

QUARTERMASTER (*without letting himself be disturbed*): There are dissenters and proselyters, who insist the Formula of Concord [12] is binding for all nonconformists, but they forget one thing—let me see! The last symbolic book, issued in 1577 at the convention in Torgau . . .

SERGEANT MAJOR: Keep your trap shut!

QUARTERMASTER: Did I say Torgau? I meant—what was it? Wait a bit, I'll soon have it. (*Speculates and counts on his fingers. Drummers beat their drums.*)

SERGEANT MAJOR (*sits down at a table, takes paper and writing utensils from a bag. A group of soldiers' wives gather on the stage*): Quiet with the drums! Provost! Come here!

(PROVOST *comes on.*)

SERGEANT MAJOR (*proclaims*): Inasmuch as a camp is now to be set up, and as, according to the articles of war, no loose women may be tolerated near it, the commanding general has provided that every woman who can't prove by means of a certificate of marriage her legal marriage to a foot soldier, a cavalryman, or a baggage man on active duty is to be driven away. Are your papers clear, women? (*The women approach the table and show their soiled papers.*)

WOMAN I: Kind sir . . .

SERGEANT MAJOR (*speaks rapidly*): Shut your mouth until I ask you! (*Looks at the paper*) Anna Margreta . . . I don't give a damn about that! Who are you married to? Småland's cavalryman, number 246. Provost. Look at the list of Småland cavalrymen: number 246.

PROVOST (*reads*): Småland cavalrymen, number 246. Married.

SERGEANT MAJOR: Go, woman. You can wash dishes in the field kitchen. March!

(WOMAN I *goes.*)

SERGEANT MAJOR (*shouts*): Number two!

WOMAN II: Dear, kind sir . . . it's number 68 . . .

SERGEANT MAJOR (*shouts*): Are you going to correct me? When I say number two, it is number two. Your husband, on the other hand, may be number 68. Let me see—Småland's cavalryman, number 68. Provost, look at the list of Småland's cavalrymen. Number 68.

PROVOST (*reading*): Småland's cavalryman, number 68. Vacant!

SERGEANT MAJOR: Vacant? Is he dead?

PROVOST: He's dead.

SERGEANT MAJOR: So, you blasted woman! Do you think this is a marriage bureau? Have you gone to war to catch a husband? Do you think that there is any military support for widows and orphans here? Out! Out! Out!

WOMAN II: He is *not* dead! He is *not* dead!

SERGEANT MAJOR: If he has run away, then, we'll hang him as a deserter, so his place will be vacant anyhow. Out! Out! Out! Woman! Provost, take the woman away! Quartermaster!

QUARTERMASTER: Oh, well. It was the religious conference of Marburg.[13]

(*The* PROVOST *takes the* WOMAN *out.*)

SERGEANT MAJOR: God save the king! But it certainly is a mess that they have to drag their women along in the baggage.

QUARTERMASTER: Paul says: It is better to marry than to burn.

SERGEANT MAJOR: As if marriage weren't burning! But won't you take the women with you and distribute the food over there? For the generals will soon be here, and then the camp must be polished like a living-room floor.

QUARTERMASTER: Know what, my son? I've made an agreement with my eyes, and woman born of woman is a firebrand from hell!

SERGEANT MAJOR: Take the provost along; he'll come with switches and scorpions, if you can't trust your flesh.

QUARTERMASTER: My flesh? For shame! Come with me, women! (*Goes accompanied by the women*)

SCHOOLMASTER (*an old soldier with a wooden leg, glasses, and a cane comes in*): God save you, sergeant.

SERGEANT MAJOR: God save you, old Powder [14] . . . What are you looking for?

SCHOOLMASTER: I'm looking for a place for my boys.

SERGEANT MAJOR: Is there such a terrible hurry about your abracadabra? Give the boys vacation from school today and let them throw stones down on the seashore. But, if they yell, you'll have to twist their necks; it's to be quiet, for the generals are coming here to sleep. (*In the background, Scotchmen have come in dancing to a bagpipe; in the middle of the stage is a Swedish fiddler.*)

SCHOOLMASTER: God save the king, but do you know, sergeant, why women and children have to be along in the war?

SERGEANT MAJOR: Because there wasn't anything to eat at home, I suppose.

SCHOOLMASTER: Is there anything to eat here? I haven't seen even the hole in a cookie yet.

SERGEANT MAJOR: Please make your reflections to yourself, and don't go about plotting, for then you'll be hung in a tree until your flesh has loosened from your rotten bones. Do you know what that was? (*Gets up*)

SCHOOLMASTER: So! That's how you treat a source of knowledge, a forest of forests, a *hortus deliciarum,* whose only desire is to be a *servus servorum eruditorum* . . .

SERGEANT MAJOR: Abracadabra, abracadabra, abracadabra, *ortus meretrikorum, in secula seculorum—Eistenueian panton ton filon;*

ḳai hapanton, ḳai panton proserḳomenon filo. Do you know what kind that was?

SCHOOLMASTER: Was that Finnish?

SERGEANT MAJOR: No, sir, that was Greek . . . For I have been at Uppsala for five semesters as *liber studiosus;* drank and fought; was drafted . . . but now I'm here. So, source of knowledge, run away to the forest of forests.

SCHOOLMASTER: *Jauseif beseiser eljaun!* Do you follow?

SERGEANT MAJOR: *Hazur tomin poolall!* Can you give me one for that? Go to the quartermaster and abracadabra with him, for big shots are coming.

SCHOOLMASTER (*going*): A pleasant midsummer day, this!

SERGEANT MAJOR: *You* would have liked to dance around the mid-summer pole!

SCHOOLMASTER: Don't ridicule misfortune! Don't you know that it is to my honor to have lost a member on a campaign?

SERGEANT MAJOR: On your campaign home from the tavern after a binge, you fell into a ditch and broke your leg. That's what it says in the official records, you see, and so you'll have to sleep on one leg like the rooster, you old soak! *Salum aleiḳum!*

SCHOOLMASTER: *Seid mauchel!* Fox! (*Goes*)

SERGEANT MAJOR: Goose!

(FINNISH ENSIGN *enters with a* DANISH ENSIGN.)

FINNISH ENSIGN (*has a Finnish accent; shouts*): Can you imagine . . .

DANISH ENSIGN (*has a Danish accent*): I've spent a lot of money, but all the same I can't say that I'm afraid my wife'll scold me . . .

FINNISH ENSIGN: Well, but can you imagine . . .

DANISH ENSIGN: Where did we stop?

FINNISH ENSIGN: I can't tell you that now.

DANISH ENSIGN: The devil, you're not going to outtalk me!

FINNISH ENSIGN: Well, well, well, well! (*Trumpet signals about the stage*) Ah, they're already sounding peace in bed.

DANISH ENSIGN: Well, then, why don't you want some fun tonight?

FINNISH ENSIGN: Well, I don't care to dance to that bagpipe as the

Scotch are doing, and they ought to have given the fiddle a gypsy pass on a holy evening, when one isn't likely to suffer from any celebration in camp. Oh, if I were only home and were free from all this papistry . . . they've certainly had their fun with me, but, hell and damnation, if I only get home, I'll stay there . . .

SERGEANT MAJOR (*has risen and signaled that the Scotchmen and the violinist are to be silent. He now approaches the* ENSIGNS): You must not talk so loudly, ensign. The generals are just coming!

FINNISH ENSIGN: Well, I don't know the generals!

SERGEANT MAJOR: Then you're going to. Attention!

(*Trumpet fanfares. The people on stage become silent; all straighten up and look to the left. The* SERGEANT MAJOR *and the* ENSIGNS *stand concealed by a tree so that the generals cannot see them. Now the defile begins, from the left in the middle of the stage to the right into the mill where the guard of honor stands.*)

(GUSTAV HORN *first; dressed in mourning*)

SERGEANT MAJOR (*to the* ENSIGNS): Gustav Horn![15] Son of Karl Henriksson Horn . . .

FINNISH ENSIGN: Horn of Kankas, the Finlander? Can you imagine that . . .

SERGEANT MAJOR: Yes, but you can do your imagining a little more quietly. Karl Henriksson Horn *was* condemned to death by Charles IX at the bloodbath of Linköping,[16] but he was reprieved.

FINNISH ENSIGN: Oh, that bloodbath.

(NILS BRAHE)

SERGEANT MAJOR: Nils Brahe!—the son of Abraham Brahe, the judge at the bloodbath of Linköping.

FINNISH ENSIGN: Really! and a cousin of Ebba Brahe.[17]

SERGEANT MAJOR: Sh! Sh! Sh!

(JOHAN BANÉR)

SERGEANT MAJOR: Johan Banér!

FINNISH ENSIGN: Surely that's the king?

SERGEANT MAJOR: No, but he looks a lot like him. The son of Kristina Sture and Gustav Banér, who was beheaded at the bloodbath of Linköping.

FINNISH ENSIGN: Can you imagine that! . . .

(FREDRIK STENBOCK)

SERGEANT MAJOR: Fredrik Stenbock. The grandson of Malin Sture and Erik Stenbock, the brother-in-law of Gustav Vasa; reprieved at the bloodbath of Linköping!

FINNISH ENSIGN: Really! Vasas and Stures!

(LENNART TORSTENSSON)

SERGEANT MAJOR: Lennart Torstensson, the son of the traitor Torsten Lennartson, who went with Sigismund to Poland.

(ERIK SOOP)

SERGEANT MAJOR: Erik Soop of the Västergötland cavalry. Saved the king's life at Weissenburg . . .

FINNISH ENSIGN: Never in my life . . .

SERGEANT MAJOR: Sh! Karl Hård of the West Goths with Axel Lillie of the East Bothnians!

(KARL HÅRD. AXEL LILLIE)

SERGEANT MAJOR: The one who's coming now you certainly recognize. Torsten Stålhandske of the Finnish cavalry.

FINNISH ENSIGN: No, I don't seem to. . . .

SERGEANT MAJOR (*holds him back*): Quiet!

(TORSTEN STÅLHANDSKE)

FINNISH ENSIGN: Thou great almighty God, isn't it as if the whole of Swedish history were marching out into the open . . .

SERGEANT MAJOR: Stop! More are coming—Åke Tott, grandson of King Erik XIV;[18] Vasa blood! The king's cousin.

(ÅKE TOTT)

FINNISH ENSIGN: Trivial things and trifles, that's all I've seen until now. Isn't that right, Dane? (*Looks about and notices that the Dane has disappeared*) Well, if that bootlicker hasn't escaped! It really hurt him to see these big shots because they weren't Danish foxes . . .

SERGEANT MAJOR: Ensign, duty makes me tell you without reserva-

tions that in the Swedish camp no one may abuse any nationality
—not even Jews or gypsies. That is our king's command, and it
must be respected.

FINNISH ENSIGN: Well, they're certainly less prejudiced here than
I'm used to. But what about the emperor's people?

SERGEANT MAJOR: They're not a nationality.

(ERIK RÅLAMB *enters, dressed in black with two feathers in his
hat, one white, one red.*)

SERGEANT MAJOR: The king's, or, more correctly, the queen's chamberlain, Erik Rålamb. His uncle was beheaded in Kalmar by
Duke Charles!

FINNISH ENSIGN: Then we can expect the king himself soon!

SERGEANT MAJOR: Certainly. Certainly.

ÅKE TOTT (*comes out of the mill with his hat in his hand; irritated*): The devil himself can't stay in there! Sergeant, what sort
of quarters have you given us? Why, it smells of fire and is as
hot as hell.

SERGEANT MAJOR: We don't have anything else, my lord; and we
couldn't help it that the Croatians had set fire to it before we
got here.

ÅKE TOTT: Set the table out here, then, and see to it we get good
wine, at least.

SERGEANT MAJOR: God save us, but there isn't a scrap of bread in the
whole camp.

ÅKE TOTT: Get out and forage, then.

SERGEANT MAJOR: My lord means that we're to *take* it from the people. In the first place, there's nothing to take, for the emperor's
forces have plundered the country, and, in the second place . . .

ÅKE TOTT: And, in the third, you'll ride the wooden mare [19] if you
let your officers go without food, you and the quartermaster; and,
in the fourth, the king will soon be here to eat dinner.

JOHAN BANÉR (*comes out of the mill, bareheaded*): I've slept in
barns and pigsties, but the devil take me if I've ever been in anything like this! Where is the quartermaster?

ÅKE TOTT: He's mustering the women, but we have the sergeant major here.

JOHAN BANÉR: Oh, then he may put up tents out here.

SERGEANT MAJOR: With your permission, but the king's tent is to stand here, and the baggage hasn't arrived.

FREDRIK STENBOCK (*comes out with his boots in his hand and throws them toward* TOTT): Is there any devil here who can brush a pair of boots?

   (ÅKE TOTT *kicks the boots aside.*)

FREDRIK STENBOCK: Do you dare to kick my boots?

ÅKE TOTT: Come here and I'll kick you! in an obvious place!

FREDRIK STENBOCK: Satisfaction! Satisfaction!

ERIK RÅLAMB (*comes out*): Gentlemen! The field marshal begs for peace and quiet. Not only has his son's recent death bowed him in sorrow, but the troubles of the trip over have affected his health as well. Peace, in Jesus' name, peace!

ÅKE TOTT: That's a nice thing to say to hungry people; you see, I'm so hungry I'm sweating way out at the tips of my hair and could eat my tongue.

ERIK RÅLAMB: Is it a new thing for you, Åke Tott, to put up with hardships in the field?

ÅKE TOTT: No, not when it's necessary, but this is carelessness on the part of the baggage people.

JOHAN BANÉR: Such a thoroughly damnable carelessness . . .

SERGEANT MAJOR: No, my lords, it isn't carelessness . . .

ÅKE TOTT: Slit his throat if he answers . . .

FREDRIK STENBOCK: I don't give a damn about the food, if I only get my boots brushed . . .

ÅKE TOTT: Fop!

FREDRIK STENBOCK: And how about you?—you glutton!

ERIK RÅLAMB: Fredrik, don't irritate the wild Åke; why, he's a spoiled child of royalty . . .

JOHAN BANÉR: You, Åke, there's a festival of some sort on at Wolgast; let's mount, and we'll ride in and get us a little midsummer bait for our money.

ÅKE TOTT: What a brilliant answer to the food problem . . . Let's go! (*Hurries out, followed by* JOHAN BANÉR)

FREDRIK STENBOCK (*pulls his boots on and hurries after them*): Wait a bit! Here I am! Åke, my friend, wait! (*Out*)

QUARTERMASTER (*has come in; turns to the* SERGEANT MAJOR): These should be the instruments of the Lord . . .

SERGEANT MAJOR: All brooms aren't clean, and some shovels still less.

FINNISH ENSIGN (*comes up*): It's all too wonderful to see the offspring and kinsmen of the executed lords getting together in one place . . .

SERGEANT MAJOR: There you see our great king's noble and conciliatory spirit; but at home in Stockholm there are still more Linköping lords: Johan Sparre, the councillor, is the son of Erik Sparre, beheaded; Per Banér, head of the chancellery, is the son of Ture Banér, beheaded; Nils Bielke, the councillor, is the kinsman of the beheaded Ture Bielke. The gentle son of the cruel Charles IX atones for the sins of his father. The quartermaster calls that *satisfactio vicaria personalis* or the personal vicarious atonement . . .

QUARTERMASTER: I? No, far from it . . . That was Anselm of Canterbury and the heretic Abelard, who in opposition to the nonconformists . . . wanted to establish, as demonstrated by the letter to the Galatians . . .

SERGEANT MAJOR: Stop! Stop right there! To think that I should go and touch that spigot! Now he's flowing . . . let's fly, ensign! Ah! Here comes a minister . . .

(FABRICIUS, *the court chaplain, enters with Secretary* GRUBBE.)

SERGEANT MAJOR (*to the* FINNISH ENSIGN): Court Chaplain Fabricius and Secretary Lars Grubbe. The king can't be far away.

FINNISH ENSIGN: No, but listen . . .

(FABRICIUS *speaks softly to* GRUBBE.)

GRUBBE (*to* ERIK RÅLAMB): His Majesty is coming. He requests that his tent be set up next to the generals' quarters.

ERIK RÅLAMB (*to the* SERGEANT MAJOR): Quickly! His Majesty's tent here under the oaks! (*The* SERGEANT MAJOR *and the* QUARTER-MASTER *go out and return with men who set up an open, blue-and-yellow-striped tent roof between the trees. It has become still darker.*)

GRUBBE (*to* ERIK RÅLAMB): His Majesty requests a meeting here with Field Marshal Horn, General Torstensson, and Colonel Nils Brahe.

(ERIK RÅLAMB *bows.*)

GRUBBE: Retreat is to be sounded at once, and the court chaplain will conduct prayers, after which there is to be silence . . . The greatest strictness with our own people, and the greatest forbearance toward the natives: that is the king's command.

(ERIK RÅLAMB *goes into the mill.*)

(FABRICIUS *speaks softly with* GRUBBE *and goes out to the right. Adjutants come out of the mill and station themselves to the right and left. Thereupon retreat is sounded, on drums and with trumpets, far and near and round about.* GRUBBE *sits down at a table, takes up writing equipment, and writes.*)

(GUSTAV HORN, LENNART TORSTENSSON, *and* NILS BRAHE *come out of the mill, sit down at the table under the* KING'S *tent.* ERIK RÅLAMB *comes out, after the others, and stands in back of* HORN.)

(GRUBBE *rises and goes out to the right. Silence; the generals look worried and embarrassed; they look at each other for a while.*)

HORN: Say something.

TORSTENSSON: What?

BRAHE: It will certainly take the king's happy self-confidence and firm faith not to be dismayed by such a bad beginning.

TORSTENSSON: I can't deny the inhabitants' decided coldness dismays me. Why don't they greet the helper and liberator with joy instead of running off and hiding themselves?

BRAHE: That could be explained by their fear of the emperor . . . perhaps even by a natural animosity toward strangers. But what can't be explained is that we've been allowed to land without seeing so much as one of the imperial soldiers. Where is the enemy? Where is Conti? [20] Where is Tilly? And, above all: Where is Wallenstein?

TORSTENSSON: No reports have yet given us answers to these questions. We know one thing: the imperial troops are scattered round about us in numbers decidedly superior to ours.

HORN: Don't worry. When the king comes, he'll blow on the skein so that it can be wound up. Where we see absolute darkness, he'll see pure light, for he brings light with himself and is born of light!

RÅLAMB (*exalted*): Well said, Gustav Horn! I always think of the sun or of gold when I see my hero approach . . . and the day I find a spot on his pure, warm soul, I'll no longer believe in what is good.

HORN: That will never happen, Erik Rålamb.

RÅLAMB: But if it should . . .

BRAHE: Quiet! The king is coming!

(*All of those seated rise and wait silently. One can see the glow of torchlight from the left. Then three torchbearers; then three bodyguards. Finally the* KING)

KING (*in light yellow with a light blue sash; in his hat he is wearing one white and one red plume, the Hohenzollern colors of the* QUEEN; *in his hand he has dispatches which he throws on the table*): Well! Now I am here. How are you? So quiet! Have you had dinner?

HORN: No, Your Majesty . . .

KING: Why not?

HORN: Because there isn't anything to eat.

KING: Then we'll have to go to bed hungry, for once; and still be thankful after such a splendid start.

HORN: Splendid?

KING: Isn't it splendid that we could complete our landing without the slightest opposition? Isn't it good fortune without compare that the enemy withdraws? I am so delighted that . . . I am afraid, afraid as always in good fortune that it won't last long . . . Does anyone know where Wallenstein is?

HORN: No. But they say Tilly is somewhere to the west.

KING (*unrolling a map*): Fine! Look at this map, and at the red line. First I'll take Stettin; then I have the key to the Baltic and the road to Berlin . . . Then I'll take Frankfurt an der Oder, and separate my cousin Sigismund from my dear brother-in-law, the Brandenburger. Then I'll get Spandau as a gift; and so at once I'll have Magdeburg in my pocket! . . . You look doubtful, Gustav. And now you're like my good Oxenstjerna, who always sees difficulties . . . he didn't like this war, but, when he couldn't prevent it, he gave in . . . Why are you so quiet? Say something, Nils; Lennart . . . say something!

TORSTENSSON: Your Majesty, the enemy that doesn't show himself is more dangerous than the one you can see . . .

KING: You speak foolishly, dear Lennart, and I'll leave you, since you want to rob me of my courage. Where is my friend Johan?

BRAHE: Banér, Tott, and Stenbock rode to Wolgast to attend a festival, where something good was to be had.

KING: Well, I have to smile. I have just come from that festival, and there's neither wet nor dry to be had; well, it was dry. They were celebrating the centennial of the Augsburg Confession with fasting and prayers, and, since the reformed church was not included in the Treaty of Passau,[21] the good people of Wolgast were at each others' throats. I'm thinking of Åke and Johan with empty stomachs and dry throats listening to an eight-hour disputation in exegesis! Ha ha! Yes, let them take it! Go to bed now, my friends; I'll stay out here under the stars.

HORN: And tomorrow?

KING: Tomorrow we'll take Stettin. Erik Rålamb, stay with me and let the guards go to bed.

HORN (*goes into the mill*): Good night, Your Majesty.

KING: I wish you the same, Gustav; and that your sorrow may not disturb your rest.

BRAHE: Good night, my king.

KING: A pleasant night, kinsman.

TORSTENSSON (*to the* KING): God's peace and blessing.

KING: The Lord be with you, Lennart, and, if you believe good of God, you'll get rest. (*Guards and torchbearers leave at a sign from* RÅLAMB. *The foreground and the* KING *are lighted by the reflection of a campfire off stage. At the back it is dusk, and in the heavens one can see the stars of Charles's Wain,*[22] *which has gradually appeared. The surf can be heard in the distance.*)

   (KING *sits down at the table, takes off his hat; a worried expression on his face.* RÅLAMB *remains standing.*)

KING: Sit down, Erik.

   (RÅLAMB *sits down, his head uncovered.*)

KING: Can anyone hear us?

RÅLAMB: No, Your Majesty. But someone sees us.

KING: Who?

RÅLAMB: The Omniscient—above the stars.

KING: Yes! May He see in my heart that my love for my fellow believers is as boundless as my hate for the papists. "I hate the unjust with a perfect hate," says David . . .

RÅLAMB: David lived under the law as the papists do, but we live in faith under the gospel.

KING: And so, you mean, I should love them! Love Richelieu? Love Wallenstein? Never . . .

RÅLAMB: Isn't there a middle way between love and hate? Can't one tolerate?

KING: I can't tolerate intolerance . . . and so I hate the Catholics . . . You know I can smell a Catholic within gunshot, and when I've had to take one by the hand I've felt as if I were taking hold of a snake! That's why, you see, my position is so clear, my task is so simple. That's why I didn't need any declaration of war, that's why I needed no alliances, because the sheep know their shepherd, and the shepherd knows the wolves. And the one who is not with me is against me! Where are you, Erik, my friend?

RÅLAMB (*on his knees*): Here at your feet, my hero and my king! And may my soul wither the day I fail you!

KING: There, there. Youngster! But if I fail, what then?

RÅLAMB: Then I'll turn my back to you, break my sword, and forever despise you!

KING: You love me, Erik! Do so always, no matter what may happen. But get up now; someone is coming.

RÅLAMB (*kisses the* KING's *hand and gets up*): My king, and my God!

(KING *draws his hand away*.)

MILLER's WIFE (*enters with an armful of willow branches in her apron and strews her path up to the* KING): "And the word of the Lord came unto me the second time, saying, What seest thou? And I said, I see a seething pot; and the face thereof is toward the north. Then the Lord said unto me, Out of the north an evil shall break forth upon all the inhabitants of the land." [23]

RÅLAMB: So says Jeremiah, woman. But Isaiah says: "I have raised up one from the north, and he shall come; from the rising of the sun shall he call upon my name; and he shall come upon princes as upon mortar and as the potter treadeth clay." [24]

MILLER's WIFE: He didn't understand. But Jeremiah says: "For lo, I will call all the families of the kingdoms of the north, saith the Lord; and they shall come, and they shall set every one his throne at the entering of the gates of Jerusalem, and against all the walls thereof round about, and against all the cities of Judah . . . touching all their wickedness, who have forsaken me!" [25] Blessed is he, who cometh in the name of the Lord!

KING (*gives her his hand*): Rise, woman. Your faith is as warm as your hand. Mine know me, as I know mine. (*To* RÅLAMB) The first Protestant who has bid me welcome. (*To the* WOMAN) Peace be with you!

MILLER'S WIFE (*as she goes, she makes the sign of the cross*): *Et cum spiritu tuo!* Amen! (*Goes*)

KING (*looks startled at* RÅLAMB *with an expression which dissolves in a smile*): What was that?

RÅLAMB: I understand nothing, but she was a Catholic!

KING: Who bids me welcome . . . ?

RÅLAMB: A Pomeranian woman, who has waited for deliverance from the Austrians. So? Wasn't her hand warm? Well, then, her heart was warm.

KING: Don't smile at me, Erik. I'll be wiser with every day that goes. (*Goes upstage with his arm about* RÅLAMB's *shoulders, stops, and looks out to sea.*) See, Charles's Wain. There is my home; there my little daughter sleeps. (*Throws a kiss*) Good night, my royal child! Good night, my queen! Good night, Charles's Wain! (*Comes back; stops, with a worried look*)

RÅLAMB: You are worried, my king.

KING: No, do you know what your king is? He is hungry! But now I want to sleep my hunger away, and you shall read me to sleep out of the Book of Books. (*Sits down, turned toward the fire. Trumpet signal in the distance; new signals ever closer; finally, beating of drums nearby; the camp awakes and gets into urgent movement.* HORN, BRAHE, TORSTENSSON, *and the other generals come out of the mill with their sashes and swords, which they put on.*)

KING: There! What's up now?

RÅLAMB: Alarm!

SERGEANT MAJOR (*comes in hastily with torchbearers*): The enemy is here! The emperor's forces have attacked the outposts!

KING: The enemy is here! Now, Torstensson, Horn, Brahe! All of you: the Swedish watchword! Take it! God is with us!

CURTAIN

ACT II

*A wealthy burgher's home in Stettin. Dark, hand-carved cup-
boards; tables with heavy cloths in solid colors; chairs of the same
style. At the back one large open window, which faces the harbor, where Swedish warships are anchored with their flags flying.
On the back wall engraved portraits of Luther, Melanchthon, and
GUSTAV ADOLF. To the left, a table that has been set for a birthday
celebration with two lighted candles, a bouquet of flowers, and
several gifts spread on the white tablecloth, which is decorated
with green leaves and flowers. RUDOLF, a student at Wittenberg,
and LUISE, his cousin, are at the window.*

RUDOLF (*sticks a Swedish flag out through the window*): The emperor's eagles have fled from the golden crosses, and the snow
king has brought coolness to this sultry July night.

LUISE (*hangs a wreath under GUSTAV ADOLF's portrait*): Hail, golden
king! who has opened our harbor so that the ships can come and
go! Think of it, Rudi, now I'll get silk from France again so that
I can finish your sash!

RUDOLF: My sash, Luise, I shall wear the day my friend Gustav
Gustavsson becomes rector at Wittenberg. Luise, I'm his friend,
the friend of Gustav Adolf's son. What a shame that he isn't a
prince!

LUISE: But his father is king!

RUDOLF: His mother's not queen, though! (*Softly*) Margareta Cabeljau [27]—his beautiful mother—who's married up in the north.

LUISE: You shouldn't have told me that; I don't know why, but—it
isn't nice to desert a woman . . .

RUDOLF: True, but the king's own mother, the dowager queen, brought them together to save the son from a great and true love for a lady at court, whose name was Brahe, I think . . .

LUISE: Please stop! Father's coming soon with his company, and then there must be wine on the table (*she takes out wine bottles and glasses and places them on the table*), happiness in our hearts, and only cheerful thoughts.

RUDOLF (*Indicates* GUSTAV ADOLF's *portrait*): Lights alone don't make you a picture, Luise. Take the shadows away from that portrait, and you'll see only a piece of white paper with some water stains which the blacking hid.

LUISE: Is it philosophy you're studying?

RUDOLF: Erotics, too!

LUISE: What's that?

RUDOLF: It's . . . woman!

LUISE: I don't like your talk and your manner, Rudolf. But times are evil when there's war, and people become animals. Take care of yourself!

RUDOLF: Listen, Luise. It's your birthday today, your seventeenth; the whole harbor's decked with flags—in your honor. Luise, won't you . . .

LUISE: Sh-h! Mother's coming . . .

MOTHER (*comes in with a feather duster; mutters to herself*): I don't like this at all.

RUDOLF: What, aunt?

MOTHER: I don't like this at all. The gunpowder smoke that ruins my curtains; the banging and shooting, which frighten the sick to death—and the whole town's full of drunken sailors and soldiers.

RUDOLF: Aunt Gertrud, forget it and think about what this day means for us, for Luise . . . Listen to me in the Lord's name . . . your Luise has her birthday today, and I, your brother's son, have come . . . (*irritated, raises his voice*) as long as . . . let me finish speaking . . .

MOTHER: Sh-h! Father's coming! And he has our guests along . . .

COOPER (*wearing his leather apron and band iron in his belt rather happily enters with the* FINNISH ENSIGN, *the* SCHOOLMASTER, *and the* PROVOST): This is where I live. And here are my new friends. My Swedish friends. This is a Finnish ensign in the cavalry— what was your name again?

FINNISH ENSIGN: Why, my name's Axel Eriksson, but I don't have the heart to walk right in like this . . .

COOPER: Erik Axelsson, oh yes! And here is the schoolmaster . . . You, Rudolf; he's in your line.

SCHOOLMASTER: Field schoolmaster, if I may . . .

(RUDOLF *looks contemptuous.*)

COOPER (*points at the* PROVOST): And here's the professor . . .

PROVOST: Good heavens, no . . .

COOPER: Hush now, and sit down to a glass of wine . . . My daughter, Luise, will pour it . . .

(MOTHER, *sullen; goes about cleaning with her feather duster; then she takes a towel and wipes the table between the guests.* LUISE *unwillingly pours wine into the glasses.* RUDOLF *approaches the* PROVOST *suspiciously.*)

COOPER: A toast to the king! On your knees! (*Three cannon shots outside. They drink while they kneel.*)

ALL (*but the* MOTHER, RUDOLF, *and* LUISE): Hurrah-h-h!

(MOTHER *wipes between the glasses and looks sullen.*)

RUDOLF (*to the* PROVOST): Professor!

PROVOST (*shouts*): No, I'm not a professor; I'm the provost! The provost!

RUDOLF (*signals to* LUISE, *and they steal out*): What a crowd!

MOTHER: I don't like this. At all!

COOPER (*pouring wine*): What are you wiping here for? And watch your tongue, Gertrud!

(MOTHER *goes out.*)

COOPER (*raises his glass*): Friends, benefactors, and liberators! In these three words, I express my sincerest thoughts. My house is

yours, and mine, everything that I possess . . . put up your feet,
ensign! Make yourself comfortable, professor!

FINNISH ENSIGN (*and the others make themselves extremely com-*
fortable): Will it be long before that beautiful girl will be back?

SCHOOLMASTER: *Puella!* Beautiful women are the soldier's reward!

COOPER (*somewhat embarrassed*): I don't understand . . .

SCHOOLMASTER (*drunk; knocks over a glass*): *Estisne preparati?*
Sumus! A cantilena! (*Sings and beats on the table*)

> Sum, sum, sum,
> Dum, dum, dum;
> Bum, bum, bum.
> Trum, trum, trum!

(*Jumps up on his chair; sings a mournful melody and dances in
accompaniment*)

> There was young Lord Sverkeling,
> He rode the horse so gray,
> He rode a hundred miles and more
> Before he looked back today.

> Between mountains and dales,
> There lie the warriors dead.
> In Sweden they leave children small
> Who cry for their butter and bread.

FINNISH ENSIGN: Listen, how can anyone sing such sad songs among
a strange people . . .

COOPER (*with restrained anger*): Get down from that chair!

SCHOOLMASTER: Listen, you Finn, watch out!

COOPER: Get away from the chair; I'm expecting company for my
daughter's birthday party!

SCHOOLMASTER: You have company, cooper, and you can't get any
better!

FINNISH ENSIGN: Listen, schoolmaster, how can you bear to be so
crude . . .

COOPER: I am distressed, and it hurts me to see an old man, who has been struck by misfortune, make such a fool of himself—excuse me, gentlemen, for saying so . . .

FINNISH ENSIGN: I imagine it was a misfortune that that old scarecrow went on a binge and broke off his leg . . .

SCHOOLMASTER: You dare to talk, but no one dares to touch me! Touch a cripple if you dare! Touch a cripple! Touch!

FINNISH ENSIGN: Yes, but listen to that everlasting scold; listen to him; that's the thanks I get for feeling sorry for you . . .

SCHOOLMASTER (*deliberately overturns a glass with his crutch*): It's marvel—ous how one can point with a whip! Sum, sum, sum, trum, trum, trum . . .

SERGEANT MAJOR (*enters; he is erect but has been imbibing*): Get away from that chair, you rascal! Are you the master of the coopers' guild? (*The* SCHOOLMASTER *goes away from the table.*)

COOPER: At your service, sergeant. Have you forgotten anything?

SERGEANT MAJOR: Yes, I have forgotten a glass . . . a couple of glasses . . . a couple of glasses of wine! *Bonum vinum infelix gaudeamus!*

COOPER: A pleasant fellow! Won't you please help yourself? (*They drink.*)

SERGEANT MAJOR: I had another errand, too, but the quartermaster can take care of it; in good company with a good glass . . . (*Empties a glass*) I don't want to cause the gloom that an unpleasant bit of news brings with it; life is short, and after death no pleasure. *Ergo bibamus!* (*General gloom*) This is the bright side of war. Yes, it is!

QUARTERMASTER (*enters*): Why are you sitting here getting drunk, sergeant? And you, ensign, provost, and schoolmaster? Are you the master of the coopers' guild? And is this your house? Well, then! (*Takes up a paper*) May I sit down?

COOPER: Sit down and have a glass in honor of the day, quartermaster.

QUARTERMASTER: No, a thousand times no!

COOPER: Won't you let me tempt you?

QUARTERMASTER: Tempt? For me there are no temptations. See, here is a glass. (*Lifts a filled glass*) Here is delicious wine, and here are my lips. Here is my nose, which smells the delicious wine. And! And I do like this! (*Puts the glass away*) I have overcome the last temptation; and now: to the point! According to the treaty between the Swedish king and the duke of Pomerania, the city is obligated to accept a Swedish garrison, and the general commandant has designated your house as royal headquarters. Enough said?

COOPER: The honor's great, of course, but the inconvenience greater; we were going to celebrate a birthday here . . .

QUARTERMASTER: Talk, talk, talk! All of you are to leave but the master of the guild.

SERGEANT MAJOR (*empties his glass*): This is the dark side of war. (*Goes out*)

QUARTERMASTER: Then the room is to be cleaned, all the little odds and ends are to be removed, and every trace of dissipation is to be swept away.

FINNISH ENSIGN (*goes out*): Nah, but listen! . . .

SCHOOLMASTER (*goes out*): Sum, sum, sum! *Preparati sumus!* We are prepared for everything—but death!

QUARTERMASTER: Be prepared for the gallows, you godless man!

COOPER (*worried*): Then I am driven out of my own house?

QUARTERMASTER: In your free translation of the word "billeting," yes! But that is the punishment for your sins. For over a hundred years you Protestants have been sinning in grace; when Luther said namely: Faith is everything and deeds nothing, you accepted faith as a dog takes a lump of sugar, but you blew away the deeds! Therefore, your degeneration has entered into its last stage, and now he who will discipline you with whips and scorpions is coming, and afterward he will give you true freedom.

(FIRE CHIEF,[28] *the former bailiff in Wolgast, enters followed by the* PROVOST, *who carries a bundle of wax wreaths.*)

QUARTERMASTER (*to the* COOPER): This is the chief of the fire brigade. On duty, chief?

COOPER (*to the* FIRE CHIEF): We have seen each other before. Aren't you the bailiff in Wolgast?

FIRE CHIEF: Have been.

COOPER: Have been the emperor's man, and are now the king's!

FIRE CHIEF: Yes. Am what they make me. Do good to me, and I'll do good to you; evil, and I'll do evil to you.

COOPER: But under all circumstances with money!

FIRE CHIEF: With money, when I have any; without, when I haven't any; but under all circumstances! . . . So, master, get your contribution together. Five hundred *gyllen* as your share of the 50,000 *riksdaler* which the city of Stettin has agreed to pay. (*Rattles a moneybag*)

COOPER (*furiously*): Contribution? Is the enemy upon us, or has the devil sent a false friend to drive us out of our homes and extort our money? . . .

QUARTERMASTER: Just keep quiet. A soldier doesn't argue.

COOPER: I am no soldier, but I can become one, and then I am going to be a Croatian! Think of it, for years our city has defended itself against the emperor's forces and has endured the siege with honor; now the liberator, the friend, comes and fools us into opening the gates of the city so that he can plunder and burn. And for these swine I open my home and extend the goblet of welcome! Ah, to hell with it! (*Throws a tray and glasses out of the window*) And for this Turk I've hoisted the flag which isn't my country's! Traitor that I was! (*Loosens the Swedish flag and throws it out of the window*) No, an emperor and a fatherland, but not the foreigner and the foreign king! (*Turns* GUSTAV ADOLF's *portrait to the wall*) But this is what we get for our dissension and for our revolt against our legal lord. Oh, my poor German land, if you had known what you did!

FIRE CHIEF (*calmly*): Shout, but pay.

COOPER: Yes, I will shout: Long live the emperor! For rather one honest enemy than fifteen thousand faithless friends!

FIRE CHIEF: Provost! Produce your wax wreaths! What are they?

They're symbols of the risk the city would have run if it had
failed to pay.

COOPER: Arsonists!

FIRE CHIEF: They're only symbols.

(COOPER *snatches the wreaths from the* PROVOST.)

QUARTERMASTER: Now you've crossed the bounds of decency! Call
for help! Guards!

(RÅLAMB *and* LUISE *enter; her* MOTHER *appears in the doorway.*)

RÅLAMB (*signals to those present to leave*): Leave this room. The
king will be here directly. (*All begin to go but* RÅLAMB, LUISE,
and her MOTHER.)

RÅLAMB (*to the* COOPER): Full justice will be done to you, and the
offenders will be punished. We've already hanged a Swede who
took a farmer's cow. So far as the levy goes, it is intended to support the troops and to fortify the city and has been levied with
the approval of the duke.

COOPER: His approval before the mouths of cannons, and with his
heart in his throat . . .

RÅLAMB: My friend, don't say anything more, for it could be . . .
that I share your opinion, and that I must not do. Go before that
happens.

COOPER: That was a friend, who spoke . . . (*Goes*)

RÅLAMB: Go, go, go! (*To* LUISE) Lovely child, the hard necessities
of war, the prevailing want, and the complaints of the soldiers
have forced us to act as we have. It isn't the best people who go
to war, but not all are the worst, either. It hurts me more than I
can tell you . . . forcing our way into a family and disturbing a
party . . . all the more as it is yours, lovely lady . . .

LUISE (*begins to clear the birthday table*): What do you know about
me and about what I deserve? *163804*

(MOTHER *goes about disgruntled, wiping up the spilled wine.*)

RÅLAMB: Miss Luise, let the table be; nobody shall desecrate this
little altar, raised by parental love for a beloved child . . . I will
keep knightly vigil by it, and, before the candles have burned

down, your house shall be yours again. Where virtue and beauty dwell, nothing evil and ugly can flourish.

MOTHER: What are you saying? Control your feelings.

RÅLAMB: My feelings, woman, are so distant and so high that your thoughts could not reach them even if they took the wings of the morning. (*Takes off his hat and polishes the red and white feathers. Martial music on the street below*)

RÅLAMB: Come out quickly. The king is here! (*Conducts* LUISE *and her* MOTHER *out*)

MOTHER: I don't like this; it isn't honest.

LUISE: Mother, perhaps we have to suffer a great deal before we can attain happiness.

(KING *enters.*)

(RÅLAMB *stands at the window and turns his back to the* KING.)

KING: Erik!

(RÅLAMB *sulks.*)

KING: Are you still ungracious . . . to your king?

(RÅLAMB *as before*)

KING: Erik! You're a spoiled child, and you misuse the power my friendship has given you!

(RÅLAMB *turns.*)

KING: You despise me?

RÅLAMB: Yes, a thousand times, yes!

KING: But I surely can't go back home just because the soldiers lack means of support; and I don't want to plunder.

RÅLAMB: What is levying contributions, then? It is: "Pay, or I'll burn your house down!" And that to friends, to fellow believers! What can the enemy expect, then?

KING (*takes his arm*): That you don't understand. Come, now, be human. Or go out and cool off.

RÅLAMB: No, I won't leave this room before it is restored, in perfect condition, to the woman who owns it!

KING: Woman? Oh, are you already faithless to the lady of your heart?

RÅLAMB (*embarrassed*): My lady? No!

KING (*sees his portrait, the front of which has been turned to the wall*): Who has also turned his back on me?

RÅLAMB: Someone who has been put in the corner.

KING (*turns the portrait right*): Erik Rålamb! The day I can become angry with you, and shall become angry with you, I will be so thoroughly angry that I fear the moment!

RÅLAMB: Let's postpone the moment, and don't be angry sooner than you must. Be good to everyone, even the humblest, and always do what's just . . .

KING: I am always just, and I haven't anything to reproach myself for yet . . .

RÅLAMB (*takes both of the* KING's *hands and looks into his eyes*): Oh, God, you believe that! You believe that!

(LARS GRUBBE *enters.*)

KING: Well, Lars, what do you have to tell me?

GRUBBE: Without circumlocution: the French ambassador is here again offering you an alliance.

KING (*sits down*): Again! And he dares do that after his latest crime against the Edict of Nantes,[29] after the siege of La Rochelle with all its horrors, where our fellow believers were starved and cut down. Bid him get back to his country and tell the cardinal that the Swedes will eat the bark off the pines of Brandenburg before they eat French rolls out of the heretic's hand!

GRUBBE: Your Majesty, may I say one word?

KING: Speak!

GRUBBE: The ambassador has 400,000 *riksdaler* along as subsidy for the first year . . .

KING: Let him consume them himself! Did Christian IV have any blessing from the Jesuit money he got? The negotiations are over! What else do you have to say?

GRUBBE: The duke's 50,000 *riksdaler* have been authorized as half-pay for the soldiers, but the troops still don't have anything to eat.

KING: What's that? Lars, go out and look at the birds, and then tell me who feeds them! That will give you a brighter view of the matter. What else do you have to report?

GRUBBE: Letters and audiences.

KING: Start with the letters.

GRUBBE (*takes an open letter from a pouch*): From the elector of Brandenburg.

KING: What does he say?

GRUBBE: He does not grant you the right to march through his territories, and he will not turn over any fortress.

KING (*opens a map*): No marching through Brandenburg for the relief of Magdeburg? Is he a friend? Oh, well. Then I'll go and take Frankfurt an der Oder; then he and I can talk about this later. A red cross on Frankfurt! What does the elector of Saxony say?

GRUBBE: He has failed to answer three letters.

KING: Good! Then he shall come three times to beg for help himself! In his own high person. Who wants an audience?

GRUBBE: The governor of Mecklenburg, Wallenstein's representative in the duchy.

KING: No, what are you saying? Wallenstein's? Am I finally to ... Let him come in right away.

RÅLAMB: Your Majesty! He might be a Jesuit!

KING: What if he were! They're people, too, just like the Mohammedans, Jews, and heathens I have in my pay. Go, Grubbe, and let him come immediately!

(GRUBBE *goes.*)

RÅLAMB: My king!

KING: Quiet, Erik! Haven't you seen that God is with us? Who can then be against us? I hate Jesuits as deeply as you do, but I fear them less. If you are afraid for me, stay. Besides, here come my lifeguards.

BANÉR (*comes in without noticing the* KING *immediately; somewhat noisy*): Isn't the old man here?

KING: Am I the one you call the old man?

BANÉR: Beg your pardon, Your Majesty; it's Gustav Horn; he's only thirty-eight, but still he's the oldest, and so we call him that.

(TORSTENSSON *enters*.)

KING: Yes, Johan, you're a fighter, not least in drinking bouts . . . but learn a little gentleness from Lennart, and I'll like you better . . . (HORN *enters*.) And a little wisdom from Gustav Horn . . . (BRAHE *enters*.) A little agreeableness from Nils Brahe . . . Come and sit down here, Nils. (*The* KING *indicates a place at the table for* BRAHE; *the* KING *himself goes to the open door and looks out*.)

KING (*comes back and sits down at the table*): Take your places. The governor of Mecklenburg is here. Bring him in, Erik Rålamb.

(RÅLAMB *goes out*.)

KING: Be serious, Johan, because this game will be serious.

RÅLAMB (*comes in again, followed by the* GOVERNOR): The governor of Mecklenburg presents his respects to His Majesty, the king of Sweden.

(GOVERNOR *enters, bows, and looks about for a chair*.)

KING (*remains seated*): Welcome, governor.

GOVERNOR: Your Grace . . .

RÅLAMB: Say, Your Majesty.

GOVERNOR: Your Grace!

KING (*angry*): Does your ignorance or your defiance deny me my royal title?

GOVERNOR: Neither. I speak and act only on the orders of my lord the duke of Mecklenburg, Albrecht von Wallenstein.

KING: And he denies me the majesty of Sweden . . .

GOVERNOR: His Majesty of Sweden, King Sigismund Vasa, resides in Warsaw . . .

KING (*violently*): What?

BANÉR (*strikes the table with his fist*): Behave yourself, Jesuit!

KING (*to* BANÉR): Quiet, Banér! (*To the* GOVERNOR) Let me inform you that I was elected king, elected by the Estates . . .

GOVERNOR: Oh! We believed Sweden ceased to be an elective monarchy when the great Gustav Vasa made it a hereditary monarchy in 1544.

KING (*to* HORN): I cannot speak with that Jesuit.

(GOVERNOR *takes a chair in order to sit down, but the chair is pulled away by* BANÉR.)

KING: State your errand quickly; tell us what your lord, the duke, has by way of plans, intentions . . .

GOVERNOR (*smiles*): Surely one doesn't tell one's plans.

BRAHE (*to the* KING): Your Majesty, don't exchange words with a papist! Let the sword speak!

GOVERNOR: Why call me a papist and a Jesuit, when I'm not?

KING: What are you then?

GOVERNOR: I am a Lutheran!

KING: And serve the duke of Friedland, the emperor's own Wallenstein?

GOVERNOR: Yes! My master is like that. Born a Protestant, he has finally put all conflicts about faith behind him, for life has taught him to have tolerance for all faiths. It amazes me that you treat me as an enemy, for my prince is an admirer of Your Grace—not to say a friend.

KING: Incomprehensible!

GOVERNOR: If I may have a chair, I'll explain more fully . . .

KING: Erik, give the governor a chair; why, he's an old man, and we're young.

(RÅLAMB *unwillingly gives the* GOVERNOR *a chair.*)

GOVERNOR (*sits down, puts on his glasses, and sizes up the company*): You gentlemen are really remarkably young, not to say extremely young.

HORN: Now he has gone too far!

KING: Let the old man talk! His insolence amuses me!

GOVERNOR (*to the* KING): Your Grace was the brother-in-law of the late Bethlen Gabor,[30] weren't you? Yes! The prince of Siebenbürgen was a vassal of the Turks, and two years ago Your Grace tried to get alliances with the Turks and with the Tartars! That wasn't nice, and it wasn't good politics. Because no matter what we Christians are, we are duty bound to stick together against heathen dogs!

(BRAHE *draws his sword.*)

KING (*to* BRAHE): Put your sword back, Nils!

GOVERNOR: My prince, my hero, Albrecht von Wallenstein (*rises and bows*), sees farther than that, and so he has made it his life purpose to unify Germany first by getting rid of princes and electors, and then to throw the Turks out of Europe, recapture Byzantium, and rebuild the Eastern Roman Empire. That is a thought befitting an emperor!

KING (*unwillingly gripped*): A great thought, indeed!

GOVERNOR: Thereby the great Muscovite power is made part of Europe, and Asia need no longer be feared. If I go back to the beginning, or the unification of Germany through the elimination of the petty princes, Your Grace (*bows*) has already appeared as the Friedlander's ally, and I end this audience by expressing my master's sympathy for Your Grace and his best wishes for your continued success (*Gets up, and hands the chair back to* RÅLAMB)

KING: No, sit down, and continue your explanation.

GOVERNOR: Impossible. Duke Bogislaw is expecting me. (*Sizes up the group, one by one*) You are Field Marshal Horn! General Banér! Colonel Torstensson of the artillery—only twenty-seven years old! Colonel Brahe (*smiles*), who always has to sit closest to the king's heart . . . all of you relatives of the king, more or less; all youngsters and splendid men, filled with faith and zeal and love of honor and love of pleasure . . . Farewell, young men; the future is yours; that is, if you learn not to underestimate your enemy! (*Goes*)

KING: What's this? Who is this man who in a couple of minutes turns my thoughts upside down? Is Wallenstein's governor a Protestant?

HORN: Yes, Your Majesty, just as his generals Hebron and Pechman are Lutherans, and half of his army is made up of unbelievers and Protestants.

KING: So I'm to fight against fellow believers! But the purpose of the war was to protect them!

HORN: The contradictions of life won't be resolved by us mortals . . .

BANÉR: Resolved, no; but cut off.

KING: Wallenstein has greater thoughts than I; he sees in the remote future unity, where I saw only disunity . . . And this archfiend, this Antichrist, says he's my friend? Can I be my enemy's friend?

TORSTENSSON: This seeming contradiction St. Paul resolved when he said, "When he ascended up on high, he led captivity captive, and gave gifts unto men. Now that he ascended, what is it but that he also descended first into the lower parts of the earth? He that descended is the same also that ascended," and so on. But, adds the apostle, "Till we all come in the unity of the faith, and of the knowledge of the Son of God, unto a perfect man . . . that we henceforth be no more children, tossed to and fro, and carried about with every wind of doctrine, by the sleight of men . . . But . . . grow up into Him in all things, which is the head, even Christ!" [31]

BANÉR: Thanks, Lennart, but I didn't come here to hear St. Paul but to fight!

BRAHE: Right!

KING: If I don't exactly agree, it's because my thoughts take their own course . . . I will try to follow them . . .

TOTT (*enters hastily*): Your Majesty, I come without being summoned!

KING: You always do, Åke Tott! Sit down.

TOTT: A refugee from Magdeburg says that our Falkenberg [32] has been surrounded and that Tilly has arrived to begin the siege!

KING: That means: everyone to his post so we can take Frankfurt an der Oder. Then Brandenburg will have to grant us the right to march through it—to Magdeburg! (*Gets up. They all get up.*)

TOTT (*puts a packet of letters on the table*): But here's a bundle of notes, overdue in Hamburg and presented by the Jew.

KING (*puts the bundle in one of his pockets*): Fine! My brother-in-law will redeem them . . . in Berlin!

TOTT: And the Jew?

KING: Take the Jew along and dine him royally. "For there is no difference between the Jew and the Greek: for the same Lord is over all," says St. Paul.[33] Right, Lennart?

TORSTENSSON: But he certainly means something else . . .

KING: Certainly, certainly, certainly! So, we're off.

STENBOCK (*enters*): Your Majesty, I'm too late!

KING: You always come too late, Fredrik Stenbock, because of your clothes! Be on your toes now!

STENBOCK: Your Majesty! The troops are dissatisfied, and threaten mutiny!

KING: Have the signals for immediate departure given, and the dissatisfaction will collapse like a worn-out horse . . .

STENBOCK: A hungry horse won't carry his burden . . . And the men want butter on their bread!

KING: They won't get it! March! (*Goes by the birthday table, where* RÅLAMB *has stood most of the time*) What are you standing there guarding?

RÅLAMB: Two young people's secret, two old people's hope and joy.

KING: I understand you, dreamer, knight of virtue and honor; go and tell your protégés that, that . . . well, think of what you're to say yourself. (*Goes out*)

CURTAIN

SCENE 2

A room in a farmhouse, cluttered with captured flags, drums, weapons, and other war materiel; the KING *is sitting at a table with a map in front of him.* HORN, TORSTENSSON, *and* BANÉR *are next to him; all of them look worried and thoughtful.*

KING (*draws with chalk on the map*): Now I'll cross out Frankfurt an der Oder with red: it is taken! (*To* HORN) What do you say, old man?

(HORN *remains silent; distressed.*)

KING: Nothing? Well, young Lennart, what does St. Paul say about this?

TORSTENSSON (*hurt*): Your Majesty! (*Someone pounds on the door.*)

KING: There, there, forgive me. (*To* BANÉR) Johan, what would you do now if you were in my place?

BANÉR: I'd rather not say!

KING: Haven't you sent Rålamb up to the palace?

BANÉR: Yes, I have, Your Majesty. (*The pounding on the door increases.*)

KING: Well, I sent him away so I could talk and act freely. That youngster has won my heart so fully that he looks after my conscience like a jealous woman. There are moments when I'm afraid of him! (*General silence answers the* KING's *speech.*) He actually tyrannizes over me . . . that's how it is; why I don't know, but that's how it is! What is that noise out there? . . . Speak out, Johan . . . you're the bravest.

BANÉR: It's the soldiers, of course, dissatisfied because they haven't been paid . . .

KING: Always their pay!

HORN: All they've had to eat during the last seventy-two hours is dry bread . . .

KING: Supplies from Hamburg are expected at any minute.

HORN: The wagons have turned back and gone to the enemy outside Magdeburg instead, because the notes haven't been redeemed.

KING: How much you know that I'm never permitted to know! How is my friend, Marcus of Hamburg?

HORN: He's not exactly suffering, for Tott is treating him to both food and drink, but he's dissatisfied and will no doubt avenge himself.

BANÉR: And he's joined forces with that Jew from Wolgast and other Israelites; and they say when there are ten of them, they'll hold divine services or read the Torah, as they call it.

KING: What is Torah? Do you know, Lennart?

TORSTENSSON: The Torah rolls? The five first books of the Old Testament, the Pentateuch, the same holy book as our . . .

KING: Almost the gospel! So they're unbelievers! I certainly can't let them celebrate divine services, can I? . . . But this noise . . . it makes me ill. Johan, go and find out about it, and have Fabricius come right away.

(BANÉR *goes out.*)

KING: My friends, you know I feel how someone has taken me by the hair to drag me where I don't want to go. Those cries out there . . . they're not the cries of want or suffering; they're the evil passions that war has let loose . . . I know where it will lead; I know I don't want to go there; but I'm being dragged there. (*Gets up, moved*) For twenty years I've been at war, but I can never get used to the horrible smoke of powder; it smells of the devil, sulphur and saltpeter, and it makes people evil as if it rose from hell to mock the thunder of heaven; but it brings only showers of blood and tears instead of blessed rain for the crops of the field.

BANÉR (*comes in with* MARCUS): Your Majesty, Marcus of Hamburg requests an audience.

KING: What do you wish, Marcus?

MARCUS: Great king, I am lost if I don't render an account for the notes to my superior . . .

KING: You will get your money, but I need time . . .

MARCUS: Time? But I don't get time.

(BANÉR *goes out; the noise increases*.)

KING: And that's why you get revenge by stopping the supply wagons?

MARCUS: Yes.

KING: Do you consider that nice?

MARCUS: It is just. More just than cutting down two thousand of the emperor's forces in Frankfurt because his forces had cut down four hundred Swedes in Neu-Brandenburg![34] And it is nicer than the levies on fellow believers.

KING (*to* HORN): Should I take this?

(HORN *remains silent*.)

KING (*to* MARCUS): Go to my secretary, Grubbe, who has charge of money matters . . .

MARCUS: No, I won't; for I just came from your secretary, who sent me over here to the signer of these notes.

KING (*sits down*): What do you ask for thirty days' extension?

MARCUS: I don't have the right to sell what I don't own.

KING (*violently*): Do you think I want you to do something wrong?

MARCUS: Yes, I do!

KING (*controls himself*): Listen, I have been told that you and yours wish to hold divine services . . .

(TORSTENSSON *makes a violent movement of impatience and rattles his sword*.)

KING: I certainly don't want to link matters of faith with money matters . . .

MARCUS: But still . . .

(HORN *gets up violently, rushes up to the* KING, *bends down, and, violently distressed, whispers to him*.)

MARCUS (*in the pause that ensues*): A Christian sells everything, even freedom of belief, and he is a happy buyer, but a poor payer.

KING: Field Marshal Horn will put up his private fortune as guarantee for the notes. Are you satisfied, Marcus?

(BANÉR *enters.*)

MARCUS: The field marshal's name is good, because he owns good estates. I accept.

KING: How gracious!

BANÉR (*takes* MARCUS *by the collar and shoves him out*): Out, devil! Out! (*To the* KING) He stirred up the troops!

KING: What do the soldiers want?

BANÉR: To plunder.

KING: I knew it! Plunder my brother-in-law's city, plunder my wife's countrymen! No! Not that!

BANÉR: No help for it! The Scotch are furious, the Irish are drunk, the Dutch and the Saxons are running about with fire, the whole army is crazy.

KING: Anything but that! I'll go talk to them!

BANÉR: Don't go! The storm is loose!

KING: I will quiet it! You stay here! (*When the others indicate that they want to accompany him*) Stay! (*Rushes out*)

HORN (*to* BANÉR): Why did he send for the pastor?

TORSTENSSON: Why, he always does when he intends to commit a wrong.

BANÉR: He's like a lovable child or a beautiful woman; everything is becoming to him, even his less attractive deeds.

HORN: That's why he has been called . . .

TORSTENSSON: Even to sin, for without sin he would become self-righteous . . .

BANÉR: A little sin is very becoming to him; otherwise, he'd not be human . . . he'd be too great and superhuman.

HORN (*listening to what is happening outside*): This won't end well, though.

BANÉR: Everything ends well for God's fair-haired boy.

TORSTENSSON: And it'll end with his taking the French money, too!

HORN: Let it! When our natural allies—the Pomeranian, the Brandenburger, and the Saxon—don't want to help, then . . .

TORSTENSSON: For shame, Gustav!

BANÉR: I think we'd be better off if we limited ourselves to serving instead of giving advice!

HORN: Exactly what I think!

BRAHE (*enters*): Where is the king?

BANÉR: Who knows? Here he is!

KING (*enters; upset, hatless, and with his clothes in disorder*): Even this! Even this! Bargain, grant, take back! They threw stones on me! See—I've lost my hat! And now they're plundering! Here are the articles of war, our good intentions, purity itself, torn to bits. (*He strews about printed sheets from a torn book.*) The Swedish soldier is no better than the enemy! Just as good drunkards! Listen to the screams of innocent people! (*Covers his ears with his hands*) Nils, sit down by me—you have something to say, I see.

BRAHE: Your Majesty, there is a way of getting out of this.

KING: Can I get out of this?

BRAHE: Yes, in one way: only one.

KING: Speak!

BRAHE: The French ambassador is here.

KING (*gets up*): He's always after me like the devil—the tempter! Let him get behind me!

BRAHE: But then Marcus won't! And Marcus is right; Marcus will be ruined; Marcus is a human being and a family man with responsibilities, feelings, and justified claims on life.

KING (*childishly, slyly*): Where is Erik Rålamb?

BRAHE (*roguishly*): He has been sent so far away that he can't hear you.

KING: Why should you be unkind to me? You all are, because I have to be lenient with you because of my father's sins . . . the bloodbath of Linköping.

TOTT (*rushes in*): Your Majesty, this is going beyond all reason.

I'm not soft-hearted, but I can't stand hearing women and children scream curses over our heads! If they were our enemies, but they're our friends and fellow believers . . .

KING: Silence, Åke . . .

TOTT: No, I can't keep still! Two thousand enemies cut down, a thousand Croatians captured, but there isn't one enemy left in the whole city . . . Why in God's name go on?

FABRICIUS (*enters*): Your Majesty has summoned me.

KING: Yes, for I have only poor councillors . . . Listen; the troops have mutinied because they weren't allowed to plunder; without troops I can't wage war . . .

FABRICIUS: The troops demanded plundering because they hadn't received their pay; if they're paid, they'll stop plundering.

KING: I have no money! (*Pause*) I can hear your thoughts in your silence . . . and I am listening . . . Advise me, Fabricius!

FABRICIUS: No, I have been sent here to comfort the sick and the dying, but not to serve as a military councillor.

KING (*to* HORN): Advise me, Gustav Horn!

HORN: No, I am the servant, and my king alone shall command and bear the responsibility.

KING (*to* TOTT): Åke!

TOTT: I don't understand politics; I'm only a soldier.

KING (*to* TORSTENSSON): Lennart?

(TORSTENSSON *remains silent.*)

KING: Nils Brahe, say it like this: of two evils, choose the lesser; but, if the two are just as evil, one no longer chooses. That was Nils speaking! So I'll go to the French ambassador now!

BANÉR (*stations himself before the door*): No! Not the king! Our king shall be as pure as the flag we follow! Gustav Horn, show us that you can wear a dirty shirt for your king . . .

HORN (*gets up*): Well said, Banér; let us touch the dirt, but not he! To the French ambassador, then! We already have the authority!

KING (*childishly happy as if he had got out of something unpleasant*): Thank you, my friends! It takes greater courage to do an evil deed than to capture a fortress! (*When* BRAHE, *too, wants to leave*) No, Nils, not you! Not you!

(HORN *and* BANÉR *leave.*)

KING (*sinks down on a chair*): That was where I did not want to go. Thy will be done, O Lord!

CURTAIN

SCENE 3

In the camp outside Frankfurt an der Oder. In the foreground the KING *is sitting by a simple table.* LARS GRUBBE *is standing beside him. In the background a part of the city can be seen.*

KING: I've signed the agreement with France,[35] and I'm waiting for the money. Now I can force the Brandenburger and the Saxon into an alliance against the emperor.

GRUBBE: The amount is large?

KING: Half a million French livres a year.

GRUBBE: And the conditions . . .

KING: I have not promised anything . . . I have only signed my name; the bullet from Dirschau [36] keeps me from writing anything more than that, you know, and the old wound has bothered me especially the last few days . . . Look, there comes the money of sin! (HORN *and* BANÉR *accompanied by the* SERGEANT MAJOR *and the* QUARTERMASTER, *who are carrying blue linen bags and are escorted by six Finnish cavalrymen led by the* FINNISH ENSIGN, *enter.*)

HORN: Your Majesty, the agreement has been ratified, and here's the money.

KING: Lars Grubbe, go and pay Marcus for the Hamburg notes;

then divide half of what's left among the soldiers; with the other half try to make up for all the damage that the plundering has done to the people of the city.

GRUBBE: Excuse me, Your Majesty, but then we'll be just as poor tomorrow . . .

KING: So be it . . . We are Christians, aren't we?—even if we're not missionaries . . . Go, and do what is right first, or we can expect no blessing.

(GRUBBE *leaves, accompanied by the escort.*)

KING (*who has observed the* ENSIGN): Ensign, stay!

(ENSIGN *stays; frightened.*)

KING: Come here! . . . What is your name?

FINNISH ENSIGN (*speaks without a Finnish accent*): Axel Eriksson of the Finnish cavalry.

KING: Any other name?

FINNISH ENSIGN: Other?

KING: I'll tell you that later. You were one of those who threw stones at me a while ago, and you were one of the leaders in the mutiny.

FINNISH ENSIGN: Your Majesty, it wasn't I!

KING: Oh! Then it was Sparre!

FINNISH ENSIGN (*on his knees*): Mercy!

KING: Axel Eriksson Sparre, your father [37] lost his life in the blood-bath at Linköping because he did not want to break his oath of loyalty to King Sigismund; your mother's name was Brahe—Ebba, at that, and her father, old Count Peter, called my grand-father, King Gustav Vasa, uncle. So you are my kinsman; that you can't be my friend, I understand. What my father did to yours you cannot forgive, but I forgive you what you have done to me. Do you want to remain in my service?

FINNISH ENSIGN: Your Majesty, I am not worthy of that!

KING: Rise, and try to be worthy of it!

FINNISH ENSIGN: I don't know . . .

KING: Don't you know if you can trust yourself?

FINNISH ENSIGN: No! I was a child when it happened in Linköping, and I was on my knees in the snow beside my mother to beg the duke for mercy when he'd ride by; we were there for hours, I cried, I froze . . . when the duke came, he wouldn't look at us, but his horse threw dirt from the street into my face . . . I vowed then . . .

KING: I understand all that, and I would have done as the poor child did; but, you see, these noble lords, Horn and Banér, kinsmen from Linköping, too, they have forgiven. Go, Sparre, and try to do likewise!

FINNISH ENSIGN: I wish I could, but . . .

KING: Just stay, and, if the temptation becomes too great for you, come to me, free yourself from hate, but do not injure me, for under my plain coat and my simple person is concealed an anointed of the Lord . . . (*Gets up*) Farewell.

(FINNISH ENSIGN *goes, after looking as if he wanted to talk.*)

KING: Why should I be reminded today of what should soon be atoned for? And why should the bullet from Dirschau, Sigismund's souvenir, begin to be uneasy again? The thorn in the flesh! It is sad, very sad to be alive—at times. There comes Lennart, half-running; something important must be up if he hurries.

TORSTENSSON: Your Majesty! Great news! . . .

KING: Quickly!

TORSTENSSON: Wallenstein has been dismissed from his command! [38]

KING: Wallenstein, our archenemy! What does that mean?

TORSTENSSON: The electors' assembly in Regensburg has demanded his dismissal, and he has given up his command, disbanded his army, and shut himself up in Gitschin, his castle in Bohemia.

KING: Is the emperor sane? To disarm before the enemy, to withdraw? What *does* this mean?

TORSTENSSON: No can can tell.

KING: Is the war over, then? Against whom am I to fight?

HORN: Tilly. Tilly is still there.

KING: He doesn't matter. No, Wallenstein was the enemy, and just the same—do you remember what the governor said?—about the imperial thought? And now he's gone! Don't you miss him?

HORN: No, but think of Tilly!

KING: I have Tilly in a sack down in the forests of Thuringia; all I have to do is to tie it up. And now I go to Berlin! Come with me, Banér. (*Goes, accompanied by* BANÉR)

HORN: What now?

TORSTENSSON: This bright, easy nature, that usually follows only his clear conscience . . .

HORN: This divine lightheartedness that makes him think everything he does is right . . .

TORSTENSSON: But you saw that what happened was unavoidable. How can one have a guilty conscience about what can't be avoided?

HORN: And just the same: in a few hours we've become not the allies of Catholic France but its mercenary troops. France has not committed itself to take part in the war, only to pay for it. What is this war *now*? Cardinal Richelieu's war against Hapsburg! But do you know France's conditions that the king did not want to read?

TORSTENSSON: No.

HORN: Well, the Swedes have promised to observe neutrality toward the Catholic League [39] and the elector of Bavaria!

TORSTENSSON: Why, that's nonsense! Or the war is over!

HORN: Do you believe that our good king clearly understands what this war is?

TORSTENSSON: Hardly, but Oxenstjerna did. Do you remember what he said in the council: "The major objective of the German war was in no way the defense of religion, the weapons for which are of a spiritual nature such as prayers and tears, but the attainment for the Swedish crown and its religious allies, the German electors, of security and independence."

HORN: Let us thank God that it is not a religious war, for our weapons at least are not those of the spirit.

TORSTENSSON: But the king, who came over here with his bright, happy faith . . .

HORN: Don't disturb him, for he'll walk securely on his rope as long as his sleep lasts, but, if you awaken him, he'll tumble into the net. I suspect that he left Oxenstjerna at home so he could be undisturbed; Oxenstjerna always has to analyze everything and tear into bits the king's wholesome power of action. Why, you can see that we're going forward, forward to something unknown, undetermined, but forward at any rate. (*Pause*)

TORSTENSSON: Do you believe that the king intends to keep the provisions for neutrality?

HORN: Today, yes, but he'll break them the day after tomorrow!

TORSTENSSON: That's called the art of politics: to promise and not to keep. (*Gets up*)

HORN: Let's stick to the art of war then, Lennart. There one does what one can. (*Gets up*) So, to Berlin!

CURTAIN

SCENE 4

The palace park in Berlin. Clipped trees and bushes, espalier, colonnades, a fountain, benches, tables. Above them can be seen the palace with lighted windows and an open balcony with formally clad people.

HORN *and* BANÉR *enter.*

HORN: The elector is certainly not expecting us at his party!

BANÉR: For him to receive twenty thousand men besides Torstensson's cannons in his drawing rooms would be expecting a lot.

HORN: That's right, but to hesitate to receive the Swedish king is an unnecessary insult.

BANÉR: There's the king. Now it will be the elector who'll be received.

KING: On the spot, promptly! Fine! (*Looks up at the palace*) Terribly ugly building, that! However . . . Johan, go up to the palace and tell the elector that his brother-in-law is receiving here in the park just now. And, if he wants to throw you out, go to a window and wave your sash; Torstensson will immediately answer with a volley, which we can say was a welcoming salute. Are you afraid, Johan?

BANÉR: Afraid? Of the glances of the lovely ladies, maybe. I'm not afraid of frightening the elector.

KING: So: forward! and upward!

(BANÉR *runs up the stairs and enters the palace.*)

KING (*sits down on a bench*): Coming, not coming; coming, not coming . . .

HORN: He'll come!

KING: Where is Erik Rålamb now?

HORN: He was sent to Magdeburg.

KING: I long for him at times, in spite of his unbearable impertinence. He was never ordinary, but his high-mindedness never depressed me, even though it made me insignificant beside him. (*The widowed* PRINCESS ANNA, *the* KING's *mother-in-law, and the widowed* PRINCESS BETHLEN GABOR, *the* KING's *sister-in-law, walk by in the background.*) No, look! My mother-in-law and my sister-in-law! And I let myself be surprised here like an apple thief in an orchard! (*Conceals himself behind a tree; the ladies exit.*) I don't like this; I'd rather have stormed the palace with my sword in my hand.

HORN: I can see Johan! The palace has been taken. (BANÉR *can be seen on a palace balcony; waves his sash; a cannon shot can be heard, and then a volley of musket shots. Movement in the palace windows.* BANÉR *disappears.*)

KING: Now he's coming!

(GEORG WILHELM, ELECTOR OF BRANDENBURG, GUSTAV ADOLF'S

brother-in-law, comes down at the back with BANÉR. *They are speaking heatedly.* KING *advances a few steps toward them; then stops, waiting.*)

ELECTOR (*irritated*): I can certainly not bid you welcome, brother-in-law, when you appear with your army in my states!

KING: You don't have to . . . I come as I come to a kinsman and ally in the faith . . .

ELECTOR (*furiously*): May I point out right now that I am not your ally in the faith, since I am a Calvinist and consequently have nothing to do with the religious peace of Augsburg?

KING: There are so many confessions of faith here that it would be best not to speak of them. On the other hand, we do have an enemy in common . . .

ELECTOR (*as before*): We had a common enemy, we Germanic peoples, and that was France, but now you've allied yourself with that enemy and that's why we can no longer be friends.

KING: That's putting it frankly, at least! Well, as an enemy, then, I demand, with the right of a superior enemy, that you surrender the fortresses of Spandau and Küstrin.[40]

ELECTOR (*beside himself*): My fortresses? Never as long as I am a liegeman of the emperor, and he has not released me from my vow!

KING: The emperor has broken his vow . . .

ELECTOR: I will not break mine because of that, and I won't be better because he has made himself worse . . .

KING (*somewhat heatedly*): Then I'll have to take your fortresses, since you don't understand what's best for you. I have to get to the relief of Magdeburg, which is threatened by our common enemy, the emperor's general Tilly.

ELECTOR: Magdeburg? What do you know about Magdeburg?

KING: More than you! And above all that Elector Johan Georg of Saxony will not give me his support.

ELECTOR: May that Saxon, the damned Lutheran, go to hell!

KING: People have told me that you Calvinists and Lutherans have split so that you treat each other like Turks and Tartars, but, when a common danger threatens both of you, obviously common interests ought to force you together.

ELECTOR (*raves and wipes the sweat from his face now and then*): Us together? No, rather with the pope in Rome or the devil in hell than with Martin Luther. You talk about the edict of restitution, the restoration of the stolen monastery and church property. Yes, but who stole and who took it? Do you know that Luther [41] left a large fortune: first, the large Augustinian cloister in Wittenberg which his heirs sold for three thousand seven hundred *gulden;* second: the little cloister which his heirs sold for three hundred *thaler;* an orchard and a hops garden for five hundred *gulden;* the estate Wechsdorf for one thousand five hundred *gulden;* the estate Zerlsdorf for nine hundred and fifty-six *gulden!* Where did he get all that? Ask, ask, ask that devil of a Mammon that made him the belly for a god! Ask the Saxon brewer, that wine sack, who hasn't been sober since he was baptized . . .

KING (*who has tried to interrupt him several times*): This is not a religious discussion . . .

ELECTOR: So, if it's political, may I send my minister, von Schwarzenberg? He has full authority and is less hot-tempered than I. I beg you to excuse me now so I can return to my guests. His Excellency will be here shortly.

KING: Wait! When you treat me as a stranger and an intruder, you forget that I am a German prince of East Prussia, which through the peace treaty of Altmark [42] was ceded to the Swedish Crown; you forget that I am the master of the customs and duties in the German harbors there; that Swedish troops have freed Stralsund, Stettin, and Frankfurt from the emperor's invaders; and that Magdeburg has declared itself on *our* side. When Magdeburg is now threatened and you can't do anything, I ask that I may man Spandau and Küstrin to protect my march through your territories . . .

ELECTOR: His Excellency will be here shortly! (*Leaves*)

KING: My brother-in-law is impolite, but he's afraid of gunfire. Gustav, hint to Lennart that he let His Excellency have a salvo when he comes down; that ought to simplify the conversation a little.

HORN (*goes out*): Certainly, Your Majesty!

KING: And you, Johan, stay here behind the bushes and witness the conversation. If Erik Rålamb should unexpectedly come along, tie him and lock him up until it's all over.

BANÉR (*conceals himself behind the bushes*): Right, Your Majesty!

KING: Now His Excellency may come when he wants to . . . (*Soft music can be heard from the palace, and couples dance by the windows.*)

(SCHWARZENBERG *comes down from the palace; he is courteous, crafty, but superior.* KING *remains standing; waits.*)

SCHWARZENBERG: Your Majesty, I do not have the privilege of being known to you personally . . . (*Volley fired outside*)

SCHWARZENBERG (*without permitting himself to be disturbed*): . . . but in compensation the Swedish king is an old, valued acquaintance of the whole German empire . . .

KING: The Protestant parts, perhaps . . .

SCHWARZENBERG: Pardon me, I said the whole empire, without regard to faith . . .

KING: Strange how little importance you give to faith.

SCHWARZENBERG: Well, yes, there are so many varieties nowadays; the faith of the heart, the faith of the mouth, and others like them . . .

KING: But may I negotiate with you, Your Excellency, as a brother in the faith . . . ?

SCHWARZENBERG: If we should dismiss the matters of faith and restrict ourselves entirely to political questions . . .

KING: No; perhaps we aren't brothers in the faith; perhaps you, like the elector, my brother-in-law, are a Calvinist?

SCHWARZENBERG: To tell the truth, Your Majesty, I'm not even that; I am still a Roman Catholic, and will remain one until I find a united Protestant faith which appeals to me more.

KING: This is beyond my understanding: you are a Catholic and are the elector's minister?

SCHWARZENBERG: Yes. We are like that, and I can delight Your Majesty with a humble greeting from the papal nuncio, who is up there in the palace right now . . .

KING: I don't accept greetings from papal nuncios . . .

SCHWARZENBERG: The Holy Father, Urban VIII, expresses through his ambassador his sincere joy over Your Majesty's great victories over the emperor's armies . . .

KING: I don't understand. Or are you joking? Aren't the emperor and the pope friends any longer?

SCHWARZENBERG: The pope has never been the emperor's friend! And never can be! The emperor is a pagan descendant of the Caesars of the Rome that is dead; the pope is the heir of the Rome the apostles Christianized. His kingdom is not of this world since Christ himself is its ruler. That's the secret of the names of Guelphs and Ghibellines,[43] and that's why, you see, we cannot appreciate your Luther, because he was the friend of the emperor and a friend of princes opposed to the pope. For that reason we call Luther, too, a pagan and an anti-Christ.

KING: What I have to listen to!

SCHWARZENBERG: Yes, Your Majesty; when one gets mixed up in . . . excuse my expression . . . foreign people's domestic affairs, one ought to find out how these people think and feel . . .

KING: Jesuit!

SCHWARZENBERG: Jesus is my master, and what you use as a term of abuse is a title of honor to us.

KING: Do you belong to the order?

SCHWARZENBERG: The order of Jesus has always been dear to me, for it has taught me humility and obedience . . .

KING: I imagine! Deceitful words that confuse the mind, intellectual tricks that rob people of their faith and their happy self-confidence! I came here to confer about your fortresses, and you

lure me into the labyrinths of thought so that I forget why I am
here . . . Do you want to talk about the forts now?

SCHWARZENBERG: No, I don't want to waste words . . .

KING: God's death, man, are you mocking me, or am I to listen to
your sermon like a schoolboy?

SCHWARZENBERG: Your Majesty, I have come to get your signa-
ture . . .

KING: On a false document? Never!

SCHWARZENBERG (*takes up a document and writing utensils*): Listen
to me! Here is the assignment of Spandau and Küstrin to you,
with the provision that they are to be returned to the elector of
Brandenburg when Magdeburg has been taken. Two Swedish
generals' signatures will do.

KING (*reads the paper*): Good! Why these long litanies, then?
(*Signs with his left hand after he has tried in vain to sign with
his right*)

KING: Banér, come here and sign this!

(BANÉR *enters, stares at* SCHWARZENBERG, *who returns his stare.*)

KING (*presents him*): General Banér!

SCHWARZENBERG: The unconquerable!

KING: Sign, Johan!

(BANÉR *signs after some hesitation.*)

KING (*signals*): Gustav Horn!

(HORN *enters.*)

KING (*presents him*): Field Marshal Horn!

SCHWARZENBERG: The wise!

KING: Sign it, Gustav; we have received Spandau and Küstrin!

HORN: Without conditions?

KING: With the condition that they be returned when Magdeburg
has been taken.

HORN (*thoughtfully*): Taken? By whom?

KING: By me! Go ahead; sign!

(HORN *signs.*)

SCHWARZENBERG (*takes the paper*): And now the elector awaits Your Majesty as a guest in his palace.

KING: Convey my thanks to my brother-in-law, but I prefer to sleep in Spandau. It feels decidedly calmer in a fort than outside a palace!

SCHWARZENBERG: His Swedish Majesty's wish is as good as a command. I have the honor . . . and take the liberty to wish that Your Majesty may be blessed on his victorious path.

KING: You don't mean that!

SCHWARZENBERG: Yes, Your Majesty, I do mean that! (*Goes*)

KING (*pleased*): That is the way to take fortresses—with a quill pen!

HORN (*serious*): The sword would have been better!

KING: But think of it. His Excellency was a Catholic just as Wallenstein's governor was a Protestant; soon we'll have to invent field badges for the different faiths. Does anybody understand this? I don't, but just keep going.

BANÉR (*shaking* HORN): You're not happy, old man! Chin up . . . tonight there'll be a celebration in Spandau!

HORN: Let me alone!

(STENBOCK *and* TOTT, *somewhat gay, come down from the palace arm in arm without seeing the* KING.)

BANÉR: Where have those birds been?

TOTT: We've been up dancing in the palace! Beautiful women, good wine . . .

STENBOCK: And an orchestra! (*Takes a few dance steps with* TOTT)

HORN: Quiet, boys!

STENBOCK: Why? Haven't we taken the palace?

KING (*steps forward*): No, *Lennart* has with his salvos . . . Have you seen Erik Rålamb?

TOTT: Yes, he's up there . . . He'll be down soon.

KING: Then I'll flee; the only person I run away from is Erik. (*To* HORN *and* BANÉR) Come! Lennart is signaling assembly. Come! (*Goes out, accompanied by* HORN *and* BANÉR)

ERIK RÅLAMB (*down from the palace*): Is the king here?

TOTT: Is that any of your business?

RÅLAMB: Is he avoiding me? Why?

STENBOCK: What the hell!

RÅLAMB: I don't want to talk with intoxicated people—I want to see my king . . .

TOTT: You can't!

RÅLAMB: Who's to hinder me as long as I tread the path of virtue and honor?

STENBOCK: I! A little question, though! What right have you to carry the queen's colors, those of Brandenburg?

RÅLAMB (*embarrassed*): Because Her Majesty has given them to me (*takes off his hat*) . . . as a reminder of my promise as a knight to watch over her consort . . .

STENBOCK: Erik, your cheeks are raising Her Majesty's colors—white and red—a little too plainly; watch out for your head—and your heart!

RÅLAMB: Blasphemer! Where is the king? His life is in danger!

TOTT: Are you starting to see Jesuits, too?

RÅLAMB: No, but I've seen Axel Ericksson Sparre desert to the emperor!

TOTT: What difference does that make? One rascal more or less?

RÅLAMB: Where did the king go?

(STENBOCK *points in the direction opposite to the one the* KING *took.*)

RÅLAMB (*hurries out in the same direction the* KING *took*): Over here, then!

STENBOCK: What a fox!

TOTT: Do you think he's in love with the queen?

STENBOCK: Who knows? He's infatuated, at least. No harm in that.

BRAHE (*enters*): The king commands that his officers assemble.

TOTT: If I were only sober!

BRAHE: You soon will be—when you get to Spandau!

STENBOCK: In Spandau, yes, but in Magdeburg we'll go on a real binge . . .

BRAHE: In Magdeburg, yes! (*The lights in the palace windows are extinguished.*)

STENBOCK (*goes up to the palace*): Good night, fair ladies. We'll soon meet again, and then . . .

TOTT: Then!

BRAHE (*drives them out with his drawn sword*): Forward! March!

CURTAIN

SCENE 5

In the fortress at Spandau. A writing room. The KING, HORN, *and* BANÉR *are seated at a table.*

KING (*points at a map*): I'll put a red X for Magdeburg.

BANÉR: Make it black, Your Majesty.

KING: Why?

BANÉR: Because the latest news is disastrous!

KING: I don't believe it!

BANÉR: A king believes only what he wants to.

KING: What can we do then to relieve the city?

BANÉR: March right up to it and get at Tilly's flank.

KING: We can't march without money, and there isn't one soldier here who'll go for nothing. (*Pause*) It didn't last long—the French gold, and it didn't bring any blessing with it. (*Pause*) And Oxenstjerna writes that Sweden has been stripped of food. (*Pause*)

BANÉR: Marcus is here.

KING: Always Marcus! He represents the House of Israel[44] in Hamburg—the same Israel who bought the church silver and the church bells from my really *great* grandfather. Isn't it strange that our Sweden bought its freedom from the Jews in Lübeck? And now Israel is to save the Protestant city of Magdeburg! Let Marcus come! I'll go to him! (*Goes out*)

HORN: Did you see the red glow in the southwest this morning?

BANÉR: That's exactly what I saw, and I think it came from Magdeburg!

HORN: I think it did! When I was walking on the ramparts this morning, I could smell the smoke of fire in the wind. When I looked up at the clouds, a piece of scorched paper fell down in front of me. It was a leaf from a printed book, and I could still make out a few letters . . .

BANÉR: What did it say?

HORN: I don't want to say, because then you'd say I am superstitious; but I took it as a message from . . . from destitute people!

BANÉR: Now that you've said A, I'll say B. While we were talking with the king, I saw a flock of storks come from the southwest; they were sooty, and their wings were ragged . . . But I heard or thought I heard a scream . . .

HORN: You, too! (*Gets up*) For several hours I've been as depressed as if the sufferings of thousands had struck at my heart . . . the same feeling I had when my little son died, even though I was far away from him . . .

BANÉR: Do you understand this war, Gustav?

HORN: No, I understand nothing, but it seems to me as if the Lord of Hosts has taken hold of our great king and led him where he doesn't want to go.

BANÉR: Is God *with* us, do you think?

HORN: Until now the Lord has helped us . . . but at what price?

BANÉR: Yes, at what a price! The king!

KING (*enters, excited*): It has happened! There isn't any Magdeburg [45] any more! Thirty thousand people cut down and burned up! Thirty thousand? Is it possible? And there's only one house left; that is the Lord's!

HORN: So it was true, then!

BANÉR: God is not with us any more.

KING: He is with Tilly!

HORN: If He is against us, what is there left to do?

KING: Do you mean that we should turn back?

HORN: I suppose we'll have to, since we have to return Spandau now.

KING: I don't see why.

HORN: No? Spandau was to be returned when we had saved Magdeburg; now Magdeburg can't be saved since it doesn't exist, so the whole agreement is void.

KING: That isn't logic!

HORN: More than logic; it is the simple requirement of honor. What do you say, Johan?

BANÉR: When the object of the agreement has been cancelled, the agreement is cancelled, and Spandau must be returned.

KING: Never!

HORN: Your Majesty, remember that Banér and I were bondsmen for the fulfillment of the agreement.

KING: Remember what the agreement said: that the fortress was to be returned when Magdeburg was relieved; Magdeburg has not been relieved and never can be; so—the fortress is not going to be returned.

HORN AND BANÉR: Sophistry!

KING: What are you saying?

HORN (calmly): The truth!

KING (haughtily): You call me sophist; you forget that I stand above your criticism, that I am the king.

BANÉR: We haven't forgotten that . . .

KING: You dare to interrupt me when I am speaking . . .

BANÉR: Yes!

KING: Get away from here, far, so far that my wrath doesn't reach you!

HORN: Then I'll go, too!

KING: Do that! I'll not be alone!

(HORN *and* BANÉR *going*)

KING: If I have fostered little kings, who think they've outgrown me, my stern father has taught me the cure . . .

HORN: Your Majesty, do not call up bloody memories . . .

KING: Counsel yourself, and not me!

(HORN *and* BANÉR *approach the door.*)

KING: Send in Nils Brahe, Lennart Torstensson, and Marcus the Jew!

HORN: The Jew!

KING (*furious*): Watch out!

HORN: When we intend to desert Christ, the Jew is right there waiting for us! Now I'm going to the elector as a personal hostage for Spandau! And that Banér will do that, too, I know, because he will keep his written word . . . he as well as I. (*Leaves, accompanied by* BANÉR)

(KING, *worried, sits down at the table; holds his head in his hands.*)

CHAMBERLAIN (*enters*): Marcus the Jew requests an audience.

KING: Let him come.

(CHAMBERLAIN *out.* MARCUS *enters.*)

KING: Magdeburg is gone, Marcus.

MARCUS: Yes, and I'm not weeping.

KING: Why?

MARCUS: Everything that happens has its sufficient cause, *ratio sufficiens*. Magdeburg, the virginal city, was founded they say by a Roman in honor of Venus—or in her dishonor. The wealth of the city consisted of the property of plundered churches and cloisters, which were to be restored to their owners; but, if that had been done, a third of the population would have been without roofs over their heads—so the thieves had everything to fear. The income of the archbishopric was wasted by sinful priests and bureaucrats, for the desecration of a sanctuary never is blessed. But this city was the citadel of intolerance as well; the Catholics were

persecuted; their divine services were disturbed, and three years
ago they murdered Father Aegidius, when he was leaving the
festival of Corpus Christi; then they plundered two cloisters. In
a word, the virginal city had become a great whorehouse and a
Sodom, and that's why it had to burn.

KING: You talk like a Catholic!

MARCUS: Do they talk in a special way?

(KING *remains silent, controls himself.*)

MARCUS: Excuse me, Your Majesty; I am not a friend of the Catholics; the Eternal God does not seem to love the one child more
than the other, in spite of His hatred of the virgin city. You see
the latest courier says that, after the city was plundered, a fire
broke out in Tilly's camp and destroyed all he had taken. Isn't
that reminiscent of King Saul, when the Lord commanded him:
"Now go and smite Amalek, and utterly destroy all that they
have, and spare them not; but slay both man and woman, infant
and suckling, ox and sheep, camel and ass." [46] But Tilly—I mean
Saul—spared them for the sake of sordid gain and unclean spoils,
and that is why he fell into disfavor with the Lord and had to
give up both his throne and his life.

KING: Are you a prophet?

MARCUS: Not at all. But Samuel was, and, if he were alive, he would
say: Go, prince from the north, and destroy Tilly, who did not
obey the voice of God, for now God has turned away from him
because he did not destroy the spoils.

KING: You are the one who speaks, Marcus, but it is as if your
voice came from someone else! How can you, who are a Jew . . .

MARCUS: Do we not all have the same Father? Has not one God
created us all?

KING: Yes, but no one knows the Father except through the Son,
and you hate the Son!

MARCUS: No, for I cannot hate what doesn't exist for me. (*Pause*)

KING: So you don't believe that human beings destroyed Magdeburg?

MARCUS: No, for the fire broke out in sixty places at the same time, and neither the inhabitants nor the enemy wanted to destroy the city! It was the angel of death who did it, but before him the Lord in His mercy had sent another angel to warn them! When Tilly held his council of war in Hameln a storm raged over Magdeburg and struck down houses and church towers; the water in the river became blood, and a possessed person rushed along the streets crying: Woe to this city; it shall be uprooted from the earth because of its pride, its injustice, and its sins!

KING: I didn't know that! Do you know what I was thinking about when you came in?

MARCUS: I am no fortune teller, Your Majesty.

KING: I was thinking of returning to my homeland, for I seemed to see God's finger raised threateningly: Back! But now you come . . .

MARCUS: . . . the Jew!

KING: Do you know that I am blamed for the destruction of Magdeburg, and that I felt the blame was so heavy until you freed me from it just now? Advise me!

MARCUS: I already have!

KING: To stay?

MARCUS: Of course . . . And, first of all, to act justly. Return Spandau!

KING: Then I can't move!

MARCUS: Doubt not, but believe! Give what is little, and you will receive what is great! Do not tempt God, but try him. Believe that God is good! Try!

KING (*after some hesitation*): Well! Let it be in the name of Christ! (*Writes something on a paper; strikes the table with his hand*)
    (CHAMBERLAIN *enters.*)

KING: Send this open letter to the nearest legate of Brandenburg. Give the order to Torstensson to signal our departure from the fortress, which we are returning.
    (CHAMBERLAIN *leaves.*)

KING: Now I have sacrificed Isaac!

MARCUS: Isaac was not sacrificed, since Abraham had shown his good will.

KING: And now!

MARCUS: Stand up and smite the Amalekites, but do not touch their cursed goods, for then you shall die! And you shall smite them on the last plain where the northlands end and the mountains of the south begin! But, when you see the mountains rising before you, turn back to the north and remain in your own land that you may justly be sustained.

KING: From where do you get that?

MARCUS: Protect yourself in success, for adversity ruins no man!

TORSTENSSON (*has entered*): Your Majesty!

KING: Well, what do you want?

TORSTENSSON: If the fortress is to be returned, the only thing left for us is to end the war and go home.

KING: Are you sure?

TORSTENSSON: Yes, because after the fall of Magdeburg, for which we are blamed, we don't have a single friend left, and we don't have a single ally yet.

KING (*to Marcus*): You, too, are an adviser!

MARCUS: Yes, and a little bit better than the others!

KING: You may go now, Marcus, but ask me for a favor first.

MARCUS: Well, then, I ask that we Jews in the camp may have permission to celebrate Passover.

KING: Outside the camp, yes.

MARCUS: Preferably outside the camp. (*Going*)

KING (*slowly*): Farewell, Marcus.

MARCUS: Is there something else?

KING: The most important thing!

MARCUS: Money is not the most important here, and it won't help any more. But patience will, and faith, and hope. Believe and hope! (*Goes*)

KING: No money, only good advice. Well, Lennart, to go back to an impoverished homeland where I would be stoned, is that to be the end of all this?

TORSTENSSON: It looks like it.

KING: Everything would go, but the most humiliating . . . (*Pause*) I have not told you that I am expecting my queen; in my last letter I asked her to come down here.

TORSTENSSON: That won't do! You may not show that you are weak, Your Majesty!

KING: And yet I was, all the same; when Erik Rålamb left me, I lost the constant approval and the untiring admiration I unfortunately need . . . And now, when Horn and Banér have left me, I feel my loneliness more cruelly . . . It is as if those two had taken my better self with them! (*Pause*) Say something!

TORSTENSSON: I may not!

KING: Speak! The Jew . . .

TORSTENSSON: Perhaps!

KING: In my innermost being I really hate him, but I believe just the same that he has a purpose in my life, and it seems to me as if the favor of the Lord were with him! It seems to me nowadays, Lennart, as if all but I were in favor, and as if my ways were not the right ways. Everything turns away from me, but nothing surrenders. Where is Wallenstein? Where is Tilly? Where is my enemy and where is my friend? Where are the oppressed that were to be defended, and where is the oppressor? I seem to have been lured into an ambush to be squeezed between felled trees and to be burned alive! (*Pause*)

TORSTENSSON: Is the fortress to be returned?

KING: It has already been returned. Go and tell Horn and Banér.

TORSTENSSON: And then?

KING (*depressed*): Home, as a defeated man, home to dishonor and oblivion.

TORSTENSSON: I don't believe it, but I'll obey. (*Goes*)

KING (*alone; folds the map and stuffs it into his pocket, puts on his*

sword; takes his hat and puts it on, as if he intended to leave.
As he approaches the door, ERIK RÅLAMB *rushes in*): Erik!

RÅLAMB: "Art thou also become weak as we? Art thou become like
unto us?"

KING: Yes, go ahead and scold, but if you had borne my burden . . .

RÅLAMB: I would rather have collapsed under it than have thrown
it down! The great goal, the holy cause, everything forgotten for
the enemy's gold! What have we become but the abomination
of our brethren in the faith and the scorn of our enemies, a band
of plunderers of strangers? Magdeburg, the great city, for the
Protestants a firm citadel, is fallen, and fallen as *our* Sodom, because we were to defend it.

KING: Reproach me, but I have acted as I could. If I hadn't had
the French gold to give to the soldiers, Frankfurt would be in
ashes as Magdeburg is . . . without . . .

RÅLAMB: Without the treaty with France the Swedish king would
have had free hands to deal with the Catholic League, the head
of which is Tilly . . .

KING: What are you saying?

RÅLAMB: Haven't you read the treaty?

KING: No, I have not read it.

RÅLAMB: No? But all Germany has read it, for it was printed, and
all Europe knows that the Swedish king has promised to be neu-
tral toward the League and the elector of Bavaria and to be tolerant of the Catholics.

KING: Neutrality? How can I wage war, then?

RÅLAMB: You have not read it?

KING: I cannot bear your contempt any longer; let's be enemies,
Erik!

RÅLAMB: No, I have sworn to the queen never to leave her consort's
side until . . . until . . .

KING: Until you have returned him to his consort. Erik, go and
fetch the queen; she should be in Stralsund by now.

ERIK (*hesitantly*): And I didn't know!

KING: You don't need to know everything! Will you go?

ERIK: Yes! Because—what I haven't been able to do, she will do!

KING: Go in peace, and let our ways part.

RÅLAMB: Where shall we meet again?

KING: That God alone knows.

BRAHE (*enters*): Your Majesty! Great news!

KING: Speak quickly!

BRAHE: The electors of Brandenburg and Saxony, frightened by the horrible fate of Magdeburg, have sent their ambassadors to plead humbly for an alliance with Sweden.

KING: God be praised!

BRAHE: Tilly is withdrawing to the south, and, if our united armies would march now, we could catch up with him before he has reached the mountains to protect himself.

KING (*to himself*): Marcus, Marcus! (*To* RÅLAMB) Where we shall meet again? In Leipzig! (*To* BRAHE) Where are Gustav and Johan?

BRAHE: Just outside the door.

KING: Are they angry with me?

BRAHE: Not at all!

(KING *opens the door.* HORN *and* BANÉR *enter.*)

KING (*embraces them, in turn*): Gustav, forgive me! You, too, Johan! And now to the south; now the war begins, against Caesar, against the apostle of the heathens!

CURTAIN

ACT III

Scene i

A churchyard on a hill in the foreground. Three Swedish cannons have been placed among the graves. A little village church to the right. The foreground conceals the somewhat lower-lying battlefield. The background at a tremendous distance represents the hills toward Leipzig, villages, and the great highway and shades off into extremely subdued colors. A feeble dawn. The church lighted so that the stained-glass panes of the windows stand out. Two GRAVEDIGGERS *are digging a grave.*

GRAVEDIGGER I: A horrible time, a horrible day! Not even the dead can rest in peace!

GRAVEDIGGER II: Well, what day is it?

GRAVEDIGGER I: Why, September 7 is St. Louis' day.

GRAVEDIGGER II: Louis? Who was he?

GRAVEDIGGER I: The priest in there explained it during mass. He was a king of the Franks, who made France a Christian land; France and Germany were one country then, the priest said. Yes, and he said Louis, who had the right Christian faith, fought the Protestants of that time. They were called Arians, and he defeated them . . .

GRAVEDIGGER II: Why did you call them Protestants?

GRAVEDIGGER I: Because they protested against the one sanctifying church . . .

GRAVEDIGGER II: Listen, don't you know that the Lutherans teach that "We believe in a holy universal church . . . the communion of saints" . . . and the like?

GRAVEDIGGER I: The Lutherans are Catholics, then, for Catholic means universal . . .

137

GRAVEDIGGER II: What the hell! That's nonsense!

GRAVEDIGGER I: Did you say nonsense? Watch out!

GRAVEDIGGER II (*holds his spade up threateningly*): You watch out! (*They fence with their spades.*)

QUARTERMASTER (*enters*): What's this? Can't old people with one foot in the grave keep peace? What are you fighting about?

GRAVEDIGGER II: That heretic says Lutherans are Catholics because they believe in a holy universal church . . .

QUARTERMASTER: My children, there is only one universal Christian church, and that one is Lutheran. In the first place, the Catholic church isn't a Christian church, since the pope is the anti-Christ, and, in the second, it isn't universal, since there are many others.

GRAVEDIGGER I: How about the reformed church?

QUARTERMASTER: That? (*Thumbs his nose*) It's nothing. Nothing at all, since it doesn't exist . . .

GRAVEDIGGER II: Yes, but our friends the Brandenburgers are reformed, so they must exist.

QUARTERMASTER: I can't stand contradictions! But, if I have to express myself fully, they're an invention of the devil, the crew of Satan, the abomination of desolation, the bones of the dead . . . Who's the grave for?

GRAVEDIGGER I: If we only knew! They say it's for the Catholics who'll die on the battlefield . . .

QUARTERMASTER: Is that church Catholic?

GRAVEDIGGER II: Yes, it's one of the few still standing in this district.

QUARTERMASTER: Are you Catholic?

GRAVEDIGGER I: Yes, a little.

QUARTERMASTER: Then you'll go to hell! Because there's neither much nor little here; it's all or nothing!

GRAVEDIGGER II: Stop! I deny that!

QUARTERMASTER: Shut up! I can't stand contradictions . . . Do you know, children, why there's such a deplorable division within the church?

GRAVEDIGGER I: No.

QUARTERMASTER: Well, because you don't accept the same interpretation.

GRAVEDIGGER II: Whose interpretation?

QUARTERMASTER: Mine! Ours!

GRAVEDIGGER I: That's what Luther said, too!

QUARTERMASTER: And Luther was right! And do you know how this deplorable division within the church can end? Well, only through this, that you all accept my interpretation, our interpretation. It would be so easy, so natural, so . . . What shall I say . . . ?

GRAVEDIGGER II: Simple!

QUARTERMASTER: Shut up! I can't stand criticism! What are they up to in that church?

GRAVEDIGGER I: Celebrating morning mass.

QUARTERMASTER: Papal inventions, human tricks, vanity, superstition, foolishness. Don't you know that mass has been abolished?

GRAVEDIGGER II: No. It obviously hasn't!

QUARTERMASTER: Then, by God, I'll abolish it!

GRAVEDIGGER I: Watch it! The elector of Brandenburg's prime minister, Adam von Schwarzenberg, is in there, worshiping . . .

QUARTERMASTER: Von Schwarzenberg, our ally . . .

GRAVEDIGGER II: Sweden's ally and our comrade in battle, who's praying for the victory of the Swedes and their allies!

QUARTERMASTER (embarrassed and bitter): Well! Well! Yes, yes! A lot's happening . . . the world's become square! . . . and what used to be in front is now in back . . . well, let it, let it . . . go to damnation! There are many ways! Many! But I wash my hands!

GRAVEDIGGER I: Mr. Lutheran, please listen to me: I'll neither contradict nor criticize; I just want to tell you something. I was born in the Palatinate as a Lutheran; that was my childhood faith. But four times I and mine were forced to accept Calvinism until Tilly finally came with fire and sword and made us all Catholics . . .

QUARTERMASTER (*busy with his own thoughts, has not listened*):
Von Schwarzenberg, His Excellency, preserve us . . .

GRAVEDIGGER I: What do you think of that story?

QUARTERMASTER: A lie, I suppose! The sum of the matter, my children, is: Do your duty! and keep your mouth shut! (*Goes to the
right*)

PROVOST (*comes in from the left, accompanied by soldiers' wives*):
Withdraw to the village of Podelwitz, women, and don't let your
innate curiosity mislead you into looking upon the vicissitudes
of battle . . . You might be hit by stray bullets . . .

    (MIDWIFE, *the miller's wife of Act I*)

PROVOST: What are you pattering about here for?

MIDWIFE: There's a baby to be delivered!

PROVOST: Pass on then, woman. (*To the* GRAVEDIGGERS) A highly
important person: she has charge of recruiting! (*To the woman*)
Pass, and see to it we get a tall cavalryman; we've got enough
infantrymen!

    (MIDWIFE *exits at right.*)

SERGEANT MAJOR (*enters with the transportation* DRIVER, *the miller
of Act I*): Driver, get going! Your team is ready for you over
in the village where the women are. Quick! They'll be shooting
pretty soon!

DRIVER (*cracks his whip*): Then I'll shoot right back!

SERGEANT MAJOR: And when the plundering starts . . . think of me
if you have space available.

DRIVER: I'll think about it. (*Leaves*)

SERGEANT MAJOR: You can't think, can you?

SCHOOLMASTER (*enters with a group of boys, one of whom is a
TRUMPETER*): There, there, there! Attention, boys!

SERGEANT MAJOR: What do you say when the king comes?

BOYS: God save the king!

SERGEANT MAJOR: And the fatherland, you rascals? Hasn't that ab-
racadabran taught you better?

SCHOOLMASTER: Look here, boys. Now I'm the king, and now I come. What do you say?

BOYS: God save the king and the fatherland!

SERGEANT MAJOR: Fine! Go to the left of the transportation people and east of the women. Wait a minute! General orders to the young. Boys are by nature a terrible lot, more given to evil than to good. Now, when the battle begins and the bullets are whistling about your ears, you boys are to throw yourselves headlong on the ground, and with your left thumb and forefinger get a good hold on the belt of your pants, while your right hand carefully unbuttons where nature has indicated the natural point of emission of the effects a powerful explosion of powder has on the human organism. Have I expressed myself plainly enough?

BOYS: No!

SERGEANT MAJOR: Well: *maxima debetur pueris reverentia.* That means: Boys should learn not only how to behave themselves, but to keep their underclothes clean as well! Go in peace! *Valete!*
(BOYS *laugh.*)

SERGEANT MAJOR: That's the dark side of war! [*Then brusquely*] March!

BOYS: Hurrah!

SCHOOLMASTER: Listen, sergeant, shouldn't you, begging your pardon, who have been a *liber studiosus,* say a serious word to the boys at an hour like this, when the weal and honor of the fatherland depend on a throw of the . . .

SERGEANT MAJOR: No, I can't say the sort of thing you have in mind; I've been at this too long and seen too much and heard too much. I've drunk and fought all my life, and that's why I'm here. Should I stand lamenting and pretending to the young people in my old age? No! You'll have to do that yourself.

SCHOOLMASTER: Incorrigible!

SERGEANT MAJOR: But I see you have a trumpeter. If he has courage, he may stand by the signal cannons up there.

SCHOOLMASTER: If he has courage! Nils, step up and blow assembly!

SERGEANT MAJOR (*horrified, rushes up and jerks the trumpet away from the boy*): No, quiet for the sake of the millions . . . Boy, you don't know what you were about to do! If you touch that tin with your dirty little mouth, the three cannons up there will fire, and then: then the dance begins, seventy-five thousand men, on horseback, on foot, Croatians and Walloons, Swedes and Saxons, imperials and Spaniards, Italians and Scotchmen, Tartars and Poles, all Europe will rush at each other down there on the plain, which you can't see. Good heavens, boy, aren't you afraid of all that?

TRUMPETER (*with a West Gothic accent*): Not really.

SERGEANT MAJOR (*speaking in the same accent*): What's that? Your tongue gives you away! You're a West Goth, just as I am! Good lord, countryman! Do you know Erik Soop, who's commanding the West Goths today? He's a real man, though he prefers cards to the psalmbook. Well, gosling, you'll stay where you're put, eh?

TRUMPETER: Yes, of course!

SERGEANT MAJOR: How old are you, Nils?

TRUMPETER: Ten, going on eleven.

SERGEANT MAJOR: You're half dry, as we say in Borås![47] Do you know what that means?

TRUMPETER (*impudently*): Yes, but, if anybody but you had dared to say it, I'd have let him have it!

SERGEANT MAJOR: Fine! Put the trumpet away; put this badge on your arm. Then you're in the army! (*Puts a yellow badge on the boy's right arm*) Now, boys, you're to go, but give your Nils a cheer first!

BOYS: Hurrah! (*Going to the right*)

SCHOOLMASTER (*to NILS*): Say good-bye nicely to your comrades, now.

TRUMPETER (*swaggers a little*): So long, kids!

SCHOOLMASTER: That wasn't nice! Not nice at all! (*Exits*)

SERGEANT MAJOR: That's right, maybe, but it was very human, above all very boyish. March, old man! (*Three artillerymen come in with cannon sponges, take their places by the cannons, which they clean.*)

SERGEANT MAJOR (*to the* TRUMPETER): Go up there to the cannons and be quiet. Don't forget that you're an important man and that Europe's waiting for you.

(TRUMPETER *goes up to the cannons and stations himself there.*)

(*Two Afghans enter from the right; they spread prayer mats and pray silently in the Mohammedan fashion.*)

(PROVOST *comes in from the right.*)

SERGEANT MAJOR: Listen, provost, what sort of crowd is that, and what hocus-pocus are they up to?

PROVOST: They're Afghan cavalrymen from Bethlen Gabor's disbanded guerrilla bands.

SERGEANT MAJOR: There are many mansions in the kingdom of the Lord . . . but I don't like to have people like them in the house! Listen, are you really a heathen?

PROVOST: I'm not baptized, but . . . I am Romany . . .

SERGEANT MAJOR: That is to say, a gypsy. What do you believe in?

PROVOST: One God who is the Father of all!

SERGEANT MAJOR: Then you can't be a heathen!

PROVOST (*softly*): Sergeant, they say that Tilly has made himself as hard as ice so that no sword can bite into him. Is that true?

SERGEANT MAJOR: They say he's in league with the devil, like all papists.

PROVOST: They're not, surely. But listen: I can silence swords and sharpen them, too. I'm looking for the cervical vertebra of a dead man in the churchyard, the third vertebra from the top, because in it is the little bone called *luz* . . .

SERGEANT MAJOR: An ugly name for a bone! Watch out for both stake and axe if you're caught at witchcraft . . .

PROVOST: Do you believe in witchcraft?

SERGEANT MAJOR: No, I don't.

PROVOST: Well, if there isn't anything to witchcraft, how can they punish anyone for it?

SERGEANT MAJOR: Oh, you're a questioner! Do you know who was the first questioner? That was the devil! Now go to hell! Because fine folks are coming! (*Exits at the right followed by the* PROVOST)

(RUDOLF *from Act II and* GUSTAV GUSTAVSSON, *both dressed in armor as cavalrymen, enter.*)

GUSTAV (*disturbed, to* RUDOLF): I am Gustav Gustavsson, but what good does that do? I'm not baseborn, but I'm illegitimate, the son of a king, but son of a concubine. My father loves me, writes to me, but may not see me. And now . . .

RUDOLF: Calm yourself, Gustav . . .

GUSTAV: That's easy to say! Mother wrote to me the other day that she has married a man I've always hated . . . So I'm alone in the world, more alone than a stepchild, for I haven't even the right to call my father's wife stepmother.

RUDOLF: Does the king know about your mother's marriage?

GUSTAV: I don't know; I don't think so, but when he finds out he'll be hurt, I think; it'll hurt him to know that another man has the woman who's my mother.

RUDOLF: What are you looking for here? What do you want?

GUSTAV: I want to see him, only look at him before he goes into battle, for he may be killed; my mother always said that he'd die young because the gods loved him.

RUDOLF: Don't believe that sort of thing. But, if you want to see him, stay here, because he'll come here to give the signal to start the battle . . .

GUSTAV: The decisive battle that you, but not I, may have a part in! I'm to sit in that church tower looking on; a spectator, not an actor—that's my saga! Where's Luise?

RUDOLF: She and her father are on their way to the Leipzig fair . . . Why do you ask?

GUSTAV: Because we're friends . . . Since we met for the first time in Stettin, her friendship has been the bright spot in my dark life . . .

RUDOLF (*thoughtfully*): Really?

GUSTAV: And, if I weren't the son of a king, I'd make her my wife . . .

RUDOLF: Oh!

GUSTAV: Rudolf, I believe you're in love with your cousin; control your feelings and don't indulge in false dreams . . . Listen, my father can't possibly recognize me; he hasn't seen me since I was four!

RUDOLF: He can't possibly. Stand in back of that tombstone—people are coming!

GUSTAV: Where? (*Goes behind a tombstone*) Here?

RUDOLF: There! And now, farewell, Gustav; your destiny isn't bright, but you're innocent, and that's a lot . . . You've been my friend, you have brought light into the monotony of my gray life . . . If we don't meet again, marry Luise, *marry* her, you hear? . . . Do you promise?

GUSTAV: I promise! But if we meet again?

RUDOLF: Then we'll meet at Auerbachshof when the battle's over, after the victory, because we will win! Farewell! (*They embrace each other.*)

GUSTAV: You're to be envied, you, who may take part in the struggle along with the people and the princes, but I, the son of a king, fatherless and motherless, I . . . (*Weeps*) Farewell!

 (RUDOLF *exits hastily.*)

 (GEORG WILHELM, ELECTOR OF BRANDENBURG, *and* JOHAN GEORG, ELECTOR OF SAXONY, *clad in armor, come in from the right.*)

SAXONY: So we've come this far!

BRANDENBURG: Forced and driven to it; forced to break our vow to our lord, the emperor!

SAXONY (*softly*): That's why I wrote to the emperor and asked for his forgiveness, since I couldn't act in any other fashion. Do you consider that reprehensible?

BRANDENBURG (*softly*): So much the less since I did the same thing myself!

SAXONY (*gives him his hand*): That delights me. But you don't have any troops or people to risk as I do . . .

BRANDENBURG: Because I've already lost them! If there weren't these unfortunate disagreements about the articles of faith among us Protestants, the stranger would already have been driven into the Baltic . . .

SAXONY (*eagerly*): Disagreements, yes! Weren't we all Lutherans once? Why did Brandenburg have to tie up with Zwinglianism?

BRANDENBURG: Because Zwingli was right!

SAXONY (*violently*): The hell he was!

BRANDENBURG: What the devil . . .

SAXONY: Cursed be the hour when German men began to search into what is secret and hidden and began to discuss matters of faith . . . People get crazy if the subject's mentioned . . . I get wild when I hear the names of Zwingli, Luther, or Calvin instead of Jesus Christ! My dream was to see *one* Christian church built on the apostolic creed, which we all confess . . .

BRANDENBURG: Who hasn't dreamt that dream! Probably that's the one that will be realized after what's going to happen down there! (*Points at the battlefield*)

SAXONY: Down there, before Leipzig, where the devil of dissension was let loose a hundred years ago, in my Leipzig, where peaceful pursuits have flourished, world commerce by the side of the sciences . . . there shall be sown with tears and watered with blood, harvests we'll not get to see . . . *one* united German people and perhaps *one* church! Why doesn't the battle begin?

BRANDENBURG: They're waiting only for the sunrise.

SAXONY: Everybody is waiting for the sun that God lets shine on the just and the unjust alike.

BRANDENBURG: May the darkness soon give way! (SCHWARZENBERG *comes out of the church, from which can be heard Catholic singing and organ music.*) There's my friend Schwarzenberg. Isn't it strange that I can take his Catholicism more easily than your Lutheranism?

SAXONY: We must all learn to have tolerance for each other. (*Men approach* SCHWARZENBERG, *climb up to the cannons, where they observe the battlefield through spyglasses.* FABRICIUS *and* GRUBBE *enter. The Afghans, who have been motionless, resume their prayers.*)

GRUBBE (*to* FABRICIUS): I've been ordered to watch the battle from here and to report it to the chancellor afterward.

FABRICIUS: Well, we'll stay together, then. But who are those people? (*Indicates the Afghans*)

GRUBBE: Some Mohammedans who were among Cochtitsky's cavalrymen but who aren't permitted to fight because they're not Christian.

FABRICIUS: So-o! What are they reciting?

GRUBBE (*listens to the Afghans*): *Al ilah, Allah . . .*

FABRICIUS: Oh, it's that prayer . . .

GRUBBE: What does it mean?

FABRICIUS: It means: "There is no god but God; the only true, great, and highest God has His being in Himself, is eternal, is not born and does not bear, is perfect in Himself, fills the universe with His everlastingness, omnipotence, omniscience, goodness, mercy, and immutability."

GRUBBE: Why, that's the same God as ours!

(FABRICIUS *says nothing.*)

GRUBBE: And they're praying for our victory!

(FABRICIUS *says nothing.*)

(MARCUS, *the* FIRE CHIEF—*the bailiff in Wolgast—and eight other Jews in white tallith or prayer shawls; two Jews carry on poles the sacred receptacle in which the Torah rolls—i.e., the five books of Moses—are kept.* MARCUS *and the* FIRE CHIEF *carry upright silver trumpets; one Jew carries a ram's horn. The receptacle is put down and opened; the Torah is taken out and is received by two men who bow and go through other ceremonies, whereupon the Torah is taken out of its wrappings.*)

FABRICIUS: What an abomination!

GRUBBE: They're Jews!

HRASAN (*the reader reads from the Torah after the man with the ram's horn has blown it*): "I am the Lord thy God that brought thee forth out of the land of Egypt, out of the house of bondage. Thou shalt have no other gods before me ... Thou shalt not take the name of the Lord thy God in vain; for the Lord will not hold him guiltless that taketh His name in vain." [48]

GRUBBE: Why, they're the ten commandments in Dr. Luther's catechism!

FABRICIUS (*putting a finger to his lips*): Slaves of the law, who can only command and curse; not one word about the happy message, not one word about peace and blessing.

HRASAN (*who has silently finished reading the ten commandments, now raises his voice*): "And the Lord spake unto Moses, saying, Speak unto Aaron and unto his sons, saying, On this wise ye shall bless the children of Israel, saying unto them: The Lord bless thee, and keep thee! The Lord make His face shine upon thee and be gracious unto thee! The Lord lift up His countenance upon thee and give thee peace!" [49]

GRUBBE (*to* FABRICIUS): Pastor, pastor, that's our benediction! And the same Lord, the same servant! One God and the Father of all!

HRASAN (*reads*): "Associate yourselves, O ye people, and ye shall be broken in pieces; and give ear, all ye of far countries: gird yourselves, and ye shall be broken in pieces ... Take counsel together, and it shall come to nought; speak the word, and it shall not stand: for God is with us." [50]

GRUBBE: "God is with us." Immanuel! Why, that's the Swedish watchword for the day!

(*The sun comes out, lighting the church. A procession of choirboys, dressed in pure white robes, comes out singing "Ave regina coelorum," preceded by one boy who carries a banner with the figure of the Virgin Mary in gold on a field of blue. Six Lutheran pastors gather beside* FABRICIUS. *The* ELECTOR OF BRANDENBURG *and the* ELECTOR OF SAXONY *point toward the battlefield and lift their*

hats; the boy blows his trumpet for the attack; drums and snare
drums reply. MARCUS and the FIRE CHIEF blow silver trumpets
while the eight other Jews cover themselves with the white
cloths; the Afghans cry: "Allah, Il Allah!" With their heads
bared and their hands lifted high, the Lutheran pastors call:
"God is with us!" The Jews answer: "Immanuel! Immanuel!"
The three artillerymen have lighted the port fires and approach
the cannons. GUSTAV GUSTAVSSON has removed his helmet, fallen to
his knees, and folds his lifted hands in prayer. The ELECTORS remain standing, but SCHWARZENBERG makes the sign of the cross
and falls to his knees; so do the choirboys. All have put on yellow
armbands.)

CURTAIN

SCENE 2

In Auerbachshof in Leipzig. The foreground is a part of the
Auerbachskeller where some of Dr. Faust's adventures are said
to have taken place. The ceiling consists of crossed arches; on the
walls are two colossal wooden paintings with motives from the
Faust story. At the back is a large portrait of Luther. Wine casks
piled along the walls; tables, chairs, benches; wreaths of leaves,
flowers, and lights are suspended from the ceiling.

Second level: a perspective of wine casks alternating with
tables and benches; at the very back bazaars with variegated
fabrics, glassware, books, engravings, etc. An orchestra gallery to
the left.

When the curtain goes up, the HOST of Auerbachshof is standing in the foreground speaking with the COOPER. From outside

*can be heard alternately chimes and the ringing of bells, horn
music, singing and organ music, fanfares, shouts of hurrah, and
shots. Note: the banquet celebrating the victory is under way in
the large banquet hall next to what is seen on the stage.*

HOST: A blessed Sunday! Tilly, the unconquerable, thoroughly defeated, wounded, half-dead, fleeing . . .

COOPER: And thirteen thousand dead on the battlefield!

HOST: Well? Through death to resurrection and life!

COOPER: And plundering! The imperial camp is being plundered
now, and the league's war chest has been captured.

HOST: Where did you pick up your prejudice against your deliverers?

COOPER: Home in Stettin where I had to pay five hundred *gyllen* as
a war levy which I couldn't afford to pay; that's why I came here
to the Leipzig Fair to collect what I can . . .

HOST: Is that why you took your wife and daughter with you?

COOPER: No, but that's beside the point.

HOST: You ought to be out with the crows on the battlefield rather
than letting your croaking disturb a joyful celebration, where all
German men with a soul and a heart can unite in paying homage
to the hero—the deliverer from the north.

COOPER: Who has delivered me from five hundred *gyllen* . . .

HOST: Shame, cooper; be ashamed of your pettiness on a day as great
as this, when the blessings of peace shall heal the wounds from
the struggles of a hundred years . . .

COOPER: The struggles about the pope's beard and the emperor's
new trousers, about election by grace and justification by faith,
about faith or deeds . . .

HOST: Out, raven! or I'll sick the people on you!

COOPER: Huh! Don't forget the words of the prophet: "Woe unto
you that desire the day of the Lord! to what end is it for you?
the day of the Lord is darkness, and not light . . . I hate, I despise your feast days, and I will not smell in your solemn assem-

blies . . . Take thou away from me the noise of thy songs; for I will not hear the melody of thy viols."[51] (*Leaves*)

(*People begin to gather: burghers, soldiers, students.*)

SERGEANT MAJOR (*enters, speaks to the* HOST): So this is the famous . . . What's the name?

HOST (*recites*): Auerbachshof with the famous Auerbachskeller. According to legend, Dr. Faust practiced here his hocus-pocus which is pictured on the walls. But the place has a greater claim to fame through a historic event which gets its full significance today. It was here in 1519 that Luther, after disputing for seventeen days with Dr. Eck, accepted his friend Auerbach's hospitality; and out of this cask—it's genuine Rauenthaler—strengthened his wearied powers.

SERGEANT MAJOR (*taps on the cask*): A beautiful piece.

HOST: Five thousand tankards!

SERGEANT MAJOR: Five thousand? Goodness!

HOST: And today the Swedish king, who has promised to honor our mass . . .

SERGEANT MAJOR: Oh, is there to be mass, too?

HOST (*irritated*): We call it *mass* when we have our annual market fair . . . The Swedish king, I say, is going to empty a goblet in honor of the victory when he comes . . . (*Furiously*) Have I put it plainly enough?

SERGEANT MAJOR: Yes, indeed, but the king doesn't empty goblets . . .

HOST: Well, a glass then, a stoup, a can, a mug . . . what in hell you prefer!

SERGEANT MAJOR (*to himself*): Five thousand tankards?

HOST (*raving*): Fifty thousand, five hundred thousand, millions, if you like! Flay me like a cod if you think I'm standing here lying; and that Dr. Luther has drunk out of it, you can get testimony on parchment for that . . . with seals, stamps, autographs, silk, and flourishes! Will that do?

SERGEANT MAJOR: Have you heard that the queen of Sweden is coming, too?

HOST: Yes, I have. She's already here.

SERGEANT MAJOR: And the students from Wittenberg are coming in carnival procession . . . The students! Do you understand?

HOST (*shouts*): Yes!

SERGEANT MAJOR: Fine! There's the quartermaster . . . and the trumpet boy!

QUARTERMASTER: A Lord's day, a blessed day!

SERGEANT MAJOR: For us, yes! But the Lord knows His own. (*To the* TRUMPET BOY) Well, you brat, you really blew in victory!

TRUMPETER: Of course!

SERGEANT MAJOR: Here you see Auerbachshof. There sits Dr. Faust, and there hangs Dr. Luther; there lies Luther's Rauenthal cask of five thousand tankards, and here's where we're going to celebrate.

QUARTERMASTER: Sergeant! Listen! . . .

SERGEANT MAJOR: I'm listening.

QUARTERMASTER: Well, I wanted to say this: It's as if something's out of place (*points at his forehead*) in here!

SERGEANT MAJOR: Have you lost your mind?

QUARTERMASTER: No, listen to this: I haven't, but something else has happened . . . I've quit searching into the mysteries . . .

SERGEANT MAJOR: And have started drinking, perhaps?

QUARTERMASTER: Not exactly, but I've quit exaggerating . . .

SERGEANT MAJOR: So there are temptations nowadays?

QUARTERMASTER: No, I won't agree to that! If drinking is an insignificant act, then it isn't a temptation . . . If I should drink, then, that is a quite simple and natural matter . . .

SERGEANT MAJOR: Well, I should think so!

QUARTERMASTER: And therefore not a temptation.

SERGEANT MAJOR: Heavens, what a Jesuit—you've been converted in reverse!

QUARTERMASTER: Through strife to peace! I've quit struggling against my passions, and desires, and . . . Now I have peace.

SERGEANT MAJOR: Just like the elector of Saxony who suddenly quit

fighting,[52] turned his back on Tilly, and fell into a running
march . . . may he have peace! You, too, you old hypocrite!
(*Goes*)

QUARTERMASTER (*leaving*): Well, you can't understand it!
  (BOYS *enter.*)

TRUMPETER (*proud*): What do you want?

BOY I: We were only going to look—at you!

TRUMPETER: Watch it, you brats, I'm His Majesty's staff trumpeter!
  and I'm the one who led the battle, that's to say, I was the one
  who started it.

BOY II: Oh, you were the one who started, Nils! Do you know what
  the starter gets?

TRUMPETER: If you call me Nils, I'll let you have it!

BOY II: Ah, listen to Nisse brag!

BOY I: Hit him on the lip, so he can't blow the trumpet right any
  more!

TRUMPETER: Watch out, or I'll tell the king. Yes, *I* know the king
  . . . he patted my head and said I was big, and now I'm to signal
  the start of the banquet, but the one who touches me will get to
  ride the wooden mare like an in—sub—ordinations—traitor!
  Know what that is?

  (BOY I *bursts into tears and runs off with the others.*)

  (ERIK RÅLAMB, *dressed in black as usual and with white and
  red plumes in his hat;* GUSTAV GUSTAVSSON *dressed as a student*)

RÅLAMB (*violently upset*): And that's why you came, just because
  of that?

GUSTAV: Just to see the man who's my father, but who may not be
  my father!

RÅLAMB: Go ahead, but you've chosen the occasion badly . . . the
  king is seeing his queen again for the first time in a year.

GUSTAV: Maybe so, but look at my situation . . . All my friends, the
  students from Wittenberg, may come here to greet the hero from
  the north; I alone may not!

RÅLAMB: But you certainly understand that you can't be anything for the queen but a reminder and a living testimony of the sin her consort committed . . .

GUSTAV: A love child, they call me, born in sin . . . for love is sin . . .

RÅLAMB: Illegal love, yes!

GUSTAV: Which I have *not* practiced, but *he* has!

RÅLAMB: And for which no human being has the right to reproach him, for he has atoned for that sin with repentance and penitence. Obey me, and keep out of sight. Let the hero celebrate his victory without being disturbed by reproaches from a past that he has rejected and just the same can't undo. Think if the queen should come . . . she's in there in the banquet hall . . . you'd have destroyed her happiness, too, perhaps her happiness in love, for most likely she'd think the king had arranged this meeting.

GUSTAV: I'll keep out of sight, but I won't leave, for I promised to wait for someone here.

RÅLAMB: Rudolf! Are you sure he's alive?

GUSTAV: I'm not sure. He got in among Cochtitsky's cavalrymen.

RÅLAMB: Who were shot down, every last man, by Torstensson's cannons . . .

GUSTAV: Are you sure? Or are you just guessing?

RÅLAMB: I know. And he's dead unless he ran away.

GUSTAV: Rudolf did not run away!

RÅLAMB: Then it's Luise you're waiting for!

GUSTAV: So you know that, too? Yes, I am!

RÅLAMB: To comfort her because you love her.

GUSTAV: Yes.

RÅLAMB: But *she* loves Rudolf, Rudolf dead or alive! Yes, life is like that!

GUSTAV: And you know that!

RÅLAMB (*looks about*): Quiet!

GUSTAV: You brought the queen here? Does she make my father happy?

RÅLAMB: Happy? Happiness? What does that mean? Yes, what's past! I once was my king's friend, but I'm not any longer since his queen came. I'm superfluous. I'm in the way, people laugh at me, my time is over. Can you imagine anything as crazy as this: I'm jealous of the queen!

GUSTAV: Just so you're not jealous of the king.

RÅLAMB: Gustav! I'm jealous of both of them! That's my secret!

GUSTAV: You're born to be unhappy, you as well as I . . .

RÅLAMB: . . . I can't bear to see my great king as a lover . . . it nauseates and disgusts me; I can't bear to have a woman touch his soul, wind her little thoughts about his; when he talks with her, every elevated expression disappears from his face; he looks foolish, lowers his voice so he'll not frighten her, and the god who generally thunders steps down and . . . lisps . . .

GUSTAV: And you love her all the same?

RÅLAMB (wildly): I saw them together this morning . . . she is beautiful, I can't deny that, and my feelings concern no one as long as I conceal them . . .

GUSTAV: Conceal them better, Erik!

RÅLAMB: Better? No one could!

GUSTAV: How old are you, Erik?

RÅLAMB: I'm twenty; so I'm a man, who has tried life, learned a little, and know a little. But you're a child, Gustav, only fifteen . . . still, when you fall in love, you'll find you'll grow up . . .

PAGE (enters): Her Majesty, the queen, awaits Chamberlain Rålamb in the banquet hall. (Goes)

RÅLAMB (to the PAGE): At your service! (To GUSTAV) At least she doesn't fear my presence. (Takes off his hat and touches up the feathers)

GUSTAV: Careful with those feathers so you don't burn them in the sun and fall to earth like a plucked bird!

RÅLAMB: Do you think they're borrowed?

GUSTAV: From an ostrich, yes! Now I'll fly, said the ostrich!

RÅLAMB: Yes, now I'll fly! (Goes)

(LUISE and her MOTHER enter; GUSTAV goes up to them.)

GUSTAV: Luise, come over here and sit down.

MOTHER: What's the meaning of this?

GUSTAV: You know me, and you know Rudolf's fate.

LUISE: Is it certain he's dead?

GUSTAV: Yes, it's certain . . .

(LUISE *sinks down on a bench.*)

GUSTAV: You probably know, Luise, that Rudolf made me promise something before he went into battle?

MOTHER: What?

GUSTAV: To ask for Luise's hand. There are certain difficulties, however, in the way of my keeping this promise.

MOTHER: I imagine!

GUSTAV: My high birth . . .

MOTHER: Listen: In the first place, I find an insuperable difficulty in your lack of manners. To start courting the girl brutally before the man she loved has become cold doesn't promise you'll make a thoughtful husband. But there's also another difficulty . . .

GUSTAV: I have the power to get rid of difficulties . . .

MOTHER: Wait a moment! According to the law of the coopers' guild, an alderman's daughter may not marry a baseborn man . . .

GUSTAV: Baseborn?

MOTHER: A concubine's son, then, an illegitimate, if you prefer!

GUSTAV: Father, why have you done this to me?

MOTHER: So that story's over! Come, Luise!

(GUSTAV, *crushed, sits down at one of the tables.*)

MOTHER: Come, Luise! Our place isn't in the banquet rooms; other duties call us to the dead.

GUSTAV: Let me follow my friend to his grave at least!

MOTHER: No!

GUSTAV: Cast out! I belong nowhere. I may share no one's joy, no one's sorrow!

(ÅKE TOTT *and* FREDRIK STENBOCK *enter, somewhat gay.*)

TOTT (*puts his arm about* LUISE *and tries to kiss her*): Happiness in love is the victor's reward!

GUSTAV (*draws his sword*): Stand, scoundrel!

TOTT (*draws his sword*): Die, boy!

STENBOCK (*goes between them*): Not here! Not here! The king
might come . . .

GUSTAV: Let him come so he can punish the villain!

TOTT: Do you know who I am?

GUSTAV: Do you know who I am?

TOTT: I don't need to, but you're to remember that I have the royal
Vasa blood; I'm the grandson of Erik XIV!

GUSTAV: Månsdotter blood, then! But I am the son of a king. I am
Gustav's son!

TOTT (*to* STENBOCK): Is it he?

STENBOCK: Apparently!

TOTT (*to* GUSTAV): Kinsman, forgive me!

GUSTAV: Your insult to me, yes, but not your insult to this lady!

STENBOCK: Quiet! The queen's coming.

(LUISE *and her* MOTHER *draw away. The* QUEEN *enters with*
ERIK RÅLAMB *and accompanied by some ladies-in-waiting.*)

QUEEN (*to* RÅLAMB): What is happening here?

STENBOCK: Your Majesty, only the renewal of an old acquaintance-
ship, called forth by the fickle caprices of war . . .

QUEEN: That's not true! Who is the girl over there with the woman?

MOTHER (*comes up; kneels*): An innocent girl's mother who begs
for justice and protection for her child!

QUEEN: What has happened?

MOTHER: This colonel . . . his name is Tott . . . has insulted my
daughter who is mourning for her lover, who fell fighting on the
Swedish side!

QUEEN: Is this true, Tott?

TOTT: If you wish!

QUEEN: Go to the field marshal and surrender your sword, Tott;
then wait for the king's commands! (*To the* MOTHER) Go in
peace. There, there. That's enough! Enough! (*To* RÅLAMB, *indi-
cating* GUSTAV) Who is the young man?

RÅLAMB: A student from Wittenberg.

QUEEN: So-o? But he has a sash that only the nobles at the university may wear.

(RÅLAMB, *embarrassed; says nothing.*)

QUEEN: And . . . (*Looks searchingly at* GUSTAV) It is he! (*to* RÅLAMB) This infamy you could have spared me!

GUSTAV: The fault is not mine if I am infamous; nor is it my fault if I disturb your banquet, Your Majesty!

QUEEN (*turns her back and goes. To* RÅLAMB): Why should I be reminded of this now, just now, when my hero is pure and high as never before? Let us go!

(NILS BRAHE *enters; comes toward them.*)

QUEEN: Brahe! Who has sent for him? I can't stand him and his dove's eyes that always remind me of his cousin Ebba! (*Turns, but goes now toward* SCHWARZENBERG, *who is just entering*) Still another! Protect me, Erik, from this man, my brother's evil spirit, the Jesuit (*whispers*) and the emperor's friend! (*Turns to the back of the stage but meets her brother, the* ELECTOR OF BRANDENBURG) And there he is, the renegade in our family, who became a Calvinist so he could rule through dissension! Take me away, Erik; why, I'm like a surrounded deer. (MARCUS *and the* FIRE CHIEF *enter.*) And these Jews! How can we join heretics at this banquet, which was to raise the spirits of our brothers in the faith through the memory of the father of our church, Dr. Luther?

RÅLAMB: Your Majesty! The king has already requested that the banquet not receive a special Lutheran character, since representatives of so many faiths are present as our friends. He refuses particularly to receive the burghers' invitation to toast the memory of our reformer because that would lead to another Bartholomew's Night! [53]

QUEEN: Schwarzenberg is coming up to me! . . . Erik, try to help me avoid him!

RÅLAMB: Impossible, Your Majesty. Brandenburg is our only sure friend, Saxony our sure enemy.

SCHWARZENBERG (*to the* QUEEN): Your Majesty, permit your servant to convey his respects and bid you welcome on German soil.

QUEEN: Thank you, Your Excellency.

SCHWARZENBERG: . . . And as an expression of my fellow believers' sincere admiration and their gratitude for the tolerance they've been granted, I present this insignificant gift as a memento of the the day at Breitenfeld. (*Hands her a diamond necklace which resembles a rosary*)

QUEEN (*looks at the gift*): Am I to wear your necklace?

SCHWARZENBERG: Maria Eleonora of Brandenburg has worn Hohenzollern jewels before this.

QUEEN: Excellent; I accept the gift as a symbol of the bonds that bind me to my old fatherland. Thank you.

SCHWARZENBERG: No, I'm the one who is grateful. (*Joins a group*)

QUEEN (*looks more closely at the necklace. To* RÅLAMB): Usch! It's a rosary! Take it away! Or . . . send it to my little Christina to play with; she likes jewels!

RÅLAMB (*receives the necklace*): An unusual toy and a strange gift!

QUEEN: Everything is strange here, so different from what I had expected. Everything and everyone. Have I come among friends who have gathered in the joy of a great victory? They look as if they wanted to bite each other if they dared. (*Softly*) I thought I'd meet a beloved husband, but I meet a cold, calculating sergeant, who reproaches me for not bringing more cannons and other military supplies. I don't understand war, but I know that there is something here that's not right. They say the king has accepted money from the Catholic cardinal Richelieu in return for not disturbing the Catholics. Is that true, Erik?

RÅLAMB: That's true.

QUEEN: Is it also true that the Swedish king has taken into his army five thousand of Tilly's Catholic soldiers?

RÅLAMB: That I didn't know, but if it's true . . .

QUEEN (*whispers*): I know it's true! And I know still more; he has negotiated for a treaty with the archenemy, Wallenstein.

RÅLAMB: We've long suspected that, but we haven't known. "Because thou hast forgotten the God of thy salvation, and hast not been mindful of the rock of thy strength, therefore shalt thou plant pleasant plants, and shalt set it with strange slips: In the day shalt thou make thy plant to grow, and in the morning shalt thou make thy seed to flourish; but the harvest shall be a heap in the day of grief and of desperate sorrow." [54]

QUEEN: Take me away from here, Erik, for my heart is heavy. Everything that has seemed great, exalted, and pure is pulled down into the dirt and the dust.

RÅLAMB (*accompanies the* QUEEN *out to the right*): I could say: It's the hard law of life that angels do not dwell on earth, that the man who wants to take the rudder out of the hands of Providence runs into the shallows, that the purest must be dragged in the filth so that they shall see that there isn't anyone who is pure. But I'll only say: "Surely men of low degree are vanity, and men of high degree are a lie: to be laid in the balance, they are altogether lighter than vanity." [55] (*Exits*)

(HORN, BANÉR, TORSTENSSON *enter; serious, thoughtful, sit down at a table downstage, away from the rest of the people.*)

HORN: Say something!

BANÉR: You mean me, I suppose . . . I always have to talk my head off! Well, then: The goal is won, North Germany and the shores of the Baltic have been cleared of the emperor's forces, of Italians, and of Spaniards; the north has driven the south back within its borders, and the balance has been restored. After a victory like this, what usually follows? Gustav?

HORN: Peace!

BANÉR: Lennart?

TORSTENSSON: Peace!

BANÉR: Johan? Peace! And if peace doesn't follow now? What can we justifiably call the victor then? Johan? A lover of fighting and honor, who likes war for its own sake, perhaps for the sake of booty, and above all for personal reasons.

TORSTENSSON: Don't talk like that; the king might hear us!

BANÉR: No, he has quit listening to us . . . ever since his wife came. And the lady of the house doesn't like us. It seems to me our best days are over, and what's coming is merely dull. Think of it . . . on this day of victory and success I look back with sorrow on the time of want and adversity, the time of young enthusiasm, when we came like tramps but were filled with courage and hope and faith.

TORSTENSSON: You're right, Johan; most people can take adversity, but no one can take success!

HORN: Does anybody know our king's plans?

BANÉR: Partly; the war is to continue; we break camp tomorrow, then through Thuringia to the Rhine and to Frankfurt.

TORSTENSSON: Why to Frankfurt and not Vienna?

BANÉR: Why, Frankfurt is the coronation city, the East Franks' old capital; the West Franks have theirs in Paris. In Frankfurt's town hall is the golden bull, and in Frankfurt there's a synagogue.

HORN: Hush, Johan!

BANÉR: Let me talk!

HORN: The one who drinks . . .

BANÉR: Dabbles in politics, yes! You see, what hurts us most about the French money is that the money of sin wasn't so crazy as it looked! France and Germany, the West Frank and the East Frank, were originally one. When Emperor Charles V, a Spaniard, a man from the south who could hardly talk German, started to stretch out his arms toward the north, he crushed Flanders in his embrace; then the Frenchman's and the German's old feeling of kinship awakened; why, Henry II made an alliance with Elector Moritz of Saxony against the usurper Charles V with the result that the French took Lorraine with Metz, Toul, and Verdun. Note Verdun, where the kingdom of the Franks was once divided to make France and Germany.

HORN (*jokingly*): Don't you want something to drink, Johan?

BANÉR: Do you think my imagination needs to be fed? Or my

tongue oiled? However, the elector of Saxony was called a traitor then, but he wasn't one, for with his help the French had shot a wedge between Spanish Flanders and the Hapsburg crownlands, and the Spanish Satan, who after the conquest of America wanted to swallow Europe, wanted to invade England from Flanders and even threatened our Gothenburg recently. Who were the ones we chased out of Pomerania, out of Mecklenburg? Spaniards and Italians: Torquati Conti, Spinola, Maradas, Colalto, Merode, Montecucculi, and the devil and his mother. Whom did we fight outside Breitenfeld-Leipzig? Colloredo, Isolani, Chiesa, Balderon, Piccolomini, Strozzi: Italians and Spaniards; and now when we got toward the Rhine, the river across which the French and the Germans should nod to each other as friends, we have Ossa, Don Silva, and whatever their names are, the Spaniards! *Summa summarum:* The French alliance is our king's greatest act as a statesman, because he then quit being a narrow-minded general for one sect and became a statesman who is a credit to his teachers, Hugo Grotius and Petrus Ramus.[56] But he should make peace now! That's to say: I don't personally have anything against war, but I hear something in one ear which tells me: So far, but no farther! Now I have to have a drink! (*Pounds on the table. The* HOST *comes.* BANÉR *gestures that he wants a goblet and a drink. The* HOST *wants to talk.* BANÉR *interrupts him.*) Yes, this is Auerbachskeller, and there is Doctor Faust with his deviltry, and there Luther is hanging with his! (*To* TORSTENSSON, *who has made a disapproving face*) Yes, the devil take Luther and the pope and Calvin and all the other wranglers; I'm a Christian and would preferably be a syncretist if I should be anything! A syncretist is one of those who think it's all one, if you can only say the Lord's prayer with a fairly clear conscience . . . I said fairly, Lennart, and you're not to quibble about my words.

TORSTENSSON: Yes, you are and always will be . . . our dear old Johan . . . but you shouldn't drink so much!

BANÉR: What would I be if I didn't drink? Not Johan! So: drink, Johan!

(HOST *places three glasses and a tankard of wine on their table.* HORN *and* TORSTENSSON *turn their glasses upside down to indicate that they do not drink.*)

BANÉR: You're hopeless! (STENBOCK *enters.*) Come here, Fredrik, and tell us the news.

STENBOCK: Gladly, for I've lost my . . . my comrade-in-arms and friend Åke Tott.

BANÉR: Heavens, where is he?

STENBOCK: Sent north to Bremen for having kissed the wrong girl.

BANÉR: Is it the queen who arranged that?

STENBOCK: Most likely.

BANÉR: Where's the king?

STENBOCK: In there with electors and dukes . . .

BANÉR: Doesn't bother about us any more. Sends for his wife as he used to send for Fabricius when he intended to do some mischief or other. So Tott's gone! That's number one! We'll be getting ours soon, I suspect!

STENBOCK: Most likely, for now he has sent for Oxenstjerna . . .

HORN: Oxenstjerna?

STENBOCK: Yes, for now there's to be big politics . . . the cardinal is furious!

TORSTENSSON: Oxenstjerna? Does that mean peace?

STENBOCK: It means war! And something else, too! Haven't you heard that the son of the elector of Brandenburg is to be engaged to Christina, the daughter of our king?

HORN: We seem to have lost our king's confidence, for we didn't know that.

BANÉR: See, the king has long-range plans. Sweden and Brandenburg! Then Denmark's done for!

HORN: Johan, Johan, how wise you are!

BANÉR: Who knows? There's young Rålamb. He looks sick enough to hang!

STENBOCK: He's already hanging . . . for the queen!

RÅLAMB: Have you heard? The king of Sweden is negotiating for an alliance with Wallenstein!

HORN: They've talked about that for a long time.

BANÉR: And why not? The religious war actually ended when Tilly's five thousand Catholics were stuck into the Swedish army. If you take the one to defeat the other, that's only good strategy!

RÅLAMB: Shame, Banér! Christian tolerance does not demand that we be our enemy's friend.

BANÉR: Stop, Rålamb! Your pitcher will soon crack; watch your ears to start with!

RÅLAMB: "Wine is a mocker, strong drink is raging and whosoever is deceived thereby is not wise." [57]

TORSTENSSON: Peace, for God's sake, peace! The king is here!

RÅLAMB: Fine! So let the ax fall!

(*The* KING *appears at the back with* FABRICIUS, GRUBBE, *the* ELECTORS *of Saxony and Brandenburg,* SCHWARZENBERG, *and* NILS BRAHE.)

BANÉR: He has sent for Fabricius. Then we can really expect something! And then he has Ebba's . . . I mean . . . Nils Brahe's eyes on him. That means his wife isn't in favor!

(*The* KING *and his companions sit down at a table to the right, while* HORN, TORSTENSSON, BANÉR, *and* STENBOCK, *who are sitting to the left, get up and greet him. The* KING *gives them a sign that they are to remain seated.*)

BANÉR: The king looks ten years older today . . . he's dropped his boyish manner. Don't you think he's grown since the day before yesterday?

HORN: Quiet, quiet!

BANÉR: But look at Rålamb; he's staring at the Jesuit as if he wanted to bite him, if only someone would say: Go to it!

KING (*to* RÅLAMB): Chamberlain Rålamb! Where is the queen?

RÅLAMB (*violently, impolitely*): She's at home weeping over her lost happiness, over broken faith, over six thousand dead and wounded, and over five thousand Jesuits, whom the Swedish king has taken under his wings! (*Amazement among those present. The* KING *embarrassed at first; then angry; finally calms himself.*)

KING: Chamberlain Rålamb has our disfavor because of his violent temper, and by way of punishment is to serve at table until he has regained our favor through a change in his conduct! Get goblets and fill them for us!

RÅLAMB: No! (*General amazement, then silence*)

RÅLAMB (*speaks vehemently and quickly*): King of Babylon! "Hell from beneath is moved for thee to meet thee at thy coming: it stirreth up the dead for thee, even all the chief ones of the earth; it hath raised up from their thrones all the kings of the nations. All they shall speak and say unto thee: (NILS BRAHE *has risen and signaled to the wings. Drums and snare drums are beaten, but* RÅLAMB *raises his voice and continues*) Art thou also become weak as we? Art thou become like unto us? Thy pomp is brought down to the grave, and the noise of thy viols: the worm is spread under thee, and the worms cover thee. (*Raises his voice still more*) How art thou fallen from heaven, O Lucifer, son of the morning! how art thou cut down to the ground, which didst weaken the nations!" [58]

(HORN, BANÉR, TORSTENSSON, *and* STENBOCK *have risen and gone toward* RÅLAMB, *who hurries out to the right.*)

KING (*has wanted to interrupt* RÅLAMB's *speech but has not been able to. When he has collected himself, he rises*): Let the banquet begin! (*Music. A procession of Scotchmen; then Wittenberg students in festival garb, and carrying banners; then Afghans, Calmucks, Turks, Poles; then Catholic priests with Virgin Mary banners, choirboys, monks; then the Jews in their white tallith, two with silver trumpets; finally, the burghers with the Protestant clergymen. The* KING *rises and uncovers his head.*)

CURTAIN

ACT IV

Scene 1

A pass in Thuringia. Wartburg can be seen in the background.
RÅLAMB *stands concealed behind an oak on a projecting rock.*
When the curtain goes up, TOTT *can be seen climbing up the cliff.*

TOTT: Erik, if you're going north with me, you'll have to quit rushing about the mountains like a doe.

RÅLAMB: I must see him; I must see Tilly, the great hated enemy I'm forced to admire.

TOTT: Go ahead, admire him . . . but at a decent distance! Tilly's cavalrymen are combing these forests, and, if they catch sight of us, we're done for!

RÅLAMB: Oh well, life isn't worth much any more, since I've lost my faith in my hero.

TOTT: *Your* faith, Erik, your faith! Do you remember how you and I used to fight in Uppsala? [59] You were on Messenius' side, I on Rudbeckius'! Now I'm on Messenius', and you on Rudbeckius'! That's life's little game of knocking skulls against each other. Now you're on a mountain in Thuringia directly opposite Wartburg, Luther's Wartburg, so you can admire Tilly! Why in hell do you have to admire everything? *Nil admirare!* I learned that from Horace, and that's the best way for me. I've never admired the king, though I've liked him, so I can't despise him as you do when he's kicked me out!

RÅLAMB: Do you remember my oration in Uppsala that caused so much talk?

TOTT: You mean the one on "Truth, the Highest Virtue, and Its Superiority over King, Wine, and Woman"?

RÅLAMB: Yes, that's the one.

166

TOTT: That almost cost you two lawsuits, the one for treason because they thought you were hitting at the king's little weaknesses, and the other for heresy because they thought you were hitting at Luther's famous "wine and women."

RÅLAMB: Why mayn't I respect Luther and Tilly at the same time? And approve the faults of the one and disapprove the weaknesses of the other? Tilly has never tasted wine, never embraced a woman; Tilly has never been cruel to anyone but himself. He was not only innocent of the destruction of Magdeburg but wept over the city so that he could have put out the fire with his own tears, and he personally saved both children and women. Luther . . . well, I don't need to sing his praises here near Wartburg . . .

TOTT: Yes, you do, and for better reasons than you sing Tilly's! Listen, Rålamb! Remember this! Your grandfather was a traitor to my grandfather, King Erik XIV, and turned Catholic with John III. Your uncle was educated by Jesuits and was beheaded by Charles IX at Kalmar. How can you have forgotten that?

RÅLAMB: Suppose I had forgotten it for a while, but now I'm beginning to recall it . . .

TOTT: Well, then, let me remind you of the Statute of Örebro of 1617, the one that exiles Catholics and Calvinists, and of Johannes Hammerus, who eleven days after the statute went into effect was tortured and beheaded because he was a Catholic. And about Behr, Anthelius, and Campanius, who were executed for the same reason in 1624.

RÅLAMB: Why should you remind me of this now? Here?

TOTT: To show you how your hero, our king, is more worthy of your admiration now that he has rejected the Statute of Örebro than he was in the ignorance of youth when he was loyal to it! It is braver to give up an error than to hold fast to it! Here in sight of Wartburg, the city of St. Elizabeth, Wolfram and Walther, and Luther, I command you, Erik Rålamb, to shout, "Long live the brave renegade, Gustav Adolf the Great!"

RÅLAMB: Silence, fool!

TOTT: And Luther! The Augustinian monk who gave up his Augustinian errors which were his childhood faith—do you want to honor his memory here? Now? You don't want to? No! You see, you're standing where I stood a bit ago, you harebrain, you self-worshiper! If you're a papist, go to hell, down to your Jesuits! Down with you! (*They wrestle.*)

RÅLAMB: Stop, you crazy Vasa! (RÅLAMB *is plunged down and disappears.*)

(*Out of the ravine come two Bavarian cavalrymen dressed in black with death's heads on their helmets—see Act I, scene 1; TILLY rides behind them on a large white horse; one of his arms is in a sling; behind him are seen a number of monks on horseback.*)

CURTAIN

SCENE 2

The terrace of a pleasure palace outside Mainz. A vine-covered, Roman colonnaded walk directly across the stage. To the right a loggia with tables and chairs, where those who appear cannot be seen by those who are strolling in the walk. At the back can be seen the Rhine River with vineyard-covered hills and the ruins of castles.

JOHAN BANÉR *and* NILS BRAHE, *sitting at a table in the loggia, observe the princes, prelates, and ambassadors who come out of the* KING's *audience room at the right.*

BANÉR (*not quite sober*): Well, young Brahe, we had never dreamt of this: Gustav Eriksson the Uppland farmer's grandson, Gustav Adolf, is sitting on a golden chair in Mainz, and all the monarchs of Europe send their ambassadors to him to ask for peace! Today it's really something to be a Swede!

BRAHE: Yes, indeed, and a Brahe is proud today to be related to Eriksson!

BANÉR: First time since the Viking Age that there have been Swedish keels on the Rhine. Slept at home for almost a thousand years, taking care of our own business with the neighbors and at home, made a few expeditions eastward, against the sun, now and then, but now we've gone west with the sun, left the blond drinks of the wort and reached the grape's . . . hm! . . . golden, golden . . . (*hastily*). You probably think I think too much about fermented drinks, but that's how it is . . . Nils: there's the Rhine; there's France! Here lives the duke of the Franks, Louis XIII. The West Frank and the East Frank extend their hands to each other. A great day, a blessed day!

BRAHE: What will happen now?

BANÉR: No one knows. After Breitenfeld the elector of Saxony hinted about the imperial crown, but our king is too wise to grasp at chimeras. He wants the shores of the Baltic to keep the emperor off and to encircle Denmark, and a unified North Germany against the emperor's South Germany.

BRAHE: You've become a great politician lately!

BANÉR: Others have said that, too! They call the king Joshua; I believe he'll be only our Moses who's to lead us about in the wilderness, but never get to possess the promised land, unfortunately. No, the Joshua who's to march in and possess—that will be Brandenburg, I suspect. That's why our king has his plans for the elector's son and his own daughter, you see. Seem to have got stuck because of that blessed religious question! Doesn't matter; the honor is ours . . . Look! There comes the Winter King, Fredrik of Pfalz, the root and the cause, as they say!

(FREDRIK *goes from right to left in the colonnade, stops for a moment, and looks out over the landscape.*)

BRAHE: He was the one who defeated the emperor and was elected king of Bohemia.

BANÉR: Exactly, and thereby started this war; that's to say: it began when the Protestants in Prague threw out the Catholics' Martinitz and Slawata through the window . . .

BRAHE: The ones who landed on the manure pile?

BANÉR: Yes, the manure pile, say the Protestants, but the Catholics write that they landed on their heads in an elderberry bush . . . That's supposed to be a little nicer! I suspect they're lying, both of them. I'm a syncretist, as you probably know. Yes, that was Fredrik of Pfalz! And I suspect he came from our king and Axel Oxenstjerna . . . you know that Oxenstjerna's in there, of course.

BRAHE: Yes, he came in the nick of time!

BANÉR: Oh, yes, of course! We, the old phalanx, are starting to thin out . . . Tott has been sent north; Rålamb was sent off, like a letter; Torstensson is sick in bed with a stone in his head at Kreuznach; Gustav Horn is mourning again . . . his wife died in Stettin . . . There come the French ambassadors. Three of them! (*The French ambassadors come from the right in the colonnade and go slowly to the left.*) Cardinal Richelieu's own brother-in-law! The one who's in back. This French thing's really amusing. Our king is as afraid of the cardinal as of the devil, but the cardinal was still more afraid of our king, and so he took Louis with him to Metz; and there they're watchfully waiting!

BRAHE: I've never understood this friendship for the French. Why, the king of France is a Catholic . . .

BANÉR (*talking big*): Of course, but he has given the Protestants freedom of religious worship. When the Protestants misused this freedom and constituted a political party and took over fortified places to oppress the Catholics, then he said, "Stop." That's why La Rochelle [60] had to be besieged . . . (*Procession of ambassadors, etc., in the colonnade*) Look at that, young Brahe! There is the Turkish ambassador! There is the Swiss Union's! Holland's!

Scotland's! Fredrik of Pfalz is married to the daughter of James I. And electors in quantity! Impressive, eh? And that eternal Pfalz again! We're sort of related to him, that bird of misfortune! Charles IX was, as you know, first married to Maria of Pfalz; our king's half-sister Katarina is the wife of John Casimir of Pfalz, the fellow who's at home in Sweden now looking after a government bureau while his woman brings up our gracious crown princess. How it's going with her education, God alone knows; little Christina's a little devil whose purpose in life seems to be to undo what her father has done. There, the audience is over. (*The boy* TRUMPETER *enters and takes his place by the colonnade.*) What are you looking for, boy?

TRUMPETER: The king is coming!

BANÉR: And you're to trumpet that forth! Listen, haven't I seen you before?

TRUMPETER: Yes, Your Excellency, at Breitenfeld.

BANÉR: He already says "Excellency"; he'll go far! Oh, you were at Breitenfeld, and we danced to your pipe. It's a little buckled now, I think. Well, do you know this excellency?

TRUMPETER: Yes, that's Colonel Brahe, or "young Brahe" as we call him; the colonel of the Yellow Brigade or the king's main cushion . . .

BANÉR: Why is he called cushion?

TRUMPETER: I can't say that!

BANÉR: Do you know who I am?

TRUMPETER: Johan Banér, the bravest of all!

BANÉR: Listen to him! Well, what do people say about me?

   (TRUMPETER *puts mouthpiece of his trumpet to his mouth.*)

BANÉR: I drink, you mean. Yes, that's the truth. But I do my job like a man!

BRAHE: Quiet, Johan! The king's coming!

KING (*enters from the right, is wearing a sort of elector's suit*): You've had to wait for me.

BANÉR AND BRAHE (*stand up*): Your Majesty!

KING: Do you want to go along on a pleasure trip up the Rhine?

BANÉR: At your service, Your Majesty.

KING: Yes, but my wife is going along. You don't like her, do you?

BANÉR (*maliciously*): Isn't Fabricius going along?

KING (*smiles*): Just as insolent as always, Johan. Tell me, why don't you like my wife?

BANÉR: Because we like her husband better!

KING (*laughs*): If my father had heard that, he would have had your head! Yes, one can take life as long as one can smile; so let's smile today, the first day of spring, for tomorrow serious business begins. Go and change your clothes now . . . You don't say a word, Nils Brahe!

BANÉR: He's talking with his eyes!

KING (*seriously*): Banér!

BANÉR: Forgive me!

KING (*sadly*): You misuse your power, because you know I can't do without you. But don't do that again! I beg you! You saw what happened to Rålamb! (*Violently*) Go! The chancellor's coming! (BANÉR *and* BRAHE *pretend to be frightened.*)

KING: You are more afraid of Oxenstjerna than of me!

BANÉR: He's so terribly serious, the chancellor, and a man who can't smile . . .

KING: Silence, and off with you! (BANÉR *and* BRAHE *go.*)

OXENSTJERNA (*enters*): One word more if it isn't inopportune.

KING: Has something new happened since we were talking just now?

OXENSTJERNA: Yes, the courier from the south has come!

KING: Won't you sit down?

OXENSTJERNA (*sits down*): In the first place: Tilly is in Bavaria, and its elector has become the ally of France.

KING: What? France, our ally, has allied itself with our enemy, Bavaria? Yet another of Richelieu's dilemmas, arranged so that, no matter how you act, you act wrong.

OXENSTJERNA: Yes. That is how it is when you have to deal with dishonorable statesmanship. You never will get out of it with clean hands.

KING: This is the judgment over my alliance with France!

OXENSTJERNA: I am reluctant to judge the acts of my king. In France there are Franks, of course, but they speak Latin . . .

KING: And understand German well. It was France that forced through the Treaty of Passau, through which the religious peace of Augsburg came into being . . . and all the same: the French gold has always weighed on my conscience like the wages of sin.

OXENSTJERNA: Do not look back, Your Majesty! and don't draw up an account against providence! You remember very well that I was opposed to this war from the beginning because it was too great for the strength of our poverty-stricken nation. Well, I knew how to adjust myself to it, and, when we now have set out on the ice, we must cross the lake.

KING: What can we do?

OXENSTJERNA: Inasmuch as Tilly and Bavaria have attacked Bamberg, they have broken their neutrality, and they have declared war in that way. For us there remains only . . . defending ourselves, and we must go down to Bavaria.

KING: Listen: Do we have the right to break a treaty just because they have broken it?

OXENSTJERNA: My king, let us leave casuistry and theory, and let us defend with the sword what we have won with the sword! I must admit that our road has not been absolutely clean, but, if one is forced to climb in the dirt, well, do it! Time enough to wash up afterward!

KING: You mean then: down into Bavaria? To the Danube and Vienna?

OXENSTJERNA: One thing at a time, depending on the opponents' next move . . . This was number one.

KING: And number two?

OXENSTJERNA: King Sigismund of Poland is dead! [61]

KING (*jumps up*): At last! God forgive me! He was my kinsman, but I can never forget the harm that miserable man has done my country.

OXENSTJERNA: No, Your Majesty! Sigismund was brought up in the Catholic faith by a pious mother. They say that even as a child he was whipped because of his Catholic faith; and a child who suffers for his faith is at once beautiful and touching.

KING: You always see beauty in ugly things!

OXENSTJERNA: I have two eyes . . . I see two sides!

KING: However: then I claim the throne!

OXENSTJERNA: The Polish crown?

KING: Yes, indeed!

OXENSTJERNA: A powerful Brandenburg will make Poland superfluous; and the Polish crown isn't a headpiece for the Swedish king. One head, one crown!

KING: But the emperor?

OXENSTJERNA: The imperial eagle is two-headed! and his wings stretch over two hemispheres!

KING: But I have three crowns in my national coat of arms!

OXENSTJERNA: Heraldry is a fine art, but government is a science. (*Gets up*) My king, permit an old friend . . .

KING: . . . to block my plans? No! No one may, not even an Oxenstjerna!

OXENSTJERNA (*sits down again*): So it's true that success has so intoxicated our king that he's begun to dream he'll be a second Alexander the Great?

KING (*violently*): Chancellor, no more!

OXENSTJERNA: King, no more . . . Stop here! and turn back to the little country where God placed your cradle.

KING: It's too limited for me!

OXENSTJERNA: Is it too limited . . . our large country, whose borders and extent no one yet knows, where there is one man per square mile who longs for neighbors? Our forefathers, the Goths and the Northmen, emigrated because they found it too limited, but they were soon crushed by the streams of emigrants, were swallowed up, and didn't leave a trace after them. No, our land is big enough for the one who has a mind and spirit great enough to fill the empty expanses, and with great thoughts to populate the empty wilderness.

(QUEEN *enters, without being noticed by* OXENSTJERNA. KING *reaches the* QUEEN *his hand behind his back*.)

OXENSTJERNA: For me this rich land with its white wheat and its yellow wine is repulsive. I long for my native land with its red cottages in evergreen forests, its black bread and its brown ale, and I shall thank God the day he lets me see again the shores of Lake Mälar, with its great silence and its deep solitude. But that is far off, I suspect. Remain in your land and support yourself honestly! (*Notices the* QUEEN; *rises and greets her*)

QUEEN: Go on, chancellor; don't let me disturb you. (*She sits down beside the* KING, *who now and then secretly presses her hand*.)

OXENSTJERNA (*sits down*): Then, Your Majesty, you'll go south and I north?

KING: I'll go to the Danube, the great river, which comes from the Black Forest and flows past the black city and empties into the Black Sea. We'll meet again? Where?

OXENSTJERNA: Yes, where? In Erfurt, in Weissenfels, perhaps in Leipzig, where we always meet and where the road home begins.

KING: Farewell, then, Oxenstjerna, until then.

OXENSTJERNA: Farewell, my king. And, when you do get to the south, don't forget the north. And, if you should, just look at the heavens some starlit night. Where the Charles's Wain is! There is our home! (*Leaves*)

QUEEN: At last! May we go now?

KING: No, my child, we have other things to think about now. Tilly is at it again, so today I must march south, toward the Danube!

QUEEN: Isn't the war over? Weren't we to have peace?

KING: Since they won't leave me in peace . . .

QUEEN: My poor Germany!

KING: Your poor Sweden! Can't you remember you're Swedish?

QUEEN: Yes, but I can't forget I am German!

KING: Your Germany will reap where my Sweden has sown! (*To the* TRUMPETER) Nils, signal assembly!

  (TRUMPETER *blows; the Swedish flag is raised on a pole below the terrace.*)

QUEEN (*covers her ears with her hands*): Again the trumpet of war, again blood and tears, murder and fire!

KING. Do you want to go home?

QUEEN: Yes, with you, darling! (*She wants to embrace him; he tears himself away. Trumpets and drums in the distance.*)

KING: First to the Danube . . . then I will go home!

QUEEN: No, now! Turn back!

KING: It's too late! Leave me, you won't help, for the generals will be gathering in a minute, and I don't want to be impolite to you.

  (FABRICIUS *and two Jesuits can be seen in the colonnade.*)

QUEEN: Do you associate with these black Jesuits, my dear?

KING: Yes, with these two, because they saved my life from two other Jesuits. There are good people and bad in all kinds of garments! I'll say "good-bye" to you for a while. We'll meet again before I leave. Nils, signal for departure! No one is coming!

QUEEN: Farewell!

KING: Farewell, beloved child! But go, for there'll be shooting here! Why doesn't anyone come at my signal? (*Goes up to the cannons, strikes fire with steel and flint, and lights a quickmatch or port fire*)

  (QUEEN *hurries out.*)

  (MARCUS *enters.*)

KING: You came at the right time, Marcus. We need money. Do you have any?

MARCUS: Yes, but I have something else, too.

KING: Good advice! Oh, well, I'm not ungrateful, but just now I don't need any. (*Waves the lighted quickmatch*)

MARCUS: No? Does Your Majesty know that Sigismund of Poland is dead?

KING: I knew that before you did.

MARCUS: No, because I knew it yesterday, and Your Majesty got the news through me today . . . Well, who will get that throne?

KING: You know that, too?

MARCUS: I ought to! (*Pause*)

KING: Is the election over?

MARCUS: Doesn't Your Majesty know?

KING (*angrily*): You are a rascal!

MARCUS: Is that certain?

KING: Well, since you do know more than I, speak out!

MARCUS: Well, then! When Your Majesty presented your candidacy for the Polish crown through Ambassador Russel,[62] the proposal for religious freedom for Catholics was received very well. But, when the codicil demanded that the Jesuit gang . . . that was the word! . . . was to be exiled, the Póles were indignant, and the document was publicly burned!

KING: How can you know all that?

MARCUS: Because my people, *unsere Leute,* are everywhere, and are the friends of everyone. We never wage war; we stick together in unity; we haven't any priests, for the congregation is its own priest; we have no kings . . . hm! . . . no armies . . . hm! So, when I get to Warsaw, I'm as much at home there as in Vienna, Lübeck, London, Amsterdam, anywhere at all! We're independent of national coinage for we have a universal coinage, exchange; we have *one* language, one faith, no sects, one God, one hope.

KING: You still hope?

MARCUS: Yes, we hope that the Messiah will come who . . . who will make all people as fortunate as we! (*Pause*)

KING: Won't you come to Sweden?

MARCUS: No, it's too hot for us there!

KING: Hot?

MARCUS: Yes, they burn people there!

KING: That was when I was young! It doesn't happen any more. Can you tell me why you always have money and we never do?

MARCUS (*slyly*): No, that's a secret that only the thrifty soul can know.

KING: Do you mean we're wastrels?

MARCUS: Yes, it's certainly waste to burn cities, tear down villages, trample fields, and feed a hundred thousand highway robbers while the industrious have to starve! (*Pause*)

KING: Will you go with me, Marcus?

MARCUS: Yes, a little way, but not far! Sacrifice myself, no; our sacrifices ended with the destruction of Jerusalem . . . May I tell the great news, the very greatest?

KING: Speak!

MARCUS: Wallenstein, the Friedlander, has risen and joined the emperor!

KING: Wallenstein, the Friedlander, who was negotiating with me?

MARCUS: Yes, Wallenstein is like that.

KING (*violently*): Why doesn't anyone come? Signal, Nils! Where in heaven's name is everyone?

MARCUS: The stay on these vine-clad hills has done the Swedes no good. The sleep of victory and drunkenness! Ring the dinner bell; then they'll come! (*He pulls on a line; a bell starts ringing.*) It's going downhill, Your Majesty! Downhill!

KING: Downhill?

MARCUS: Yes, downhill!

CURTAIN

Scene 3

*The market square in a village near Ingolstadt on the Danube;
the backdrop a Danube landscape. On the square, a Maypole;
near it a bandstand with music holders. To the right a tavern
with tables and benches outside.* FABRICIUS *and* GRUBBE *are standing on the bandstand observing the battlefield with spyglasses;
the housetops are covered with spectators. The school children
with the* SCHOOLMASTER *stand in a group by themselves. The* SER-
GEANT MAJOR *and the* QUARTERMASTER *in the foreground. The boy*
TRUMPETER *below the stand. Noise in the distance.*

SERGEANT MAJOR: Are you going up to look at the battle?

QUARTERMASTER: N-o, I can't stand to look at butchering; never have
been able to. How about you?

SERGEANT MAJOR: I'm not so happy today, either. We've come too
far south . . . I've begun to long for home. And this Danube carries one down to the Turks; it looks dark and disturbing . . .

QUARTERMASTER: I notice you don't joke any more.

SERGEANT MAJOR: I'm tired, tired of this game that never leads to a
result. Didn't we thoroughly defeat Tilly at Breitenfeld? Now
he's on his legs again, dancing around with his Walloons down
in that hollow.

QUARTERMASTER: Well, what are we here for? Why, this is a Catholic country . . . there's hardly one Lutheran church.

SERGEANT MAJOR: Who talks about churches any more since we have
five thousand of Tilly's soldiers in our army? How crazy it all is
—Tilly's fighting against his own men today! (*Shouts from the
spectators on the rooftops*) There! Something's happened! (*Shouts
of hurrah and screams of joy from housetops*)

VOICE: Tilly has fallen!

SERGEANT MAJOR: Is he dead?

VOICE: He's dead!

SERGEANT MAJOR: Then I say: Hurrah! (*Embraces the* QUARTER-
MASTER)

QUARTERMASTER: Will we get to go home now?

(FABRICIUS *and* GRUBBE *shake hands. The schoolboys toss their
caps into the air and shout hurrah; then they dance in a ring
around the Maypole when the* SCHOOLMASTER *has gone out to the
left.*)

(*The transportation* DRIVER, *the miller of Act I, and the* MIDWIFE,
the miller's wife, enter.)

DRIVER: Why are you crying?

MIDWIFE: Tilly's dead!

DRIVER: Is that something to cry about?

MIDWIFE: Yes, for me, for us.

DRIVER: Now I don't understand this any more. Woman, as a midwife aren't you part of the Swedish army? Haven't you delivered
soldiers' wives without considering person, rank, nationality, and
religion? And now you're crying over a defeated enemy!

MIDWIFE: He was a holy and pious man . . .

DRIVER: Fine, then you have still less reason to weep over him, because then he has gone to his eternal rest without fear . . . Well,
since we don't have any common agreement on these vital matters . . . Yes, I'm serious. Look, old woman, go ahead and cry. I
shan't laugh so you see it. Every one is saved in his own faith,
now as before. But, when peace is concluded, I intend to retire
with a good sum that I've collected!

MIDWIFE: Where have you collected it?

DRIVER (*strikes his coat*): Here!

MIDWIFE: Yes, but where?

DRIVER: Everywhere! Everywhere it rained on the priest, it dripped
on the sexton! Didn't I tell you from the start that my taking
part in the war was dictated solely by my unwillingness to be
plundered? I preferred to plunder! But I had another motive,

too: revenge! Our daughter, whom Wallenstein's Croatians ruined . . .

MIDWIFE: I don't want to hear any more! But I'll say one thing. If you have collected anything unjustly, restore it at once. For one thing is certain: you haven't stolen anything from any heretics, your friends.

DRIVER: Heretics? Listen: I thought there wasn't to be any more talk of heretics and nonheretics.

MIDWIFE: Many believe that, or pretend to! (*Goes*)

(*Shouts from spectators on roofs*)

VOICE: Duke Kristoffer of Baden has fallen!

FABRICIUS (*turns away*). No, Grubbe, I can't look at this!

GRUBBE: He lost his head; yes, that is upsetting. An unfortunate day for some!

(PROVOST *enters; goes up to the* DRIVER.)

PROVOST: Tilly has fallen. Do you know what that means to us?

DRIVER: No.

PROVOST: It means that Munich is ours. You know, *ours,* for Munich is to pay a war levy to us. And, since the man in charge of the levy is ours, we'll be the winners.

DRIVER: Can we depend on the Jew?

PROVOST: We've been able to so far. In Würzburg, Mainz, Nuremberg, he took care of us like an honorable man . . . sh, there he is!

FIRE CHIEF (*enters, speaks to* DRIVER): How many wagons do you have charge of now?

DRIVER: Six wagons, and twenty-four horses.

FIRE CHIEF: Get twice the number, for the capital of Bavaria is to be sacked.

DRIVER: How much will I get?

FIRE CHIEF: A fourth, as usual.

DRIVER: No, I don't want that; I'd rather work on my own.

FIRE CHIEF: You want to be independent?

DRIVER: Yes!

FIRE CHIEF: You can't . . . you're mine, hide and hair.

PROVOST: Wait a minute! Shouldn't I be in on it, I who represent the law . . . I don't dare to say justice?

FIRE CHIEF: Isn't it just that we get the money when those fellows who are fighting down there get the honor? Shouldn't our peaceful activities be rewarded? We don't hurt anyone; we don't kill anyone; we gather honey like the bees . . . without stinging anyone . . .

(Shouts from spectators on housetops)

VOICES: The king has fallen!

GRUBBE: The king! God be merciful to us!

FABRICIUS: Eternal God and Lord! (*All hurry out, except the boy* TRUMPETER.)

TRUMPETER (*puts the trumpet on the ground and falls to his knees*): Dear God, help our gracious king so that he may not die!

Curtain lowered for a moment

(*The* KING *enters, spattered with blood, without a hat and with one boot soleless and heelless. He leans on* HORN *and* BANÉR; TORSTENSSON *comes in behind him. The* KING *sits down on a bench.*)

KING (*to* BANÉR): No, Johan, I can't joke any more, for I have walked through the valley of death. I thought when Tilly fell that he alone was in our Lord's disfavor, and that I was the chosen one, but then I had to learn better. My time has not yet come, but I'm grateful for the warning.

HORN: Turn back, Your Majesty; don't go farther.

KING: To Munich, first; then I will turn back.

BANÉR: Tilly is dead; let's rejoice!

KING: That's what I did, but, when my bullet came, I remembered the words of the preacher: "Rejoice not when thine enemy falleth, and let not thine heart be glad when he stumbleth: Lest the Lord see it, and it displease Him, and He turn away His wrath from him." [63] Gustav Horn, we will part now. You are to turn back and go north to protect the way home, because even I long

for home. I am tired, and I feel that it's going downhill . . .
downhill, Marcus said in Mainz. But first to Munich; farewell,
Gustav Horn; you were my best man . . . no one can take amiss
my saying so! Sorrow has been your faithful companion, and
that's why you became better than we. What my father did to
your father you have atoned for, not I. Farewell, Gustav. Embrace me, my friend.

HORN (*moved, with uncovered head, embraces the* KING): Farewell,
my king; and forgive me if I have not always obeyed you without
protest, but I have protested because I have not always understood my king's plans and objectives . . .

KING: *My* plans, *my* objectives, which haven't been mine and which
I'm just beginning to understand . . . as I understand that I have
been only a blind subordinate of the Lord, whose plans we are
never permitted to understand. God be with you, Gustav; when
we meet again . . . *if* we meet again . . .

HORN: Since we never shall meet again . . . (*On his knees*)

KING: You feel that! Well, well . . . I do, too! Farewell forever,
then! And go now, before . . . (*Turns away to conceal his
feelings*)

HORN (*gets up, embraces* BANÉR): Johan Banér, we'll meet again.
But . . . be a little more serious!

BANÉR: Seriousness comes; it comes with the years, old man!

HORN (*embraces* TORSTENSSON): Lennart Torstensson . . .

BANÉR: Don't look so sad, Lennart; life is bad enough anyway!

HORN (*hurries out. The* KING, BANÉR, *and* TORSTENSSON *wave to him
with their hats and shout*): Long live Gustav Horn!

KING: Now things begin in earnest! Where is Wallenstein?

BANÉR: The inscrutable one is still invisible and silent.

KING: What do you know, Lennart?

(TORSTENSSON *with a gesture and a look indicates that he knows
nothing.*)

KING: You've got out of the habit of speaking, Lennart?

BANÉR: In tongues, yes. But with cannons he's always the one to speak the loudest word! (*To the king*) He has lost his hearing a little . . .

KING: But he listens to voices, which we do not hear, and his tender conscience still speaks stern words, apparently. Let's signal assembly and breaking camp. And then, to the south, the last stop!

CURTAIN

SCENE 4

In Munich. In the foreground a little market square; to the right a Catholic chapel. A narrow street with medieval houses decorated with flags and banners ends at the square. In the background at the end of the street can be seen the palace and its gates. On the left side of the square is a little palace with a stone balcony outside the lower floor. This balcony extends all the way to the footlights. On the right side of the square is a large open window of a print shop. It is dusk; the setting sun casts a red glow upon the palace at the back, but there are black clouds above the palace. The street and the square are deserted. When the curtain goes up, a window in the street to the right is opened; an expensively dressed burgher's wife sticks her head out as if she were checking on the weather. A window, directly opposite to the left, is opened, and another woman sticks her head out there.

VOICE I: Hi!

VOICE II: Hi!

VOICE I: Has the apostate come?

VOICE II: The apostate has come, the one who deserted the faith of his fathers; from the land of Gog and Magog has he come! Abaddon, Apollyon! [64]

SEVERAL VOICES (*one after another from windows along the street*):
Apollyon!

(*The* SERGEANT MAJOR *and the* QUARTERMASTER *come down the street; they are very serious; they stop outside the* PRINTER'S *shop.*)

SERGEANT MAJOR: Did you hear voices in the air?

QUARTERMASTER: Yes, but I don't know if they are human voices. The sky is black as ink, and the thunder isn't far off. If I were to admit the whole truth, I'm filled with anxiety.

SERGEANT MAJOR: You, too? You know, this town depresses me; I feel as if we had no business being here. It's a foreign country, where everything is foreign, even the gods . . . But the king has promised the soldiers that they may plunder; he had to promise them that, or they'd have rebelled!

QUARTERMASTER: It's terrible! But since it has to be . . .

SERGEANT MAJOR: To our credit is the king's new proclamation of capital punishment for anyone who disturbs a Catholic church service or in any way upsets a divine service.

QUARTERMASTER: You can't go further, and shouldn't, either . . . the one who closes his eyes, gives his consent.

SERGEANT MAJOR: Don't speak so loudly! Why, the king has his quarters over there!

QUARTERMASTER: I ought to know . . . I cleared the house of Jesuits!

SERGEANT MAJOR: Well, then you know where the printer lives, too . . . the one who's printing the proclamation.

QUARTERMASTER: Let's see; it should be here by the square. Yes, there's the man.

(PRINTER *appears in his doorway.*)

SERGEANT MAJOR: How do you do, my good man?

PRINTER: What do you want?

SERGEANT MAJOR: Have you printed the proclamation?

PRINTER: I don't print any proclamations for enemies!

SERGEANT MAJOR: If the enemy is the victor, and the victor is your master, you are your master's servant! Do you understand that?

PRINTER: If a foreign people invades a city whose inhabitants have never injured anyone's rights, then the foreigner is a bandit, an oppressor, and a villain!

SERGEANT MAJOR: Have you read what you were to print?

PRINTER: Yes, I read that you intend to set fire to the city if it doesn't pay 400,000 *thaler,* which we don't have.

SERGEANT MAJOR: Then you've also noticed that our gracious king has granted the unlimited right to Catholics to worship in their own way.

PRINTER: *Very* gracious! Wasn't it your purpose to secure religious liberty for everyone?

SERGEANT MAJOR: Do you think I came over here to dispute with you?

PRINTER (*throws a paper on the street*): Be ashamed and go! We're good-natured people, but we acknowledge obligations even to ourselves, and printing this document violates the liberty of our conscience!

SERGEANT MAJOR: Pick up the paper, or we'll destroy your house!

PRINTER: It won't be destroyed!

SERGEANT MAJOR (*takes a piece of red chalk and writes a "D" above the entrance to the house*): Absolutely!

(QUARTERMASTER *picks up the paper.*)

PRINTER: This house will not be destroyed! (*Goes in, closes the door and the shutters*)

QUARTERMASTER: I can't help it, but the fellow's right. I'd have behaved in the same way.

SERGEANT MAJOR: The dark sides of war are manifold, but it's your duty to close your eyes. (*Lightning*)

QUARTERMASTER: There's thunder in the air! Let's go!

SERGEANT MAJOR: Are you afraid of the thunder?

QUARTERMASTER: Yes, since it's dangerous, I am afraid. And, since I'm not a soldier, I have the right to be afraid. And now I'm (*peal of thunder*) very effectively afraid! (*Hurries toward the chapel*) I want to get inside!

SERGEANT MAJOR: Listen, don't go in there; it's dangerous for Protestants to go into Catholic churches.

QUARTERMASTER: Dangerous? (*Looks into the church*) Yes, but it's beautiful.

SERGEANT MAJOR: That's what it is, exactly. Watch out so you don't stay!

QUARTERMASTER: I? No, no, not I. For the one who's been along at Breitenfeld, there aren't any dangers, any temptations. (*Goes into the chapel*)

SERGEANT MAJOR: Ha-ha!

(*The* SCULPTOR *and the* PAINTER *come in from the street, the* SCULPTOR *with a sculptor's stand, the* PAINTER *with a palette, stand, etc.*)

SCULPTOR (*to* SERGEANT MAJOR): Is this where the king of Sweden lives?

SERGEANT MAJOR: No, but he intends to stay here. What do you want?

PAINTER: We intend to do his portrait.

SERGEANT MAJOR: I see you're a painter, but I need to know something else. Excuse me for asking a very personal question.

PAINTER: A personal question won't be forgiven before the questioner has had his face smashed in. (*Shakes his fist*)

SERGEANT MAJOR: Young man . . .

SCULPTOR: Let that bastard ask first; we can always hit him afterward.

SERGEANT MAJOR: You talk as if you were masters in this city.

PAINTER: Aren't we?

SERGEANT MAJOR: No, we are.

SCULPTOR: You were, but you aren't any more, since the Swedish king spared the city from the fate of the conquered. And it is this generous, noble-minded act that we want to celebrate by recording forever the features of the great hero.

SERGEANT MAJOR: Is the city spared?

SCULPTOR: Yes, for a suitable ransom. What was it you were going to ask?

SERGEANT MAJOR: Well, before anyone is received in audience by the king, we have to know if . . . he is a Catholic.

SCULPTOR: What's that? Well, can't you tell what we believe by looking at us, by smelling it out? Well, the king just received a delegation of Capuchins, and is right now in a Jesuit meeting, and then plans to attend mass here in the Chapel of Our Lady . . .

SERGEANT MAJOR: That's a lie!

SCULPTOR: Shall we hit him?

PAINTER: Nah! It'll only cause trouble, and as philosophers we should really be above that.

SERGEANT MAJOR: Now I don't understand any more.

PAINTER: Have you ever understood anything? Does the shoemaker need to understand anything but his last?

SERGEANT MAJOR: Now I'm going home to bed. (*Goes up the street; meets the* SCHOOLMASTER, *who is drunk*)

SCHOOLMASTER (*sings*): Sum, sum, sum! Dum, dum, dum!

SERGEANT MAJOR: Where are you going?

SCHOOLMASTER: Who knows? Where's all this going? The king's with the Jesuits and . . . can you imagine . . . they say a Capuchin . . . has converted him!

SERGEANT MAJOR: To papism?

SCHOOLMASTER: Papism or Catholicism: the great schism!

SERGEANT MAJOR: It's a lie, of course!

SCHOOLMASTER: Of course it is, but what business does he have at mass?

SERGEANT MAJOR: Is he already at mass?

SCHOOLMASTER: They say he's in the Chapel of Our Lady!

SERGEANT MAJOR: Here?

SCHOOLMASTER: Here or there, what do I know?

SERGEANT MAJOR (*to the* SCULPTOR *and the* PAINTER): The king is in there? Then he went in the back way.

SCHOOLMASTER: Who are those birds?

SERGEANT MAJOR: Two philosophers!

SCHOOLMASTER: What are they philosophizing about?

SERGEANT MAJOR: Well, that's hard to tell, since they're above everything like that!

SCHOOLMASTER (*approaches the chapel*): What sort of inn is this? Oh, it's one of those papist cottages! (*Sings*) Sum, sum, sum! Brum, brum, brum!

CANTOR (*comes out of the chapel*): Don't disturb the services, man!

SCHOOLMASTER (*lifts his crutch*): Behave yourself!

SERGEANT MAJOR (*to the* SCHOOLMASTER): Think of what you're doing!

SCHOOLMASTER (*strikes the crutch against the church door*): Trum, trum, trum!

QUARTERMASTER (*comes out of the church*): Who's disturbing divine services? So it's you, you old good-for-nothing! Don't you know the king's in there?

SCHOOLMASTER: What the devil! So it's true he's turned Catholic?

QUARTERMASTER: No, it's not!

SCHOOLMASTER (*to the* CANTOR): Go to your Virgin Mary, go, and don't stand here playing the saint! (*With his crutch lifts down a wreath which has been hanging at the foot of the image of Mary; tosses the wreath out onto the stage*)

CANTOR (*shouts*): Sacrilege! Desecrator!

VOICES (*from the windows along the street*): Apollyon! Abaddon!

SERGEANT MAJOR: Voices in the air again! Now I am afraid!

(BANÉR, TORSTENSSON, FABRICIUS *appear in the street.*)

BANÉR (*comes forward*): What's going on here? Why the shouts?

CANTOR (*points at the schoolmaster*): An anti-Christ, a godless man, who desecrates the holy . . .

BANÉR: Explain, explain . . .

(*The* KING *appears at the entrance of the chapel with* SCHWARZENBERG *and* FREDRIK V OF PFALZ.)

KING (*angry*): What's going on? Who has disturbed the holy act?

SCHOOLMASTER (*on his knees, sober*): Mercy!

KING: So it's you, teacher of the young, who dishonor me and the Swedish name! (*To the* SERGEANT MAJOR) Take him away to the punishment which the articles of war and our circular prescribe: Death!

SCHOOLMASTER: Most merciful king . . .

KING: No, I am unmerciful to lawbreakers and desecrators! Take him out of my sight! He shall die! Fabricius, look to his soul. You hesitate, you who today have preached tolerance and freedom of conscience!

(SERGEANT MAJOR *takes away the* SCHOOLMASTER, *and* FABRICIUS *goes along, unwillingly.*)

CANTOR (*on his knees before the* KING): Great King, may a humble servant of the Lord who well understands an unchallengeable judgment beg for mercy for a criminal who has acted out of ignorance?

KING: No! May his misfortune bring others to better understanding and, above all, to obedience! Go in peace!

(BANÉR'S, TORSTENSSON'S, *and* FABRICIUS' *facial expressions reveal their dissatisfaction with the harshness of the sentence.* CANTOR *goes into the chapel.*)

KING (*to the* QUARTERMASTER *after he has observed the red mark above the* PRINTER'S *door*): Why have you marked this house with the sign of confiscation?

QUARTERMASTER: Because the owner refused to print the proclamation.

KING: Bring the man out and let him be heard.

(QUARTERMASTER *knocks on the door.* PRINTER *comes out.*)

KING: Why didn't you obey the order?

PRINTER: Because carrying out the order went against my conscience.

KING: Is it against your conscience that I grant freedom of conscience?

PRINTER: No, most merciful king, not that. But the first part of the proclamation, that about the levy on the innocent city, I couldn't bring myself to print.

KING: Well, bring the document.

QUARTERMASTER (*hands it to the* KING): Your Majesty.

KING (*reads the document, folds it in two, draws his sword, and cuts the paper into two parts; then gives one part to the* PRINTER): Then we'll do it like this! Take this half and print it; then your conscience will be free and mine, too.

PRINTER (*on his knees*): Great king, who knows how to heal the conscience . . .

KING: Get up! (*To the* QUARTERMASTER) Spare his house.

(QUARTERMASTER *erases the red mark on the entrance.*)

SCULPTOR: The judgment of Solomon!

PAINTER: The judgment of Solomon!

KING: What do you wish?

PAINTER: We long to record forever in a portrait the Swedish king; and just as we were arguing about the first moment of the conception, we mean the allegorical presentation, Your Majesty himself deigned to give us the subject which our friend has so beautifully formulated: The judgment of Solomon!

KING: I am no Solomon as you mean it, and I can't pose. Thank you for your kindness, but I have neither the time nor the inclination. Farewell. (*The* PRINTER, *the* SCULPTOR, *the* PAINTER, *the* QUARTERMASTER *go; the* KING *stands in the foreground with* SCHWARZENBERG *and* FREDRIK OF PFALZ. *In the background are* BANÉR *and* TORSTENSSON, *both depressed.*)

KING (*to* SCHWARZENBERG): Yes, Excellency, I have now fulfilled your reasonable request, I have seen and I have heard . . . But I haven't found occasion to change my opinion, except in minor matters.

SCHWARZENBERG: Minor matters that are major matters!

KING: Not at all! However, there are many mansions in the kingdom of the Lord, and for everyone his own. Your cult is very beautiful, very attractive, and very expensive . . . suitable for your wealthy countries. But for our poor man's country a poor man's religion is more suitable. For you, wine; for us, ale; for us, homespun; for you, velvet. That's approximately what I've learned while walking about in your temples. And now I'll return to my work. Thank you for good company. Farewell.

SCHWARZENBERG: Is that all?

KING: That's all I have learned from you! Do you want to learn something from us? No, *non possumus!* So: farewell, Excellency!

SCHWARZENBERG: Your Majesty!

KING: Enough! I won't be converted . . . you know that!

(SCHWARZENBERG *leaves unwillingly.*)

KING (*goes up on the veranda; sits as close to the front of the stage as possible. Asks* FREDRIK OF PFALZ *to sit down*): Well, kinsman, what do you have to tell me? (*They see candles lighted in the palace.*)

FREDRIK OF PFALZ: Kinsman and king! Now that we have captured the elector's capital, we have at the same time blown up the stronghold of the Catholic League, for Maximilian of Bavaria was the head of the league, and Tilly its arm. May I urge you to have the city uprooted from the earth, as I have promised and you have promised the army?

KING: Kinsman, when both the head and the arm have been shot off, what good does it do to mistreat the corpse?

FREDRIK: You have promised, and the soldiers will revolt if you don't hand the city over to them for plundering.

KING: The Lord had promised Jonah that the city of Nineveh would be destroyed, but He took mercy upon the great city, and Jonah became angry unto death. Do not be angry, Fredrik of Pfalz! and don't let your hatred pronounce the judgment over yourself! You were once king of Bohemia, and you misused your royal power to plunder the churches and to oppress the Catholics, but your intolerance deceived you into cruelty against Protestant sects other than your own. To me, you have never been a martyr, and your exile, your sufferings I have always considered the clear results of your acts. This whole terrible war, this irreconcilability, this beastly hatred which we ascribe to the enemy really stem

from you. Simply think of some of the better emperors! Ferdinand I, Charles V's brother, became so tolerant of Protestants
that Pope Paul IV did not even want to recognize him. Remember Maximilian II, who was brought up by Wolfgang Stieler, the
disciple of Luther and Melanchthon, and who, because of his
Protestant sympathies, was hated and threatened by Pius V. Remember that when the empire and Maximilian II were attacked
by the Turks, who had already taken Hungary, it was the Protestants who refused to help and showed themselves to be poor
patriots. All the same, Maximilian went so far in making concessions that he granted the worst dissidents the Communion cup
at the Lord's Supper and let the priests get married! What concessions did you make in Bohemia? Not to speak of the Catholics, but of the Lutherans! You made no concessions, as no Calvinist has yet done!

FREDRIK: Your Majesty, you talk the way the enemy usually talks!

KING: I have finally heard the defendant, something I ought to
have started with; and I have learned something! Out of those
unsolvable contradictions in which I had been caught at the beginning of this war, I have finally worked my way; I have
found myself and my task, which I didn't understand until now.
This has restored my strength of decision and courage of action.

FREDRIK: I'm glad to hear about the latter, and I suppose we'll at
last be marching against Vienna.

KING: No, because the simplest concept of the art of war, which
you've never understood, says that I shall not turn south when
my enemy is in the north. Wallenstein and Maximilian are right
now in Prague, your Prague, and are ready to strike at us here. So,
northward; and, if I had to explain my actions to you, then ... Munich will be spared ... it has ransomed itself, and the soldiers have
released me from my promise by accepting two extra *gyllen* per
man. I'd like to say farewell to you now that we've reached our
common goal: the headquarters of the league; and I'll say good
night to the head of the union, for neither league nor union exists

any more. From now on it will be the deliverer against the oppressor!

FREDRIK: Or like this: Gustav Adolf *with* the Catholics!

KING (*furious, gets up*): Go, liar, go quickly! And may oblivion and shame ever go with your name!

(FREDRIK, *who at first had been sure of himself because he had not believed the situation was serious, now becomes frightened and leaves.*)

KING: Well, don't cry now, you wretch! You could light the fire, but you left its extinction to me!

(TORSTENSSON *and* BANÉR, *who have disappeared for a short while up the street, now come toward the* KING. *Both look very serious.*)

KING (*harshly*): What do you want?

BANÉR: Our king's ear!

KING: Speak!

BANÉR: Your Majesty's too hasty promise that the city was to be sacked has aroused certain hopes in the soldiers, hopes that can't be disappointed without danger of revolt.

KING: Do you think so, too, Torstensson?

TORSTENSSON: Yes!

KING: And now you want to advise me to imitate the destruction of Magdeburg, which we wept over together! Then you are bad councillors, and as such you have my disfavor!

BANÉR: We'll have to bear that disfavor, but first beg for mercy for a poor devil . . .

KING: My schoolmaster? No, he'll get no mercy from me!

TORSTENSSON: Your Majesty, it has awakened amazement and sorrow that a brother in the faith, a Protestant, is to suffer death because of a frivolous attack on the papists' superstition . . .

KING (*beside himself with fury*): Torstensson! Is the schoolmaster a Protestant, he, who has had only the devil's name on his lips, who has looked upon the war only as a bacchanal? Leave me!

Cease to be my friend, and limit yourself to being in my service, to the welfare of your fatherland! Go! (*Pause*)

(TORSTENSSON *goes slowly.* BANÉR *follows him.*)

KING: Stay, Johan Banér!

BANÉR: No! I'm going. I, too!

KING: Little kings, watch out! Remember the Folkungs,[65] the Stures, the lords at Linköping!

BANÉR (*furious*): Watch out, Vasa! Snow King! The Winter King has a successor!

KING: Is it Johan Banér that says that?

BANÉR: Yes, Johan Banér, born in legal marriage bed of Gustav Axelsson Banér, the national councillor who was beheaded in Linköping by the traitor Charles the Bloody . . . my father by your father! My father, because he kept his royal vow! And my mother, Kristina Sture! There you have the Stures again, Vasa! Yes, it's Johan Banér speaking!

(TORSTENSSON *pulls at* BANÉR's *arm;* KING *remains speechless.* BANÉR *goes with* TORSTENSSON. KING *sits down, distressed and thoughtful.*)

(*The palace doors to the veranda are opened. The* QUEEN *comes out, accompanied by attendants who stop in the doorway.*)

QUEEN: My king is not happy!

KING: Distressed . . . unto death!

QUEEN: And sitting in the dark!

KING: The shadows are thickening, and it's a summer evening, too. It isn't true that you find the sun in the south; at home it shines all night this time of year.

QUEEN (*signs to attendants, who carry out two large candelabra which they put on the* KING's *table*): Nothing in life is like what one expects.

KING: No, indeed. It's like a dream for me that I'm in the capital of Bavaria and that I've just dismissed Fredrik of Pfalz, the root and cause of this incomprehensible war.

QUEEN: The ways of Providence are incomprehensible.

KING: Maximilian and Fredrik! Bavaria and Pfalz!

QUEEN: What do you have to do with Fredrik?

KING: You may well ask! He was supposedly the head of the Protestant Union and so the one I had to be closest to; and just the same I have to fight him, since he's a Calvinist and I'm a Lutheran. Bavaria and Pfalz! We . . . Swedes . . . once had a king who came from Bavaria; his name was Christopher,[66] and he was the nephew of Erik XIII. My father, Charles IX, was first married to Maria of Pfalz. My brother-in-law, Count John Casimir of Pfalz, is at home in Sweden in charge of a government bureau, and his son Charles, now ten, is the playmate of my seven-year-old daughter Christina!

QUEEN: Where are your thoughts going?

KING: I don't know, but it's as if I'd always expected something fatal from this Pfalz. How my father from his remote country could find a princess of Pfalz I don't understand. But . . . you probably don't know . . . when my grandfather, Gustav I, had to put down the great Dacke rebellion,[67] the chieftain was supported by, among others, a Fredrik of Pfalz, who hoped to get the Swedish throne! That happened a hundred years ago! And now . . . well, you understand.

QUEEN: You mean that our Christina and John Casimir's son might through marriage some day . . .

KING: Who knows? Providence sometimes uses a hundred years to carry through a plan. And everything does repeat itself. Just think of it: Johan Banér, my friend and kinsman, too, suddenly stepped forward just now and revealed himself as a Sture! You know about the Stures and the Vasas.

QUEEN: Was Banér's father beheaded in Linköping by your father?

KING: We don't like to talk about that, but it's true. And Johan Banér's mother was Kristina Sture. But the saga of the Stures is so interwoven with the saga of the Vasas that I can't quite grasp it in what they call a natural way. As regents, the oldest Stures established the independence of the kingdom, but Gustav Vasa got the crown. Erik XIV had Stures killed for reasons that weren't fully clear. My father, Charles IX, beheaded the lords at Linköping and hit the Sture clan at the same time, probably without intending to . . . No fewer than six Stures got sorrow that day. Hogenskild Bielke was married to Anna Sture; Ture Nilsson Bielke to Margareta Sture; Ture Pederson Bielke with Sigrid Sture; Erik Stenbock with Malin Sture; Gustav Banér with Kristina Sture; and Krister Horn was the brother-in-law of Mauritz Sture. That's the blood guilt I've carried, and that's why I have put up with more from my friends Horn, Banér, and Stenbock than from any other human beings!

QUEEN: Was that why you've let these friends, whom I've never been able to bear, come so close to you?

KING: Yes, but I haven't regretted my patience, for they were dear and devoted to me until just now. Still . . . you know . . . I'm sitting here asking myself: Why did the Sture ghost rise up now? And in Banér? His face was transformed; his usually friendly eyes glowed with a hatred that has been growing for two hundred years; his voice wasn't like his own; and he uttered words that weren't his, but which crushed me.

QUEEN: What did he say?

KING: He said that Vasa has no heir to the throne but that Pfalz has.

QUEEN: Why did he say that just now?

KING: That's exactly what my conscience is trying to answer. Did he mean, did he prophesy that my child would not inherit the throne?

QUEEN: Isn't our Christina heir to the throne?

KING: Yes, and no! According to the Statute of Succession of 1544, only men could succeed to the throne. This was later changed arbitrarily.[68]

QUEEN: Well, that is news!

KING: But there is other injustice that walks abroad like a bad omen.

QUEEN: Why these dark thoughts, my dear?

KING: Because it's darkening! Don't you see that it's going down-hill, that time is getting short?

QUEEN: But, dearest, we weren't going farther south; tomorrow we'll turn back home to the north.

KING: ... My father was a usurper, not because he dethroned Erik, not because he forced Sigismund aside, but because he passed by Duke John, who was the heir to the throne.

QUEEN: But Charles IX was elected by the Estates ...

KING: Yes, but Sweden was no longer an elective monarchy ... And I, too, am a usurper, for the same John was still the legal heir to the throne.

QUEEN: But didn't Duke John renounce his claims?

KING: Yes, he did, after Charles IX had forced ... forced! ... him into an unhappy marriage with his cousin. The marriage ended in insanity—a genuine soul murder.[69]

QUEEN: Why dwell on what is past?

KING: Because the past comes back!

QUEEN: It came back after Breitenfeld in Auerbachshof! But then it went to rest!

KING: Since you have brought up the subject, I want to say some-thing. An unhappy chance . . . perhaps something else . . . brought you before my son, Gustav ... You have believed I was cruel enough to arrange the meeting. I've let you think so badly of me because I felt I ought to. But I tell you now that I was innocent in that matter at least.

QUEEN: *Your* son! Not ours! We don't get any!

KING: That is my punishment. Why you should suffer for my sin, I don't know. Can you forgive me?

QUEEN: I already have.

KING: Then we'll not say anything more about that.

QUEEN: But about something else since you've at last found time to take care of your affairs of the heart ... There's a man whose constant presence pains me very much!

KING: Nils Brahe! Do you demand that I sacrifice him, too?

QUEEN: I don't demand; I ask.

KING: He is my kinsman, though; he doesn't say much . . .

QUEEN: But his eyes tell me a saga that ought to be forgotten now! [70]

KING: That's right! I'll do it! (*Gets up*) It gets ever emptier about me, and more desolate. At last it will be only you and I!

QUEEN: As it should always have been!

KING: Perhaps! Tott, Rålamb, Horn, Banér, Torstensson, Brahe . . . gone!

QUEEN: You miss them!

KING: Yes, but I find myself again . . . and you! Friends give much, but they take more. (*Music can be heard from the palace; shadows flicker.*) Is there a party in there?

QUEEN: Yes, you're the host.

KING: I had forgotten! One more word . . . after the warning I got at Ingolstadt, I've had a keen desire to set my house in order, whatever that may mean afterward. And my thoughts are most often with my daughter. Tell me, do you think it wise to let John Casimir, a Calvinist, bring her up?

QUEEN: No, I've never thought so—the Calvinists I saw at close range at home were worse than the Jesuits. And if we were to have quarrels about faith in our family . . .

KING: Exactly! The thought that my child could accept another faith than the Lutheran makes me despondent; and Christina's spirit of contradiction isn't promising; you know she said black whenever I said white!

QUEEN: Her stubbornness and her insistence on having her own way are boundless. But why be disturbed? A seven-year-old doesn't understand either the truths of religion or its errors.

KING: That's exactly why I'm afraid. But I'll leave it to Providence. Join the guests, dear; I'll follow.

QUEEN: Don't sit alone—your heavy thoughts may make you despair.

KING: *Not* alone?

(NILS BRAHE *comes hastily down the street with a dispatch in his hand, which he gives to the* KING.)

QUEEN: Now I'm going. (*Goes in*)

KING: He'll soon go, too.

BRAHE: Important news, Your Majesty!

KING (*opens and reads the dispatch*): Wallenstein! Finally! Wallenstein's in Saxony and has cut off our road home! That inscrutable, dark man, who believes nothing but who's always lucky in the saddle. So I'm to meet him at last! Nils Brahe, for reasons I can't state but that you may suspect, don't go into this festive hall, where you've been invited. Go back to camp and get your troops into order.

BRAHE: Is this the declaration of disfavor?

KING: No! And believe me when I say that.

BRAHE: I don't have the right to ask further . . .

KING (*touched*): But I have the right to demand of a friend that he would understand and believe . . .

BRAHE (*distressed*): I believe . . . but I don't understand. Farewell, my king. (*Goes*)

KING: Alone! . . . alone with you, my Lord and my God!

LEUBELFING (*out; kneels before the* KING): Majesty and most gracious king!

KING: Who are you? So! The queen's page! What's your name?

LEUBELFING: Leubelfing, from Nuremberg; at your service, Your Majesty.

KING: Oh! What do you want of me, child?

LEUBELFING: To serve a king that I worship next to God in heaven!

KING: Not that! You shall worship the Lord your God alone! I once had a young friend who worshiped me, but, when he saw that I was only a weak human being, full of faults, he left me and spat behind him! Since then I've been afraid of the young.

LEUBELFING: Don't be afraid of me, great king; I will be faithful to you unto death; I will follow you like a dog . . .

KING: Tell me: You were brought up a Catholic?

LEUBELFING: Yes, great king, and in a cloister, but when I saw how wicked the papists were . . . what miserable people . . .

KING: Wait a bit . . . if you think that Protestants are angels, you're deceiving yourself. Go into my camp and look at the wretchedness; you'll see that it's six of one and half a dozen of the other. And among Christian people you'll meet hardly one who's as fine a man as my friend, Marcus the Jew. No, my little friend, we've seen through all that! And, besides, people have received their nationality and their religion from God, so they ought to keep them. You look at me . . . and you have kind eyes. What can you do?

LEUBELFING: I can saddle a horse, read aloud, play the lute . . .

KING: Can you play? Will your queen give you up?

LEUBELFING (*embarrassed*): Yes, I think . . .

KING: Perhaps she sent you?

LEUBELFING: I wasn't to say that!

KING: Well, since you are a gift from the woman I love, stay with me. I shall take it as an omen, that you fell down like a ray of sunshine when I was alone in the darkness!

LEUBELFING (*kisses the* KING's *hand*): Now I've realized the beautiful dream of my childhood: I may serve the gold king. And I'll get a horse?

KING: A big horse! But . . . (*takes* LEUBELFING *by the ear*) you mustn't fall in love with the queen like the other pages.

(LEUBELFING *embarrassed*)

KING (*gets up*): Come, David, and play for your Saul!

(QUEEN *appears in the doorway*.)

CURTAIN

ACT V

The camp outside Nuremberg. The city can be seen to the left at the back; Alte Veste to the right. Tents in the middle of the stage with streets between them. The KING's *tent to the right. Tables and chairs outside his tent. A telescope on a tripod in front of the* KING's *tent. Autumn sky with dark clouds and a blood-red streak on the horizon.*

The SERGEANT MAJOR *and the* QUARTERMASTER *are on stage.*

SERGEANT MAJOR: Sixty days of this dog-day heat without getting into battle! I can't understand it!

QUARTERMASTER: You don't count the storming of Alte Veste [71] this morning.

SERGEANT MAJOR: Well, we're not sure that didn't fail, and that Wallenstein isn't ready to announce his victory up there.

QUARTERMASTER: Yes, Wallenstein! That faithless dog who worships himself alone is irresistible, but the pious Tilly was literally hacked to death bit by bit! Who's the God of Hosts today?

SERGEANT MAJOR: The same as yesterday and in the dawn of time, whose designs neither you nor I can fathom.

QUARTERMASTER: Why, you're getting serious.

SERGEANT MAJOR: Not too soon, I think; and not too late, I hope.

QUARTERMASTER: Wallenstein! Who can ever understand him? Did you know he was born and baptized a Protestant?

SERGEANT MAJOR: Of course, I know that.

QUARTERMASTER: Did you know, too, that when he was a child he fell out of a window on the third floor without injuring himself?

SERGEANT MAJOR: Yes, indeed. Just like Johan Banér of Hörningsholm—he, too, fell out of a third-story window without injuring

202

himself . . . The third story seems to be the maximum. Martinitz
and Slawata [72] were thrown out from the third story in Prague
. . . this whole war seems to have started on the third floor . . .
and will end, most likely, down in the cellar!

QUARTERMASTER: Sh-h! Now they're really making music up in the
Friedlander's old stronghold . . .

SERGEANT MAJOR (*goes over to the telescope*): Imagine if one could
only get to see him once, that invisible, immovable person who
sits up there on the cliff like an imperial eagle! (*Adjusts the
telescope*)

QUARTERMASTER: I'd give a lot to see him!

SERGEANT MAJOR (*looks into the telescope*): Wait a minute!

QUARTERMASTER: Can you see anything?

SERGEANT MAJOR: Quiet! He *is* there!

QUARTERMASTER: All right, but what do you see?

SERGEANT MAJOR (*twists and turns the telescope*): Just a minute! I
had his cape just then, but . . . now . . . I . . . want to see him . . .
under . . . his eyelids!

QUARTERMASTER: Most likely he's black and looks evil, like the devil!
And he's not good; but he's terribly rich; they say he owns
twenty-two thousand farms in Bohemia, all of them confiscated
estates . . .

SERGEANT MAJOR (*turns away from the telescope*): I saw him! He
was bareheaded, had a black beard . . . that's all I could see before he disappeared. But I saw something else, too . . . Something
blue and yellow . . .

QUARTERMASTER: Swedish prisoners . . .

SERGEANT MAJOR: Yes, they were Swedes . . . A misfortune has happened!

QUARTERMASTER: Many misfortunes have happened since we came
into this Catholic land, where we probably never should have
come. It isn't the Friedlander who has killed twelve thousand of
our men and eight thousand of our horses during the last two
months. I've counted them. It isn't Wallenstein who has starved

us to death; it isn't he who has turned disease and vermin loose upon us.

SERGEANT MAJOR: Who is it, then?

QUARTERMASTER: It's the angel of death, the one who came with the plagues of Egypt, the one who destroyed the army of Sennacherib [73] . . . The Lord is against us!

SERGEANT MAJOR: But He's also against the Friedlander! He has suffered just as much!

QUARTERMASTER: Then He's against both, because we should have made peace now.

SERGEANT MAJOR: Are you in the Lord's confidence? Do you get His secrets before the rest of us? Shame!

QUARTERMASTER: I'm ashamed, but not because of that; but because we've become a disgrace to Sweden, because from having been the soldiers of the Lord in discipline and honor we've become as bad as our enemies. All vices, all crimes flourish in our camps, and we have just as many pagans as Christians, but we have still more corpses than we have living men. The whole country about us stinks, and our friends curse us! (*At the back of the stage goes a procession of green stretchers for the living and black stretchers —covered with white—for the dead, carried by white-clad attendants.*) The angel of death's procession of triumph! (FABRICIUS *can be seen in the procession.*) And the chief priest . . . who has to bury both Christians and pagans. All become alike in the great pit! (*The* QUEEN *can be seen in the procession; she is dressed in white and is carrying a little child in her arms; a crowd of white-clad children follows the* QUEEN.)

SERGEANT MAJOR (*moved*): The queen!

QUARTERMASTER: The good angel of mercy and suffering! The mother of the abandoned children! Yes, the deserted and the orphans! Not an accurate birth certificate any more . . . only "parents unknown." The king strikes, and the queen heals; he punishes, and she comforts. Bless her! (*The* QUEEN *goes by; chil-*

dren tug at her skirt; the procession is continued by wounded with bandages and crutches.)

SERGEANT MAJOR: The dark sides of war. You know, I can't remember the bright ones any more . . . Everything smells, everything tastes of the dead! even the wine in the goblet! (*A procession of ragged people*)

QUARTERMASTER: There come the hungry. No bread and no money.

SERGEANT MAJOR: It's as if there were a curse on the French money; it never lasts.

QUARTERMASTER: And these Jewish notes, that never do anything but fall due.

SERGEANT MAJOR: All notes do, I suspect, if they get the time.

QUARTERMASTER: Where's the king?

SERGEANT MAJOR: At a council of war with the dukes of Lauenberg and Weimar and their excellencies Schwarzenberg of Brandenburg and Arnim of Saxony.

QUARTERMASTER: None of ours there?

SERGEANT MAJOR: No, because only dukes and electors have votes in the election of the emperor.

QUARTERMASTER: So it's the emperor's crown again?

SERGEANT MAJOR: Who knows? There's so much talk . . . (*The procession has continued; at the very last come the* PROVOST, *the* FIRE CHIEF, *and the* DRIVER.) See! There we have the wolves!

DRIVER: I've driven around half of Germany, and I'm tired . . .

PROVOST: And satisfied!

DRIVER: And I'd like to retire . . .

FIRE CHIEF: With a tidy little sum . . .

DRIVER: I used to be miller at Usedom . . .

FIRE CHIEF: When I was bailiff in Wolgast . . .

DRIVER: But then came the edict of restitution and took the mill away from me. Still . . . times have changed, and the mill has been returned. Should we say good-bye?

FIRE CHIEF: To each other or to the military?

DRIVER: I'll say good-bye to you.

PROVOST: You may, just so you leave the wagons.

DRIVER: The wagons? Yes, take them.

FIRE CHIEF: So they're empty? (*Takes the* DRIVER *by his collar*) Man, if you've cheated us, you're done for!

DRIVER: Wait a minute! Don't get so excited . . .

PROVOST (*grabs hold of the* DRIVER): Thief, traitor, poor comrade . . .

DRIVER: Help! He's killing me!

MIDWIFE (*comes in from right; waves*): No, you won't be murdered, but you'll die for your crimes, you plunderer of the dead, you desecrator of graves!

BRAHE (*enters with three guardsmen; says softly and quietly to the watch*): Take these three men to the gallows and let the executioner hang them. But wait with the chief of the fire brigade until new orders arrive.

(*Watch leads out the* PROVOST, *the* DRIVER, *and the* CHIEF.)

BRAHE (*to the* MIDWIFE): Go, woman; your act was not pretty; after all, he was your husband! What are you up to now?

MIDWIFE: I used to wrap newborn children; now I wrap the dead, because living children aren't born any more.

BRAHE: I don't believe human beings are born any more, only wild animals. Go, woman!

MIDWIFE: General . . .

BRAHE: You may not speak! But go and wrap your husband in his shroud, and see to it he gets into a decent pit!

MIDWIFE: That . . . heretic . . .

BRAHE: We're all heretics to each other nowadays, so we won't talk about that . . . Go! In the pit we'll all be alike!

MIDWIFE: I thought so once, but I don't think so any more . . .

BRAHE (*to the* QUARTERMASTER *while the* MIDWIFE *says the preceding speech and the ones that follow*): Where is the king?

QUARTERMASTER: In the council of war.

BRAHE: With the dukes?

QUARTERMASTER: Yes, general.

MIDWIFE: And I believed every one was saved by his own faith . . .

BRAHE (*without listening to the woman, says to the* QUARTERMASTER):
It's a disgrace to our army and our country that our Protestants
should behave as badly as the enemy . . .

MIDWIFE (*at the same time*): And I believed the deliverer had
come . . .

BRAHE (*turns to the woman*): And he has! You were right that
time! For once! Go to the gallow's hill, and you'll see! (*The*
QUARTERMASTER *takes her arm and forces her off stage.*)

SERGEANT MAJOR (*looks to the left*): The king!

(BRAHE *goes to the right.* QUARTERMASTER *and* SERGEANT MAJOR
go toward the back of the stage.)

(KING *enters from the left, followed by* MARCUS.)

KING: Sit down . . . I mean . . .

MARCUS: Stand! I know my place, Your Majesty, and I don't abuse
anyone's kindness.

KING: Will you take the notes?

MARCUS: No, king, because our paths divide here. As long as you
fought on the side of the oppressed, I was with you, against the
pope in Rome's worldly dominion, but, when you go actively
against the emperor alone, I can't go with you.

KING: Why?

MARCUS: Because . . . I am German, and you are a foreigner; because the emperor keeps the German empire together; and
because I have a debt of gratitude, I and my people, to Hapsburg.
Emperor Charles V gave us, the Jews, human rights, the first
time at the Congress of Augsburg, the second time at the Congress of Regensburg. Augsburg and Regensburg, the Protestants'
two strongholds: 1530 and 1541; Protestantism's year of birth and
year of confirmation. Do you understand now why I and mine
are Protestants? Because we're children of the same years as the
Protestants.

KING: Can you be grateful, *you?*

MARCUS: A Jew can be everything a Christian can be, in good as in
evil.

KING: What would you do now if you were in my place?

MARCUS: Conclude an honorable peace, or accept the offer of peace from the emperor.

KING: It's too late!

MARCUS: Never too late to do what is right!

KING: And you know what is right?

MARCUS: When the pagans who do not have the law know what the law requires, why, even I can know that!

KING: Tell me. Why are things going badly for me now?

MARCUS: Because your camp is polluted by sins and by crimes, by stinking cadavers and by vermin! As it says in the Fifth Book of Moses: "For the Lord thy God walketh in the midst of thy camp, to deliver thee, and to give up thine enemies before thee; therefore shall thy camp be holy: that He see no unclean thing in thee, and turn away from thee!" [74]

KING: The Lord has turned away from me. Yes, that is certain. What shall I do?

MARCUS: "If thou return to the Almighty, thou shalt be built up, thou shalt put away iniquity far from thy tabernacles . . . For then shalt thou have thy delight in the Almighty, and shalt lift up thy face unto God . . . Thou shalt also decree a thing, and it shall be established unto thee: and the light shall shine upon thy ways." [75]

KING: Are those beautiful words yours?

MARCUS: How have you read your Bible, Your Majesty? It was Eliphaz from Teman who spoke thus to Job.

KING: Job? "And the Lord said unto Satan, Behold, all that he hath is in thy power." [76] Marcus, why don't you believe in the Saviour? Is it because you cannot believe in Him?

MARCUS: I don't know. Maybe because I'm not allowed to . . . I'm careful not to look into that! (*Noise outside*)

KING: One other matter before we part. You know that your kinsman, the fire chief, has been convicted of having unjustly extorted some property. For that reason he has been condemned to death according to our laws. But I want to ask you what your laws say about that.

MARCUS: He shall die so that he may not pollute your land, because you shall put evil away from you, and all Israel shall hear it and be afraid! So say our holy laws. And may the rotten limb be cut off so that the whole body may not be infected; kill him so that he will not be a curse to all our people!

KING: Let it so be . . . And now when our paths part: where are you going?

MARCUS: Who knows? East today, west tomorrow; among the pagans it was said about them: "Here they may no longer dwell." The Lord Himself dispersed them.

KING: Farewell, Marcus; thank you for what has been!

MARCUS: What has been was great and splendid; what is coming . . . May the Lord bless you and keep you, Your Majesty, all the days of your life! (*Goes*)

(STENBOCK *enters.*)

KING (*mildly, sadly, humbly*): Is your news Job-like?

STENBOCK: Yes, Your Majesty.

KING: Speak!

STENBOCK: Torstensson has been taken prisoner . . .

KING: And Banér?

STENBOCK: Wounded . . . in his arm.

KING (*as before*): The Lord took . . . Is there still more?

STENBOCK: We have caught a prisoner.

KING: Is he important?

STENBOCK: Yes!

KING: Bring him in.

(STENBOCK *signals to someone outside.* SPARRE *brought in; in Polish uniform*)

KING (*gets up; upset*): Sparre!

SPARRE: Sparre from Linköping, from the bloodbath of Linköping! Yes, it's I!

KING: I see you've become Polish!

SPARRE: I have always been, because the Sparres are faithful to their vows and their kings; and, when my father followed his master Sigismund to Poland, I was received there as in a new fatherland.

KING: Sweden is not Poland!

SPARRE: No, but they are one; and since Vladislav [77] was proclaimed king of Sweden I'm as good a Swede as a Pole! And you, Your Majesty, who claim the Polish crown on the basis of the right to inherit from your cousin, possibly may one day wear the same costume as I without being a traitor.

KING (*to* STENBOCK): I believe it's the late Erik Sparre himself speaking . . . (*Violently*) Take him away! I don't want to exchange words with the dead! Let him return to the place he came from. He's my kinsman, Stenbock, and yours, and I don't want to wear mourning for that rascal. Take him away! And let him go!

SPARRE (*to* STENBOCK): There were five Stenbocks who were allowed to go free from Duke Charles's butcher's bench . . . but you came back and kissed the bloody hand . . .

KING: Take him away!

SPARRE: I certainly won't wear mourning for that fellow! (*Is led out*)

KING (*to* STENBOCK): Fredrik, tell me, was he right or wrong? I seem to have come to a point where everyone else is right.

STENBOCK: I can't answer a two-edged question without splitting my tongue.

KING: You have never liked me; you have always been like ice that I couldn't melt. Is it because your grandmother was a Sture? Is it?

STENBOCK: Perhaps. Perhaps because Malin Sture had to die in a cruel exile; perhaps even because Carl Stenbock . . .

KING: . . . was reprieved in Linköping . . .

STENBOCK: . . . on the place of execution! Because he was faithful to his king as I am to mine. Faithful . . . I'll be unto death, but love him . . . never!

KING (*disturbed*): Do you see how alone I have become, Fredrik

Stenbock? Only the twelve thousand bodies of dead men and six thousand dead horses about me. Why do people flee from me and avoid me?

STENBOCK: Probably one of the dukes can tell you.

KING (*violently*): So it's the dukes you're angry about? But your reply was discourteous.

STENBOCK: Oh, it will do between kinsmen.

KING (*excited*): Kinsmen! Yes! But I am the king, and I could have had many crowns! I could have had the Russian crown, which was offered my brother Charles Philip; [78] I could have the Polish one by right of inheritance through my cousin, Sigismund; the Bohemian crown, which Fredrik of Pfalz offered me; and the Hungarian one after my brother-in-law Bethlen Gabor. You know that! But you don't know that after the battle of Breitenfeld the elector of Saxony handed me the imperial German crown! Yes!

STENBOCK: You child! Why didn't you accept what was offered? Gösta . . . we used to call you that . . . at your own request . . . is it a wagonload of crowns you're dreaming about? Look after your own, to start with . . .

KING (*frightened*): What do you mean?

STENBOCK: Just what I said!

KING: Has Fabricius betrayed me? Has he told . . .

STENBOCK: He hasn't said one word.

KING: Do you know I'm tortured by evil dreams?

STENBOCK: I could guess that, since the blond king has become so dark.

KING (*uneasy*): In the silence of the night, when my senses flicker out and my mind becomes dull, the tempter comes . . . Why do I tell you this, you who don't understand it? Why should I let myself be lured into boasting? . . . If I had never said it! If only I could get it unsaid! Fredrik, advise me!

STENBOCK: What's the use? You ask advice from everyone, but follow no one's.

KING: Command me, then, and I will obey. For two months I've been here as if bewitched, unable to move. I want to get away, but I can't. It's as if Wallenstein were a sorcerer—who could silence swords and people and people's will power! I don't possess myself; I can't control myself. You know, the worst . . . God, whom I used to reach in prayer, has turned His back to me, and I cannot find Him any more!

STENBOCK: Really? Turn home to your tabernacles, Israel, for you have gone astray!

KING: That's what Oxenstjerna, too, said in Mainz. Well, then, I will go home to my fatherland, to my lakes and forests, to my child . . .

STENBOCK: Fine! If only the road to Leipzig is open . . .

KING: Gustav Horn is guarding that.

STENBOCK: Yes, but Pappenheim has occupied the pass in Thuringia.

KING: Pappenheim! Yet another shadow in my way!

STENBOCK: And what's worse: Wallenstein has assembled twenty thousand men on the Saxon border . . .

KING: Am I blocked, then?

STENBOCK: A question that only tomorrow can answer! Ultimatum: wait for the couriers who'll arrive at daybreak, and get a good night's rest.

KING: Thank you, Fredrik. Why don't you speak to me more often, you who are so wise?

STENBOCK: Why don't you ask us a little oftener—us, your old friends?

KING: I don't know. It's as if someone were separating me from everything that has been dear to me.

STENBOCK: That could be. But don't depend on the German princes any more. They've had enough of the Swede; they fear and hate the foreigner.

KING: We can't deny them that . . . the country is theirs.

STENBOCK: No, but we should consider that the country is theirs. I must say good night; the sentries have to be posted.

KING: Good night, Fredrik.

STENBOCK: Good night, my king. Sleep well . . . without dreams about crowns!

KING (*goes into his tent*): Live well.

(*During the preceding scenes the red along the horizon has faded away, the clouds have disappeared, and the stars have gradually begun gleaming. During the scene that follows, the stars of Charles's Wain become more pronounced with extensive spaces between the stars.*)

CURTAIN

SCENE 2

The TRUMPETER *and* LEUBELFING, *who have been in the background, now come forward; the* TRUMPETER *looks ill and has his left arm in a sling.* LEUBELFING *is carrying a lute and supporting the* TRUMPETER.

TRUMPETER: It isn't fun any more to be in a war!

LEUBELFING: Why did you get into it, boy?

TRUMPETER: I was born on a drum in Livonia, sir; I was cradled on a transportation wagon through Poland, and I finally got under the schoolmaster's cane in . . . let me see . . . Brandenburg.

LEUBELFING: And your parents?

TRUMPETER: You don't ask a soldier anything like that. I haven't even seen my own country once . . . I dream about it sometimes . . . a great blue lake called Väner, and I see a large, long mountain—like a church roof, but it doesn't have a tower because it was built by the giants . . .

LEUBELFING: What are giants?

TRUMPETER: Giants? They're very large heathens who don't like churches and church bells, and they're soft as wool mittens, for they don't have any bones in their bodies, and that's why you never find any of their remains in the ground. Our sergeant major is from Västergötland—and he calls me a gosling—that's a boy; but he didn't ever do that after the battle of Breitenfeld, after I had blown my trumpet to start the battle! I think I'll have to lie down. My head's very heavy . . . and I want to go home. (*Lies down;* LEUBELFING *rolls his cape together and puts it under the* TRUMPETER's *head; wants to free him from the large trumpet, but the* TRUMPETER *holds it firmly.*)

LEUBELFING: You're sicker, lad, than I thought!

TRUMPETER: I'm very warm, and it feels good, for we have frozen so much . . . no, you may not take my trumpet! Sir, I should say! Do you think, sir, the king is in his tent?

LEUBELFING: I don't think so. Why do you ask?

TRUMPETER: Well, he hasn't even looked at me lately. I suppose he has his worries and longs to get home . . . he, too. (*Dozes*)

LEUBELFING: Yes, everyone is longing to get home . . . Are you asleep, lad?

TRUMPETER (*awakens*): Was I asleep? Strange, I'm lying looking at the stars . . . It looks like the queen's black velvet cushion, the one with the diamond pins in it. Do you like the queen, sir?

LEUBELFING: Maybe you want to sleep.

TRUMPETER: Am I not asleep? (*Falls asleep*)

(LEUBELFING *is silent for a while and then picks at his lute.*)

TRUMPETER (*awakens*): Sir!

LEUBELFING: Yes, lad.

TRUMPETER: Where am I?

LEUBELFING: You're just outside the king's tent.

TRUMPETER: Wonderful! I like to lie there . . . Were you playing?

LEUBELFING: Shall I play some more?

TRUMPETER: Yes, but I'd like to look at your picture book first, the one that looks like a psalmbook.

(LEUBELFING *hands him a small book of devotions.*)

TRUMPETER: Who painted this?

LEUBELFING: Angels!

TRUMPETER: No-o. I don't believe that.

LEUBELFING: You don't understand it, boy!

TRUMPETER: I don't understand? Huh! Play a little, sir.

LEUBELFING: Does it hurt, boy?

TRUMPETER: No, it's wonderful here! Please play. (*Falls asleep*)

(LEUBELFING *plays an adagio.*)

(*The* KING *appears in the tent opening; stands motionless, observing the two children without their seeing him.*)

TRUMPETER (*who has fallen asleep with the book in his hand lets it fall; the noise awakens him*): Sir!

LEUBELFING: Boy!

TRUMPETER: Do you think I'm dying?

LEUBELFING: Are you afraid to die?

TRUMPETER: No, why should I be? I haven't done anything wrong!

LEUBELFING (*puts his hand on the boy's forehead*): You, boy!

TRUMPETER: Do you think I'm going to die?

LEUBELFING (*weeps*): Yes, I do.

TRUMPETER: Don't cry . . . I'll manage! (*Falls asleep*)

KING (*goes up to them, falls to his knees, feels the* TRUMPETER's *pulse*): Nils! (*To* LEUBELFING) He's running a fever, and there isn't any doctor, any medicine! There's nothing to be done! Nothing!

TRUMPETER (*awakens without recognizing the* KING, *throws his arms around the* KING's *neck, thinking he is* LEUBELFING): Sir, may I kiss you? But turn your face away afterward, because I'm ashamed . . . I've never got nor given one caress! (*He kisses the* KING *without seeing who it is; dozes off again.*)

(KING *gets up; tries to conceal how touched he is.*)

TRUMPETER (*awakens*): I want to look at pictures . . . Sir, play some more for me . . .

(LEUBELFING *plays the same adagio as before.*)

TRUMPETER (*awakens; gets up without seeing the* KING): I want to go home . . . I want to go home!

KING: Where, my child? Where do you want to go home, my little child?

TRUMPETER (*without recognizing the* KING): I want to go home! (*Falls back on the ground, his trumpet in his arms*)

KING (*on his knees beside the dead boy*): Dear child! How is it? That was death. (*Gets up*) Now I want to go home, too!

   (LEUBELFING *on his knees, silently praying*)

QUEEN (*enters from the left, dressed in white, bareheaded, accompanied by ladies-in-waiting and guards*): Who's lying there?

KING: Little Nils, the trumpeter from Breitenfeld.

QUEEN: Haven't we soon had enough deaths?

KING: Yes, soon. Tomorrow we start our journey home.

QUEEN: Blessed be the hour when that decision was made . . . Is the child to lie there? (*Approaches the corpse*)

KING (*to* LEUBELFING): Go and arrange an honorable funeral for the boy. He was dear to me, for he always reminded me of my greatest day—Breitenfeld! Leipzig! (*To the* QUEEN) Let us go to Leipzig again and then north, home!

QUEEN: Home!

CURTAIN

SCENE 3

At Lützen. A run-down shed which contains a smithy, open at the back; beyond it three windmills half invisible in fog; the wings of the windmills are standing so that they form three crosses. To the left in the shed is the hearth with bellows; fire in the forge. The KING's *large white horse with brilliant saddle and*

housing and full trappings stands at the back. LEUBELFING *is holding the horse by the bridle; the grooms* ERIKSSON *and* JÖNSSON *are
holding up one of the horse's hind feet; the* SMITH *strikes one last
blow on the shoe, whereupon the horse is led out. The smith's
boy stands by the bellows. A member of the watch looks in at the
opening of the shed at the back, where the highway to Leipzig
goes. Another member of the watch is within the smithy. Noise
in the distance.*

SMITH: Now the Swedish king can race with the dead and the
devil! . . . That was the first seal! "And I saw," says John in the
Book of Revelations, "and behold a white horse, and he that sat
on him had a bow, and a crown was given unto him, and he
went forth conquering, and to conquer." [79] (*To the boy*) Blow
on the fire. It's cold in here this morning.

SENTINEL I (*outside*): Halt! Where are you going?

RATCATCHER (*with equipment, stops*): To Leipzig.

SENTINEL I: You can't pass here. Get in—for your examination.

RATCATCHER: Oh! What's up?

SENTINEL II (*examining him*): You are a ratcatcher?

RATCATCHER: Yes, indeed, but I haven't caught one rat this morning;
it's as if even the innocent animals have been frightened by the
thunder and noise of the marching armies so that they have crept
down into the earth. You know, the earth's shaking so that my
teeth are chattering; and this fog, ugh, it goes through clothes
and skin. It's terrible; that's the truth!

SENTINEL I: Halt! Where to?

(FARMER *with a cart of vegetables;* FARMER'S WIFE *shoving at the
back of the cart*)

FARMER: To Leipzig.

SENTINEL II: Come in.

FARMER: Why?

SENTINEL II: To be examined.

FARMER'S WIFE: Good heavens, we have to be in the square in good
time or we won't get to sell a thing!

SENTINEL II: No one will get to Leipzig today, and there'll be other things than buying and selling here . . . Don't you know the armies have marched up for battle?

FARMER: Eh?

SENTINEL II: Stay right there!

SENTINEL I: Halt! Where to?

MILLER (*enters*): Where to? I was going down to my mills, of course.

SENTINEL II: So they're your mills; we'll set fire to them right away.

MILLER (*wild*): Set fire?

SENTINEL II: Of course. And, if you scream, we'll make you quiet. Out of the way!

MILLER: He's going to set fire to my mills! Why? What have I done?

SENTINEL II: Shut up, man!

(LEUBELFING, *leading the* KING's *red horse, accompanied by* ERIKSSON *and* JÖNSSON, *appears in the opening of the shed. The* SMITH *goes up to them; looks at the horse's feet without lifting them.*)

SMITH: The king's number two! without flaw and defect, approved, can go to a ball in Auerbachshof! (*Lifts one of the horse's hind feet and kisses the shoe*) I kiss your foot, enviable creature, that is allowed to carry His Majesty from the north. "The second seal: And there went out another horse"—it's from Revelations, too—"that was red, and power was given to him that sat thereon to take peace from the earth and that they should kill one another." [80] No, that doesn't fit. Blow on the fire, boy.

(*The horse is led away.*)

(STENBOCK *and* BRAHE *come in, accompanied by the* QUARTERMASTER *and the* SERGEANT MAJOR, *who carry the* KING's *armor.*)

BRAHE (*to* SENTINEL II): Get the people out of here. The king's coming!

(SENTINEL II *takes out the* MILLER, *the* RATCATCHER, *the* FARMER, *and the* FARMER's WIFE.)

STENBOCK (*points*): Over there are Breitenfeld and Leipzig.

BRAHE: And here is Lützen.

STENBOCK: What do you mean?

BRAHE: This is the place where it will happen . . . The battle, I mean . . . It's a horrible hole, where the ground is like waves as after an earthquake . . . I wish we were somewhere else.

STENBOCK: What is horrible . . . is this terrible darkness . . . Why, the sun has been up two hours, and it's still dark. It's the last of the plagues of Egypt; the first were the flies and the angel of death at Alte Veste.

BRAHE: So you, too, have thought of that? But it's as if things were bewitched in this darkness and fog that postpone the battle. If we could start before Pappenheim gets here from Halle, the game would be ours . . . Did you see the king?

STENBOCK: Yes, I saw him. He had slept in his carriage for a couple of hours. But it wasn't any fun to look at him. The bullet from Dirschau was moving, and he was freezing so that he shook. Ugh, this fog! And it smells like lye. Have you noticed that?

BRAHE: Like salted cod, I think! (*Pause*)

(*They go up to the fire to warm their hands.*)

BRAHE: What are you thinking about?

STENBOCK: And you?

BRAHE: I'm not happy.

STENBOCK: It does look a little difficult.

BRAHE: If Duke Bernhard is to form the left wing with nothing but Germans, and I'm to command the center . . . then I don't feel as confident as I'd like to feel . . .

STENBOCK: That may be, but you'll have the king to your right and, with him, me, Axelsson, Sack, Soop, and Stålhandske . . . It will go well, you'll see . . . oh, yes . . . and we'll all meet tonight in Auerbachshof . . . I hope the host has his *boniments* about Luther's cask of five thousand tankards, or whatever it was . . . and . . .

BRAHE (*listening*): What's that?

STENBOCK: Your . . . anxiety!

BRAHE: Perhaps!

STENBOCK: Nils!

BRAHE: Fredrik! What was that?

STENBOCK: Listen, my friend, you're making me anxious.

BRAHE (*abruptly*): Can one depend on Kniphausen?

STENBOCK: Absolutely!

BRAHE (*paces the floor*): Four, five, six . . . Six! (*Speculates*)

STENBOCK: What is it?

BRAHE: Nothing, nothing. Imagine, I can hear my watch ticking inside my coat!

STENBOCK (*puts his arm about* BRAHE's *shoulder*): Is it your heart?

BRAHE: Well-l. I just happened to think about Margaretha . . . and little Elsa whom I haven't seen yet.

STENBOCK (*brusquely*): You have the right to have one thought only today. One! (*Slaps him on the shoulder*) Chin up, Nils, or we're marked by death.

BRAHE: Just so I get on horseback, I'll manage . . .

SENTINEL I: His Majesty, the king.

(KING *enters; pale as death; hollow-eyed; his beard, wet because of the fog, hangs down. He is followed by* LEUBELFING *and the* grooms.)

BRAHE (*horrified*): God in heaven!

KING (*goes up to the fire; nods to* BRAHE *and* STENBOCK; *speaks to the smith's boy*): Put some wood on the fire. (*To* STENBOCK *and* BRAHE) I'm freezing 'way into the marrow. Did you get frightened, Nils? Fredrik, we've changed our plans so that you'll get Ysslar, Beckerman, Bulach, Goldstein, and Duke Wilhelm back of you. You don't like the duke, but you'll have to put up with him! And then . . . We could certainly have used Torstensson and Banér, but we'll have to get along without them; it is almost better, I think . . . almost better. I miss Gustav Horn more . . . but it'll go anyway, no doubt . . . (*To the* QUARTERMASTER *and the* SERGEANT MAJOR) Take that away . . . I can't wear armor today, and it helps so little. That blessed bullet's on the move again . . .

Leubelfing, give me my cape; this horrible fog and this darkness . . . Imagine if Pappenheim gets here . . . think of it if he gets here before we've started! (*Dries his beard; sits down on a bench; feels a little happier*) Well, shall we have supper in Leipzig today? . . . and dinner in Wittenberg tomorrow? It will be fun to see Wittenberg. No, this is terrible! The sun is gone, and the great darkness has come!

(SMITH *comes up, falls to his knees, and kisses the* KING's *foot.*)

KING (*gets up, furious*): Get up, man, or I'll strike you!

SMITH (*to the others*): He is a martyr and a saint!

KING: Saint? I thought only Catholics believed in saints! I'm a poor, miserable sinner, I'll have you know! So go to your hearth! . . . Leubelfing, get the horses ready.

(FABRICIUS *enters.*)

KING: What it is, Fabricius? You look as if you wanted to prepare me for death!

FABRICIUS: I believed Your Majesty had something to say to me.

KING: Thank you, my friend; I said it all to you last evening. (*More calmly*) Everything that oppressed my heart and spirit . . . Now I only want to take your hand . . . and place it on my head. (*Takes* FABRICIUS' *hand and places it on his head*) It is a good hand, and it gives warmth. (*At the back, the three windmills with their three crosses can be seen—in flames.*) What's that? The three crosses! Is it Golgotha? Into Thy hands I commend my spirit, Lord Jesus! (*Goes up to* BRAHE; *embraces him and kisses him on the cheeks*) Farewell, Nils. God protect you and keep you! (*Gives* STENBOCK *his hand*) Fredrik, no rancor, no grudges any more, and forgive my hard words!

(STENBOCK *kisses the* KING's *hand. A shot in the distance*)

KING (*in anguish*): The battle begins! The horses, the horses! (*Falls to his knees at the back with hands folded*) Oh Jesus, our Saviour, who has conquered death and the kingdom of death, have mercy upon us, have mercy upon us all!

CURTAIN

Scene 4

The castle church at Wittenberg, Romanesque style with triumphal arch and apse; stairs lead to the altar; the altar is at first concealed by a curtain. Below the stairs and on the stairs stand tripods with fires; to the right in the foreground is a chapel, where BRAHE's *coffin stands with* LEUBELFING's *and the boy* TRUMPETER's *coffins on either side. The coffins are closed;* BRAHE's *is made of oak, the other two are white; all three are covered with flowers and wreaths. On the* TRUMPETER's *coffin lies the trumpet; on* LEUBELFING's *a lute and a sword.*

Soft violin music backstage.

All the actors are dressed in mourning.

SERGEANT MAJOR *and* QUARTERMASTER *come on stage, in the foreground.*

SERGEANT MAJOR: So we've come to Wittenberg, but not to Leipzig. What's the name of this church?

QUARTERMASTER: It's the castle church. Didn't you know that?

SERGEANT MAJOR: No.

QUARTERMASTER: A holy room with great memories. Down here in the arch lie Luther and Melanchthon, Fredrik the Wise, and John the Constant. On the door of this church Luther put up the ninety-five theses against absolutions, and outside the Elster door Luther burned the pope's bull of excommunication. These paintings are the work of the masters, Lucas Cranach and Albrecht Dürer. The chancellor could never have selected a worthier place for the funeral.

SERGEANT MAJOR: Where . . . is the king?

QUARTERMASTER (*points at the curtain*): There!

(SERGEANT MAJOR *uncovers his head and prays silently.*)

QUARTERMASTER (*points toward the chapel*): And there Nils Brahe is resting . . . between the page Leubelfing, in whose arms the king died, and the little trumpeter from Breitenfeld . . .

SERGEANT MAJOR: Brahe followed his king into death . . . And Stenbock barely escaped with his life. It is a day of sorrows but the day of great joy as well, for the way home is free, and all these German people bless the deliverer.

QUARTERMASTER: Of course. Think of it, I hardly feel sorrow; for me, this act is the most beautiful and the most worthy celebration of victory, for the hero has given himself as the sacrifice of thanksgiving to the God of Hosts.

SERGEANT MAJOR: Yes, yes. That's how it is.

(HORN *and* BANÉR *enter; look about—they do not know the church.*)

HORN (*to the* QUARTERMASTER): Where . . . ?

QUARTERMASTER (*points at the curtain*): There!

(HORN *and* BANÉR *fall to their knees and pray silently, briefly; then go over to the chapel.* FABRICIUS *and* GRUBBE *kneel by the curtain; rise. Two chamberlains enter, each carrying a large wreath with ribbons and inscription, which they hand to* GRUBBE.)

GRUBBE (*reads the inscription on the first wreath*): From the elector of Brandenburg. "To the Germans' deliverer from Rome!"

FABRICIUS: Record that, Grubbe, with a gold pen.

GRUBBE (*gives the wreath to the* SERGEANT MAJOR, *who hangs it on the first tripod to the left*): Brandenburg has understood our king's achievements best, and is the one who will best understand how to make use of them. (*Reads the inscription on the second wreath*) The elector of Saxony. "To the restorer of freedom of conscience. The colors are seven but the light one."

FABRICIUS: The good Saxon has really hit it, even he. The seven colors of the rainbow out of one and the same light! That is nicely said about the different religions.

GRUBBE: Considered as a dream! (*Hands over the wreath as before*)

(*Two other chamberlains enter, carrying several wreaths.*)

GRUBBE (*reads*): From the Turkish ambassador. "To Alexander the

Great, Conqueror of the king of the Persians." (*Hands it over, et cetera*)

FABRICIUS: The king of the Persians! That's the emperor! *Recte tu quidem!*

GRUBBE (*reads*): "To the good blond man from a Catholic woman."

FABRICIUS: Ah, that's the midwife from Wolgast. Give it a place of honor.

GRUBBE (*hands it over as before*): "The good blond man!" What a tribute from an enemy! (*Reads*) "To King Solomon the Wise. From a poor printer of Munich." (*Hands it over as before*)

FABRICIUS: Also a Catholic; I remember him.

GRUBBE (*reads*): What's this? "To a beloved father, from a fatherless and motherless son. Gustav Gustavsson."

FABRICIUS: What are we going to do with this one?

GRUBBE: Respect a son's justified sorrow and forget a great man's less justified frailty! (*Hands it over as before*)

FABRICIUS: But the queen?

GRUBBE: The queen is accustomed to put up with everything, suffer everything, give up everything. (*Reads*) "A foolish young man, Erik Rålamb, who kneels at his fatherly friend's bier and with tears of humiliation begs for forgiveness for his lack of understanding."

FABRICIUS: Erik Rålamb! The youngster with the great heart and the hot blood!

GRUBBE: In a word, the youngster with the high standard for low things!

FABRICIUS: With fresh memories from the heavenly home of man that make him dissatisfied with old people's feeble attempts to establish heaven on earth.

GRUBBE (*reads*): "King Erik XIV's grandson to Duke Charles's son." That's Åke Tott! Proud even in the presence of death! Away with the insult! (*Throws the wreath away*)

FABRICIUS: A crow doesn't change!

GRUBBE (*reading*): "To Israel's Gideon! Marcus, on behalf of the Jews."

FABRICIUS: Yes! "We are by nature Jews and not sinners to the heathen!" says Paul . . . I believe, Lord, help my disbelief!

GRUBBE: We have come far, Fabricius, far from exiles and the edict of heresy.

FABRICIUS: We must wander through the desert to get a glimpse of Canaan.

GRUBBE: We haven't arrived yet.

FABRICIUS: But those who come after us shall see the Promised Land!

(*Chief marshal enters with staff, accompanied by the* ELECTORS OF BRANDENBURG AND SAXONY, SCHWARZENBERG, *the dukes of Weimar, Lauenberg, etc. Then* Stålhandske, Soop, Hård, Lillie, *other generals and commanders of various branches of the military; Scotchmen, Frenchmen, Russians, Turks, Hungarians, Calmucks, Italians, Jews. They place themselves in open rows before the stairs.* RÅLAMB *and* GUSTAV GUSTAVSSON *can be seen in the chapel. On a signal from the chief marshal the curtain is drawn aside. Organ and violin music. The* KING's *open coffin can now be seen up in the sanctuary.* QUEEN MARIA ELEONORA *enters from the left and kneels by the coffin.* AXEL OXENSTJERNA, *bowed with sorrow, comes through the open rows down on the stage; he is followed by* HORN *and* BANÉR *to the foot of the stairs; goes up the stairs alone. When he has gone up into the sanctuary, he observes the* KING's *face; places his right hand on the* KING's *forehead and covers his own face with the left.*

During this scene GUSTAV GUSTAVSSON *has wanted to rush up into the sanctuary but is held back by* RÅLAMB, *who places his arm about him.*)

CURTAIN

Notes

1. Usedom is the German island off the coast of Pomerania on which the Swedish forces landed at midsummer, 1630.

2. Strindberg says twelve years, but the miller and his wife have a son who is at war and a daughter who has been raped and carried off by the Croatians.

3. Albrecht von Wallenstein (1583–1634) was Gustav Adolf's major opponent—as the brilliant commander of the emperor's forces—during parts of the three years Gustav Adolf participated in the war (1630–1632). Wallenstein was also duke of Friedland and Mecklenburg, hence the many references to him as the Friedlander. His negotiations with Gustav Adolf for a personal alliance at one time led to no results.

4. Wolgast is a small city in Pomerania.

5. Jean Tserklas de Tilly (1559–1632), one of the ablest of the imperial generals and a fanatic Catholic who apparently allowed his forces to treat Protestant enemies as they wished, was defeated by Gustav Adolf at Breitenfeld in 1631 and at Lech in 1632.

6. Denmark's Christian IV (1588–1648) was badly defeated by Tilly at Lutter am Baremberge near Wolfenbüttel in 1626. For all practical purposes the defeat ended Denmark's participation in the Thirty Years' War.

7. The Augsburg Confession of the Lutheran churches was formulated in Augsburg, Bavaria, in 1530, and was duly recognized and approved in the so-called religious peace of Augsburg in 1555.

8. The battle of the White Mountain (1620), southwest of Prague, was one of the Catholics' and Emperor Ferdinand's great victories. It resulted in the exile of Fredrik, the "Winter King" of Bohemia, and in the destruction or exile of the Bohemian Protestants.

9. See note 7.

10. Vineta, the city of the Wends, was destroyed by the Danes in 1148. There are numerous legends about its sinking into the sea; a most attractive available literary treatment of the Vineta legends is "The City at the Bottom of the Sea" in Selma Lagerlöf's *The Wonderful Adventures of Nils* (Garden City, N.Y.: Doubleday, Page & Co., 1907, 1911; New York: Pantheon Books, 1947).

11. Gustav Adolf went on board ship May 31, 1630, to lead the expedition to Germany. Contrary winds kept the Swedish fleet from progressing farther than the coast of Öland by June 16; since a much shorter journey had been planned for, food supplies had to be secured by levy in Öland and the neighboring east-central area on the mainland.

12. The Formula of Concord (1580) was the result of conferences on fundamental Lutheran Church doctrines. It was not accepted by non-Lutheran Protestants. The quartermaster's allusion to election by grace is highly apropos; Lutherans do not accept the doctrine of predestination.

13. The religious conference of Marburg apparently refers to Luther's and Zwingli's debate on transubstantiation there in 1529.

14. The schoolmaster's name—*Krut* (Gunpowder or Powder)—is a typical soldier's name.

15. For information about Gustav Horn and the other military leaders, see the notes on pp. 232-233.

16. Sigismund I (1566–1632), the oldest son of John III and his Polish-born queen Katarina Jagellonica, was brought up as a Catholic, was elected king of Poland in 1587, and became king of Sweden as well upon his father's death in 1592. His uncle Duke Charles, a devout Protestant, defeated him in battle in 1598, secured the dethronement of Sigismund the following year, and had himself made regent. In 1600 Duke Charles brought some of King Sigismund's loyal councillors to trial at Linköping, obtained their condemnation, and had several of them beheaded. Sigismund never relinquished his claim to the Swedish throne.

17. Ebba Brahe (1596–1674), member of one of the most powerful families of the Swedish aristocracy and one of the most beautiful and ablest women of her time, was the woman Gustav Adolf loved. The queen mother objected to her son's marriage to a Brahe, apparently

encouraged his affair with the Dutch Margareta (Cabeljau) Slots, and arranged Ebba Brahe's departure from court.

18. Princess Sigrid, daughter of King Erik XIV and Queen Karin Månsdotter, married Henrik Tott; their son Åke is the Tott in this play; their grandson Klas Tott (1630–1674) was one of Queen Christina's favorites. See Strindberg's *Queen Christina*.

19. The wooden mare was a studded device on which soldiers were punished.

20. Torquato Conti, an Italian, was one of the emperor's generals; he was generally considered the most unscrupulous and cruel of the enemy commanders.

21. In the Treaty of Passau, Bavaria (1552), Charles V recognized the Protestants and granted them religious tolerance.

22. Charles's Wain consists of the seven brightest stars of the Great Bear constellation.

23. Jeremiah 1:13-14.

24. Isaiah 41:25.

25. Jeremiah 1:15-16.

ACT II

26. Stettin was one of the most important of the Pomeranian ports.

27. In the summer of 1615, a Dutchwoman Margareta (Cabeljau) Slots became Gustav Adolf's mistress for a brief period; their son, Gustav Gustavsson, was born in May, 1616. Margareta later married an army engineer, received an estate in Uppland, and was comfortably supported from royal funds. See also note 17.

28. The chief of the fire brigade was also in charge of the collection of special levies.

29. The Edict of Nantes (1598) assured French Protestants both religious and political freedom. In 1628, under the leadership of Cardinal Richelieu, the French concluded victoriously their siege of La Rochelle, stronghold of the Huguenots. The treatment of the Protestants was, as the king suggests, exceedingly cruel.

30. Bethlen Gabor (1580–1629), Prince of Siebenbürgen, was a Hungarian war leader, an opponent of the emperor (the Hapsburgs), and married to Queen Maria Eleonora's sister.

31. Ephesians, 4:8-10, 13-15.

32. General Ditrich von Falkenberg, Swedish commandant of Magdeburg during the long 1630 siege by Pappenheim and Tilly, was shot to death toward the very end of his brilliant defense of the city. The city was plundered and then burned to the ground.

33. Romans 10:12.

34. The popular accounts substantiate Marcus' accusation. SB says: "The plundering continued almost all night, but contributing to it were both the soldiers' lack of food for three days as well as the memory of the enemy's behavior in Neu-Brandenburg" (IV, 315).

35. The agreement with France was signed on January 16, 1631.

36. On August 8, 1627, near Dirschau, East Prussia, Gustav Adolf was shot in the right shoulder close to the throat. The Polish bullet was not removed and frequently caused the king a great deal of pain.

37. See note 16. Erik Sparre was beheaded at Linköping.

38. Wallenstein was dismissed from his command in 1630 largely because of the envy of the princes.

39. See note 34. In return for the subsidy from France, Gustav Adolf did promise to observe neutrality toward the Catholic League and the elector of Bavaria so long as neither made any hostile move against him.

40. Spandau, at the junction of the Spree and Havel rivers, and Küstrin, at the junction of the Warthe and Oder rivers, were two of the most important fortified cities in Germany.

41. The accounts of Luther's fortune vary. Arthur Cushman McGiffert in his *Martin Luther, the Man and His Work* (New York, 1911) says that after Luther's marriage he acquired a house in Wittenberg as well as an orchard and a hop garden and other pieces of land on which farming was carried out on a small scale (pp. 293-294). Later he bought a farm from his brother-in-law. At his death, according to McGiffert, he left property amounting to 8,000 *gulden*.

42. The Treaty of Altmark (1629), which ended the war between Sweden and Poland, included the provisions cited by Strindberg.

43. The Guelphs and the Ghibellines were opposing political factions in Italy from the twelfth to the fifteenth centuries. The Guelphs, the church party, opposed the German emperors' control of Italy and supported the papacy's independence of the emperors. The Ghibellines favored the emperors' control.

44. Herman Israel of Lübeck was one of the Lübeck councillors who helped make it possible for Gustav Vasa to establish Sweden's independence by 1523. As Strindberg says in *Master Olof* and *Gustav Vasa,* the king confiscated much of the church silver and many of the church bells and sold them to Israel. Sweden was on the verge of bankruptcy when Gustav I came to the throne; the reformation helped make it possible for the king to finance his program.

45. The destruction of Magdeburg took place on May 20, 1631.

46. I Samuel 15:3.

ACT III

47. Borås is a city in Västergötland.

48. Exodus 20:2-3, 7.

49. Numbers 6:22-26.

50. Isaiah 8:9-10.

51. Amos 5:18, 21, 23.

52. Some fifteen thousand of the Saxon forces fled from the field early in the battle.

53. Bartholomew's Night (August 24, 1572) witnessed the massacre of the Huguenots (French Protestants) who had gathered in Paris because of the marriage of Henry of Navarre and Margaret of Valois. Extended throughout France, the massacre cost about twelve thousand Protestants their lives.

54. Isaiah 18:10-11.

55. Psalms 62:9.

56. Hugo Grotius or Huig de Groot (1583–1645) and Petrus Ramus or Pierre La Ramée (1515–1572) were two of Gustav Adolf's favorite philosophers. Grotius, generally considered the founder of the science of international law, was in the Swedish diplomatic service (1632–1645).

57. Proverbs 20:1.

58. Isaiah 14:9-12.

ACT IV

59. During the early years of Gustav Adolf's reign, conditions at the University of Uppsala and in the university city were anything but quiet. Faculty members quarreled in words and in physical acts; two of

the well-known professors—Messenius and Rudbeckius—not only engaged in open feuding themselves but encouraged the students to par-
ticipate in their controversies. King Gustav Adolf finally settled their
feuding by dismissing both from their professorships and assigning
them to positions elsewhere. Rudbeckius was an enthusiastic defender of
Lutheranism; Messenius was rightly suspected of pro-Catholicism.

60. See note 29.

61. King Sigismund, Gustav Adolf's cousin as well as a predecessor
on and claimant to the Swedish throne, died on April 30, 1632.

62. In 1630, according to Anders Fryxell's *Berättelser ur svenska historien* (Stockholm, 1900 edition), Gustav Adolf commissioned Ambassador Jakob Russel to work actively for Gustav Adolf's election as successor to his cousin Sigismund on the Polish throne (VI, 317). Russel's
approach was tactless, and the matter led, as Strindberg suggests, to no
favorable results.

63. Proverbs 24:17-18.

64. In the Bible Gog and Magog are princes who will appear just before the end of the world. Abaddon and Apollyon are Hebrew and
Greek names for the Devil, the Destroyer. See Revelations 9:11, 21:8.

65. The Folkungs were the most famous of the great families of the
Swedish nobility in the middle ages. Both before and after its accession
to the throne, the Folkung family and dynasty was marked by bloody
strife both within and without the family. See Strindberg's *The Saga of
the Folkungs*. The Stures, leading rivals of the Vasas, were generally
considered the greatest noble family in the fourteenth, fifteenth, and
even the sixteenth centuries.

66. Christopher of Bavaria (1418–1448) was king of Sweden from
1441 to 1448, of Denmark from 1440 to 1448, and of Norway from
1442 to 1448.

67. The Dacke rebellion raged in 1542 and 1543 and was led by the
Småland chieftain, Nils Dacke.

68. The change which permitted women to succeed to the throne
came after the deposal of Erik XIV.

69. Duke John's marriage was, according to the popular accounts, exactly what Strindberg calls it. See p. 11.

70. Nils Brahe was Ebba Brahe's cousin. See note 17.

ACT V

71. Alte Veste was the imperialists' principal fortification on a height outside Nuremberg. The Swedish attempt to storm it failed; Johan Banér was seriously wounded, and Torstensson was taken prisoner.

72. Martinitz and Slawata were Emperor Ferdinand's Catholic "regents" and councillors in Prague who, on May 23, 1618, were thrown out of a third-story castle window by Protestant and Catholic Bohemian lords and commoners largely as a protest against Austrian (or imperial) encroachment against Bohemian liberty.

73. The army of King Sennacherib (705–681 B.C.) of Assyria was, according to legend and uncertain Assyrian records, destroyed by pestilence about 683 while he was campaigning against the Egyptians.

74. Deuteronomy 23:14.

75. Job 22:23, 26, 28.

76. Job 1:12.

77. See the section on the Polish Vasas, pp. 10–11. In 1632, on the death of Sigismund, Vladislav was proclaimed king of Sweden as well as of Poland.

78. In 1611 Charles Philip was elected ruling prince of Russia by segments of the Russian nobility; before his position could be secured, Michael Romanov succeeded in getting the Russian crown. It is not at all unlikely that Gustav Adolf himself had aspired to the Russian crown.

79. Revelations 6:2.

80. Revelations 6:4.

THE KING'S COMMANDERS

Johan Banér (1596–1641) was until his death one of the generals who made it possible for the Swedish armies to retain and extend their gains under Gustav Adolf. Many of the details about Banér in the play Strindberg got from the semipopular sources, Stärback and Bäckstrom's and Fryxell's books.

About *Nils Brahe* (1604–1632) the sources agree that he was an excellent soldier who was respected and loved both by the king and by the soldiers under his command.

Gustav Horn (1592–1657), field marshal, assumed command of the Swedish armies after the death of Gustav Adolf at Lützen. He served his country not only as a military leader but in various political capacities, especially during the reigns of Queen Christina and her successor, Charles X Gustav.

Fredrik Stenbock (1607–1652) made an honorable record for himself both as a military commander and later in various official government positions at home in Sweden.

About *Åke Tott* (1598–1640), SB says: "Violent, daring, impulsive, he stormed ahead like wildfire, was a great warrior at the University of Uppsala and a superb warrior on the battlefield. The king appreciated him according to his good qualities, rewarded his courage and bravery, but was not blind to his arrogance and intolerance" (IV, 173).

Lennart Torstensson (1603–1651), Count of Ortala and the leading Swedish general during the last phase of the Thirty Years' War (1641–1645), was nicknamed *Blixten* (Lightning) because of his ability to speed up movements of his troops both in and out of battle. That and his earlier command of the Swedish artillery made him one of the most feared and respected commanders during the war.